Knowledge for Social Change

LEE BENSON, IRA HARKAVY,

JOHN PUCKETT, MATTHEW HARTLEY, RITA A. HODGES,

FRANCIS E. JOHNSTON, AND JOANN WEEKS

Knowledge for

SOCIAL CHANGE

Bacon, Dewey, and the Revolutionary Transformation of Research Universities in the Twenty-First Century

TEMPLE UNIVERSITY PRESS

Philadelphia • *Rome* • *Tokyo*

TEMPLE UNIVERSITY PRESS
Philadelphia, Pennsylvania 19122
www.temple.edu/tempress

Library of Congress Cataloging-in-Publication Data

Names: Benson, Lee, author.
Title: Knowledge for social change : Bacon, Dewey, and the revolutionary
    transformation of research universities in the twenty-first century /
    Lee Benson, Ira Harkavy, John Puckett, Matthew Hartley, Rita A. Hodges,
    Francis E. Johnston, and Joann Weeks.
Description: Philadelphia, Pennsylvania : Temple University Press, 2017. |
    Includes bibliographical references and index.
Identifiers: LCCN 2016050224 | ISBN 9781439915189 (hardback : alk. paper) |
    ISBN 9781439915196 (paper : alk. paper) | ISBN 9781439915202 (e-book)
Subjects: LCSH: Community and college—United States. | Universities and
    colleges—United States. | Universities and colleges—United States—Public
    services. | Research institutes—United States. | Education, Higher—Social
    aspects—United States. | Service learning—United States. | Social justice—
    Study and teaching. | Education—Philosophy. | BISAC: EDUCATION /
    Educational Policy & Reform / General. | EDUCATION / Philosophy
    & Social Aspects.
Classification: LCC LC238 .B46 2017 | DDC 378.1/03—dc23
LC record available at https://lccn.loc.gov/2016050224

∞ The paper used in this publication meets the requirements of the American
National Standard for Information Sciences—Permanence of Paper for Printed
Library Materials, ANSI Z39.48-1992

Printed in the United States of America

9 8 7 6 5 4 3 2

To Barbara Netter and in memory of Edward Netter

Benefactors, colleagues, friends

Contents

Preface

Knowledge is power.

—FRANCIS BACON,
Religious Meditations: Of Heresies (1597)

Serious mismanagement of the world as a whole exists today as
it has for centuries. As concerned scientists and world citizens,
we are deeply alarmed, particularly in a time of so-called peace.
We do not understand (or cannot accept) why so many people
are starving, illiterate, diseased, hopelessly bound by political
forces; why the ecology of the world is threatened by major
pollution and the lack of serious conservation efforts; why wars
are still used to "solve" international problems; why racism,
homelessness, and child abuse are still common; or why there
is such widespread neglect of the plight of future generations.
. . . Hence, the major axiom of this article is: we ought (in an
ethical sense) to create a science that knows how to manage the
world of human affairs better.

—C. WEST CHURCHMAN AND IAN I. MITROFF,
"The Management of Science and the Mismanagement
of the World," *Knowledge and Policy* (1994)

We strongly accept the validity of the two axioms quoted above, from
works written by Francis Bacon at the turn of the seventeenth century and C. West Churchman and Ian I. Mitroff four hundred years
later. To accept the validity of their axioms, however, poses a remarkable paradox for democratic-minded academics:

1. Never before in human history have human beings possessed so
   much knowledge that *potentially* gives them the power to produce
   truly good lives for *all* human beings.
2. Never before in human history have so many human beings lived
   so long and yet experienced so vast an array of disastrous conditions that produce such human misery.

How can we explain that paradox? More significantly, what can and should democratic-minded, pragmatic academics *do* to eliminate it? We propose a solution, greatly oversimplified here and developed at length below. Following the brilliant lead Bacon provided in *The Advancement of Learning* (1605), democratic-minded academics should form a worldwide movement to eliminate the paradox by working systematically to radically transform the research university to *radically advance the advancement of learning and knowledge*. Such a movement, we contend, is both possible and capable of producing and *implementing* the knowledge needed to enable *all* human beings to enjoy long, healthy, active, peaceful, virtuous, and happy lives.

Are we suffering from a bad case of delusionary utopianism? Obviously, we do not think so. This book's primary goal is to help develop a neo-Baconian movement to produce the knowledge needed to implement John Dewey's powerful theory that participatory democracy is the best form of human society—the "organic" form of society capable of realizing the "Good Life" for all human beings.

As is well known, Dewey greatly admired Bacon's theory that the continuous advancement and implementation of scientific learning and knowledge were the key means to realize societal progress. He regarded Bacon as "the real founder of modern thought," and yet he radically disagreed with Bacon's elitist, top-down, antidemocratic theory of society. Instead, Dewey theorized that only a society based on bottom-up governance (participatory democracy) could transform the world into a "Great Community" of integrated, interactive, interdependent, truly collaborative, truly democratic societies dedicated to achieving Bacon's fundamental goal, "the relief of man's estate"—that is, the continuous improvement of humanity.[1]

Dewey's crusade to advance participatory democracy was, in our judgment, the greatest of his many theoretical contributions. To quote Robert Westbrook, one of his most insightful biographers:

> Among liberal intellectuals of the twentieth century, Dewey was the most important advocate of participatory democracy, that is, of the belief that democracy as an ethical ideal calls upon men and women to build communities in which the necessary opportunities and resources are available for every individual to realize fully his or her particular capacities and powers through participation in political, social, and cultural life.[2]

In a previous book, however, three of us observed that despite his passionate belief in, and advocacy of, participatory democracy, Dewey never actually developed, let alone implemented, a comprehensive strategy and program capable of realizing his powerful general theory in real-world practice.[3] In this book, therefore, we try to strengthen Dewey's major contribution to a better world by placing his participatory democratic theory in larger historical perspective. To do that, we begin with Bacon's seminal works and conclude with contemporary efforts (highlighting the case we know best—the work of the University of Pennsylvania's Netter Center for Community Partnerships) to radically advance the learning necessary to achieve the worldwide Great Community brilliantly envisioned by Dewey.[4]

Dewey published *The Public and Its Problems* (1927) to counteract the antidemocratic ideas and movements gaining strength in the United States and elsewhere during the 1920s. Reflecting a dominant tendency in European and American social theory, he asserted that the disintegration of local communities had severely negative consequences for human well-being. If human societies are to function effectively, they must be based on *face-to-face local communities* that function effectively. "Democracy," he famously wrote, "must begin at home, and its home is the neighborly community."[5] While we strongly agree with Dewey's brilliant, far-reaching proposition, we also argue that today democracy's home is the engaged neighborly college or university and its local community partners.

We do not claim that we prove that proposition. To the contrary, our primary purpose is movement development through stimulating creative counterproposals, serious debate, and informed action. To put it another way, we hope that this book contributes, in some small way, to the formation and development of an interactive, international network of democratic-minded academics determined to radically transform research universities in order to realize Bacon's fundamental goal, "the relief of man's estate," as well as Dewey's inspiring utopian vision of a worldwide, organic Great Community composed of truly participatory, democratic, collaborative, and interdependent societies.

Introduction

University-Assisted Community Schools and the Expanding Global Movement of Democratic, Civically Engaged, Modern Research Universities

The philosophers have only interpreted the world, in various ways; the point is to change it.

—KARL MARX, *Theses on Feuerbach* (1845–1846)

The university, I maintain, is the prophetic interpreter of democracy; the prophet of her past, in all its vicissitudes; the prophet of her present in all its complexity; the prophet of her future, in all its possibilities.

—WILLIAM RAINEY HARPER, "The University and Democracy" (1899)

Karl Marx was wrong; John Dewey was right. In modern societies, the economic system is not the strategic societal subsystem; the schooling system is. Karl Marx was wrong; William Rainey Harper was right. In modern societies, the factory is not the strategic organization; the research university is.

To develop and support those propositions, we have written this book, whose title summarizes our basic argument: *Knowledge for Social Change: Bacon, Dewey, and the Revolutionary Transformation of Research Universities in the Twenty First Century*. We argue for radically transforming research universities to function as democratic, civic, and community-engaged institutions dedicated to advancing learning and knowledge for social change and "the relief of man's estate"—an iconic phrase by which Francis Bacon, writing in the early seventeenth century, meant the continuous betterment of the human condition. To support that argument, we focus on some of the significant contributions to learning made by Bacon, Benjamin Franklin, Seth Low, Jane Addams, William Rainey Harper, and John Dewey, as well as past and current efforts, including our own, to create and sustain democratically engaged colleges and universities for the public good.

We also discuss *university-assisted community schools,* our approach for effecting a radical transformation of research universities and contributing to more democratic schools, communities, and societies. Our own experiences and the work of a number of significant thinkers helped us develop the idea of the university-assisted community school, which is one of this book's two major themes. Most directly, the idea was shaped by Dewey and Harper. To introduce the concept of university-assisted community schools and sketch out our plan for this book, we turn to two concrete examples of their contributions to the advancement of learning.

Until his appointment to the University of Chicago in 1894, Dewey had only a minor interest in how schooling systems functioned and how they might be improved. For complex reasons, the Chicago appointment radically changed his interests. During his ten years in Chicago, Dewey became convinced that revolutionizing the schooling system was the best means to transform America into the participatory democratic, "organic" society he had envisioned as early as 1888 in a lengthy essay entitled "The Ethics of Democracy."[1]

In Chicago, Dewey came to believe that a major component of that schooling revolution would be the transformation of American public schools into *community schools*—that is, schools that would function as the social centers of the communities in which they were located. Although he did not invent the concept of community schools, he extended the work of other scholars and added his own distinctive interpretation. He envisioned neighborly organizations that would help educate democratic citizens by bringing together people of diverse backgrounds for continuous lifelong education and social interaction in collaborative ways that would surmount the barriers of race, class, and religion. He came to the community school idea largely as a result of his close association and friendship with Jane Addams and her colleagues at Hull House, the famous social settlement Addams and Ellen Gates Starr had founded on Chicago's poverty-stricken West Side. The practical activities of the women of Hull House, and the powerful theories and insights these passionate activists derived from their work, helped Dewey to understand the central role that local communities played in American society and also to see that public schools could function as strategic agencies to help develop participatory democratic communities.

In 1902, inspired by Hull House and settlement houses in other cities, Dewey presented a highly significant, prescient address, "The School as Social Centre," at a National Education Association conference. Viewed in historical perspective, the talk clearly anticipated some of the community school movements that episodically rose and fell in the United States after 1902, and are now strongly rising again. The current community school movement, in particular, builds on and extends Dewey's idea that since public schools "belong" to all members of the community, they should "serve" all members of the community—and are particularly well-suited to function as neighborhood "hubs" or "centers," around which local partnerships can be generated and developed. When they play that innovative role, schools function as community institutions par excellence, providing a decentralized, democratic, community-based response to rapidly changing community problems. In the process, they help young people learn and develop skills through action-oriented, collaborative, real-world problem solving.

Dewey's 1902 address and the various community school movements that it inspired would, in complex ways, eventually lead to the development of the theory and practice of university-assisted community schools in the twenty-first century. The university-assisted community school logically extends and updates Dewey's theory of the school as a social center. In our neo-Deweyan conception, the neighborhood school becomes the core institution that provides comprehensive services, galvanizes other community institutions and groups, and helps solve the myriad problems that communities confront in a rapidly changing world. Dewey rightly recognized that if the neighborhood school is to function as a genuine community center, it requires additional human resources and support. In this vein we emphasize "university-assisted" because community schools do indeed require far more resources than traditional schools and because we are convinced that, in relative terms, universities constitute the strategic and most powerful sources of broadly based, comprehensive, sustained support for community schools.

Our second major theme is the advancement of learning by means of *modern research universities.* William Rainey Harper played a leading role in the evolution and eventual development of the modern research university. In 1890 he became the first president of the University of Chicago, which formally began operations in October 1892. Thanks to Harper's "messianic" vision of the role research universities could play in modern societies, as well as the huge amounts of money he persuaded John D. Rockefeller to give him to realize it, his new university was quickly successful. A detailed historical account of the "Chicago pragmatists" described its astonishing rise: "By the time the university celebrated its decennial year, it had won widespread (if sometimes grudging) recognition as one of the leading research institutions in the world, and within its walls were being developed theories whose impact was felt in both academic and the outside worlds."[2]

It helps to explain Harper's grand vision of the role of research universities in modern societies that at an early age he became a leading biblical scholar in the United States. He not only passionately studied the Old Testament; his "fundamental vision" for the University of Chicago was inspired by it. In his messianic vision, the university was the "prophet of democracy"—the strategic organizational innovation that would help realize and fulfill the promise of American democracy. The complex environments of urban universities would enable them to make especially significant advances in knowledge and learning, Harper contended; these advances would come through the practice of *cosmopolitan localism*—our term for his innovative concept.[3] His own university would fulfill its prophetic role by striving to ameliorate the severe problems confronting its dynamically growing city, in particular the problems of its public schools.

Harper's theory of democracy in industrial societies, which was to powerfully influence Dewey, identified the schooling system as the leading societal subsystem, whose continuing development and *effective integration* at all levels (elementary to university) is mandatory to produce significant democratic progress. Assigning to universities the role of "Messiah," the "to-be-expected deliverer" of democracy, Harper theorized that their major responsibility was to ensure the quality of their country's schooling system. If that system did not powerfully accelerate "democratic progress," then its universities must be performing poorly—no matter what else they did successfully. "By their [democratic] fruits shall ye know them" was the pragmatic, Baconian, real-world performance test Harper prescribed for American and European universities.[4]

With his messianic philosophy, activist temperament, extraordinary organizational skills, and experience, Harper applied his societal theory and Chicago's strategic location in the midwestern communication system and economy to make his university the active hub of an integrated network of midwestern schools, academies, and colleges dedicated to fulfilling democracy's "mission to the world."[5]

Having sketched the critical roles played by John Dewey in the development of university-assisted community schools and William Rainey Harper in the evolution and development of the modern research university, we now turn to a historically and empirically grounded analysis of those two radical contributions to the advancement of learning. Our historical analysis begins with the revolutionary work of Francis Bacon at the turn of the seventeenth century.

Knowledge for Social Change

I

The Advancement of Learning for "the Relief of Man's Estate"

1

Francis Bacon and
the Advancement of Learning

There is another great and powerful cause why the sciences have made but little progress; which is this. It is not possible to run a course aright when the goal itself has not been rightly placed.

—FRANCIS BACON, *Novum Organum* (1620)

Bacon was writing at the beginning of the seventeenth century, when religious wars were raging in Europe, when Pilgrim fathers filled with Abrahamic hopes were building a new world in America, when Puritan divines filled with visions of Jeremiad doom were preaching hellfire and damnation. He offered a third alternative to the certainties of heaven and hell: the alternative of patient inquiry. He told us to ask questions instead of proclaiming answers, to collect evidence instead of rushing to judgment, to listen to the voice of nature rather than to the voice of ancient wisdom.

—FREEMAN DYSON, "The Case for Far-Out Possibilities," *New York Review of Books* (10 November 2011)

In the Preface we cite John Dewey's unequivocal assessment of Francis Bacon as "the real founder of modern thought" in one of his major books, *Reconstruction in Philosophy* (1920). Among many insights we gained from Dewey, he helped us see much more clearly that despite Bacon's elitist and authoritarian orientation, his pioneering efforts to integrate and advance learning, knowledge, and power provided a brilliant model for contemporary democratic-minded academics. Dewey wrote:

Francis Bacon of the Elizabethan age is the great forerunner of the spirit of modern life. Though slight in accomplishment, as a prophet of new tendencies he is an outstanding figure of the world's intellectual life. . . . The main traits of his thought put before our mind the larger features of a new spirit which was at work in causing intellectual reconstruction. . . . The best known aphorism of Bacon is that Knowledge is Power. Judged by this pragmatic criterion, he condemned the great body of learning then extant as *not*-knowledge, a pseudo—and pretentious—knowledge. For it did not give power. It was otiose, not operative. . . . In a certain sense it aimed at power, but power over other men in the interest of some class or sect or person, not power over natural forces in the common interest of all. . . . In contrast, his new method had an exceedingly slight opinion of the amount of truth already existent, and a lively sense of the extent and importance of truths still to be attained. It would be a logic of discovery, not a logic of argumentation, proof and persuasion.[1]

Dewey emphasized that in Bacon's view:

Active experimentation must force the apparent facts of nature into forms different to those in which they familiarly present themselves; and thus make them tell the truth about themselves. . . . [To Bacon] progress . . . [was] the aim and test of genuine knowledge. . . . A logic of discovery . . . looks to the future. Received truth it regards critically as something to be tested by new experiences rather than as something to be dogmatically taught and obediently received. . . . The great need is the organization of co-operative research, whereby men attack nature collectively and the work of inquiry is carried on continuously from generation to generation.[2]

For our own analysis of Bacon's main contributions to the advancement of learning, we choose, for clarity's sake, to divide his works into two main periods, from 1592 to 1621 and from 1621 to 1626, skipping over the years from 1561 to 1592, when he was concerned with developing his professional career in the law and his political career.

Francis Bacon was the youngest son of an aristocrat, Nicholas Bacon, the Lord Keeper of the Great Seal under Queen Elizabeth I. Details of his childhood are murky. When he was twelve years old, his father sent him to Cambridge University, where he studied for two and a half years. What the youthful Bacon actually learned at Cambridge and what lifelong dispositions he formed at the university are matters of scholarly dispute. Some biographers contend that it was at Cambridge that he formed and cultivated his lifelong disdain for Aristotelean scholarship as "good only for disputations and barren in the production of works for human betterment," as well as his passionate commitment to the advancement of learning and the development of modern science.[3]

Yet John E. Leary Jr., whom we regard as Bacon's most astute observer, disagrees. Other biographers' descriptions of Bacon's dislike of Aristotle in his Cambridge years rely, he demonstrates, on Bacon's own vainglorious stories about "his intellectual precocity and artful charm." Leary flatly asserts, "We know little about Bacon at Cambridge." Critically examined, Bacon's biographies present little evidence that contradicts Leary's conclusion about Bacon's Cambridge experience or his argument that after Bacon left Cambridge, he concentrated for a quarter-century on law and politics before turning seriously to philosophy.[4]

1592–1621: Developing a Philosophy of Learning and Science

When did Bacon's philosophical project begin in earnest? Leary argues for the year 1603, notwithstanding a 1592 letter from Bacon to his uncle Lord Burghley (William Cecil, Queen Elizabeth I's perennial chief advisor), in which he asserted his desire to "take all knowledge to be my province."[5] Despite this grandiose assertion, Leary contends that Bacon's writings from 1592 to 1603 were "mostly occasional pieces connected to his professional or political interests."[6] In those years Bacon suffered many painful disappointments in the process of advancing his political career, along with numerous distressing and psychologically disturbing difficulties in his personal relationships. In 1603 Queen Elizabeth died, and James I, "reputed to be a man of learning," succeeded her. Bacon sought to gain favor with the new king by writing *The Advancement of Learning*, embarking on a "new phase" of his career. This development was distinguished by "a remarkable burst of creative energy," as Bacon took on "a host of schemes and projects, some political, others philosophical, but all crammed together—the work of a busy man." Apparently, Bacon had moved beyond the career anxiety he had experienced in the 1590s. "Far from suffering from his active involvement in affairs of state," Leary writes, "his philosophical projects seem to have drawn energy from his rising sense of self-esteem and growing self-confidence as a political actor."[7]

Out of all of these philosophical projects, which was fundamental? Which was aimed at realizing his ultimate goal? Bacon identified that goal in a phrase, "the relief of man's estate," by which he meant the continuous betterment of the human condition until all human beings could enjoy Good Lives in a Good Society.[8] How could that condition be brought about? Dewey, as we have seen, cited Bacon's well-known aphorism "Knowledge is power" and observed: "Judged by this pragmatic criterion . . . [Bacon] condemned the great body of learning then extant as *not*-knowledge, as pseudo—and pretentious—knowledge." That is, Bacon came to see that he had to bring about a continuous advancement of learning capable of developing the true knowledge mankind needed to gain the power required to achieve "the relief of man's estate."

To achieve that goal, Bacon had to engage in a truly revolutionary enterprise: demolish all previous systems of learning and replace them with the radically new system he was painfully, painstakingly, and undauntedly developing and promoting. His biographer Perez Zagorin suggests the sweeping nature of Bacon's vision and enterprise: To succeed in his primary and most ambitious intellectual project, Bacon had to overthrow the "old regime" of knowledge and dedicate "his entire life . . . to the task of persuasion."[9]

Zagorin characterizes Bacon's primary project as "the reconstruction and hence renewal of philosophy as a form of inquiry, chiefly in relation to natural philosophy." Bacon aimed at "the achievement of a systematic, continuous progress of knowledge in all the sciences of nature and the discovery of its secrets"; this progress, he believed, was essential to ensuring continuous improvements in the human condition. Achieving this goal necessitated "the reformation of the methods of investigating nature by the introduction of a new logic of discovery or procedure for acquiring and testing scientific knowledge."[10]

What was the "old regime of knowledge" that Bacon regarded as the major impediment to realizing his philosophical project? Zagorin describes it as "a number of values, assumptions, attitudes and beliefs that were a heritage of classical antiquity, Christianity, medieval scholasticism, and of several strains in recent Renaissance thought as well. The old regime of knowledge revered the past, especially the culture of Greece and Rome, and was very respectful of its authority. Its highest ideal was contemplative rather than active. It had no realization of the transformative potentialities of science. It took no interest in innovation and discovery and their deliberate promotion. It did not possess the idea of progress either mental or material."[11]

Bacon harshly condemned the old regime for its fundamental neglect of practical works to improve human life. Instead of focusing on *works* designed for human benefit, he charged, adherents of the old regime engaged in endless angry disputes based on *words* designed to win abstract arguments and aggrandize the scholarly reputation and status of individuals. We can summarize the conflict by saying that the old regime of knowledge was built on words, while Bacon's proposed "new regime" was built on works.[12]

1605: *The Advancement of Learning*

The Advancement of Learning (1605) was the first publication to reflect Bacon's new philosophy of knowledge and science. It consisted of two books, published in English rather than the traditional Latin for "the practical purpose of making . . . [Bacon's] ideas known to a comparatively wide audience of native readers."[13] The title conveys precisely what Bacon passionately hoped all his works—and words—would accomplish.

He had one particular reader in mind: James I. Bacon's extraordinarily ambitious and revolutionary vision of learning would cost a great deal of money. Hoping that the scholarly king might be persuaded to provide it, Bacon dedicated both books of the *Advancement* to him, extravagantly praised his intellectual abilities, and compared him favorably to King Solomon.[14]

In the view of Rose-Mary Sargent, the editor of Bacon's *Selected Philosophical Works*, Book 1 of the *Advancement* essentially eulogized the dignity and "Excellency of Learning" and "defended learning against those who maintained that it could be religiously, politically, or socially dangerous."[15] Leary adds that it was also "an attempt to analyze various distempers which had corrupted . . . [learning] from within."[16] Zagorin amplifies their assessments: "In book 1, Bacon set himself to refute various criticisms of learning, following which he took notice of several 'distempers' and errors in learning that he believed had contributed to its discredit. . . . Bacon did not look upon knowledge from a narrowly utilitarian standpoint. The end to which he dedicated the achievements of the human intellect was also moral insofar as it served religion and the welfare of mankind by showing through discoveries in natural philosophy the greatness of God's works."[17]

Book 2 of the *Advancement* identifies, in very general terms, "the works or acts which pertain to the advancement of learning," specifies serious "defects" in the existing learning system, and suggests remedies for them. It begins with a lengthy dedication to James I. Praising the king for the "luster" he had already bestowed on his age, Bacon then offered him advice on adding significantly to his fame by extending his care to the "further endowment of the world with sound and fruitful knowledge."[18]

The works or acts that concerned Bacon were bound up in three "objects of learning," which he designated as "the places of learning, the books of learning, and the persons of the learned." The *places of learning* were universities, colleges, and schools, without which "knowledge . . . would soon perish and vanish into oblivion." Principal works or acts associated with these institutions included buildings, endowments, "grants of franchises and privileges," and government ordinances. Works associated with the *books of learning* were (1) libraries, which Bacon likened to "shrines wherein all the relics of the ancient saints of full or true virtue are preserved" (a reference, presumably, to scholars of the medieval scholastic schools), and (2) "new editions of authors, with more correct impressions, more faithful translations, more profitable commentaries, more diligent annotations and the like." Works associated with the *persons of the learned* included "the remuneration and designation of lecturers in arts already extant and invented; and the remuneration and appointment of writers and inquirers concerning those parts of learning not yet sufficiently labored or prosecuted."[19]

Having identified in very general terms each of the three types of works or acts that were integral to the advancement of learning, Bacon then severely criticized the way in which they actually functioned in the real world: "Among so many noble foundations of colleges in Europe, I find it strange that they are all dedicated to professions and none left free to the study of arts and sciences at large." As he saw it, the professions were being deprived of the "sap and strength" that contact with the arts and sciences would provide. Failure to attend seriously to these subjects not only dissipated the professions but was "prejudicial to states and governments"; polities lacked knowledgeable leaders who were schooled in "histories, modern languages, books of policy and civil discourse," subjects "whereby they might come better prepared and instructed to offices of state." Bacon particularly deplored the poor remuneration of "lecturers in sciences" (whose lectures were public), lamenting that these positions failed to attract eminent scholars who would function as "the keepers and guardians of the whole store and provision of learning, whence the active and militant part of the sciences is furnished."[20]

Other major defects in the works or acts necessary to the advancement of learning were the stinginess of funds for experiments; lack of consultation with "governors of universities" and "princes" about whether "scholastic exercises anciently begun" should be discontinued and better ones substituted; "too great and mischievous a divorce between invention and memory" of past advances in knowledge; and failure to develop "*a closer connection and relationship* between all the different universities of Europe" (emphasis added).[21]

Bacon then identified the last of the major defects in the traditional learning system, with a highly significant recommendation for how to remedy it: "The last defect I complain of . . . is that there has not been, or very rarely been, any public designation of fit men either to write or make inquiry concerning such parts of knowledge as have not been already sufficiently labored. To which point it will greatly conduce if a review and census be made of the sciences, and account be taken what parts of them are rich and well advanced, and what poor and destitute."[22]

We characterize Bacon's recommendation as highly significant because he identified *himself* as among the men to remedy that defect: The remainder of Book 2 was devoted to Bacon's work on his own "survey" of knowledge and what remained to be learned. It is not our purpose to revisit Bacon's survey—Zagorin provides a useful sketch of it.[23] With Leary, our interest in the *Advancement* is based on "its character as a practical proposal . . . to James I."[24] As Leary puts it: "The *Advancement* is a rich work and a virtuoso performance by Bacon, summing up what must have been several decades of private reading and reflection, but in its practical face the *Advancement* was a call for reformation of the educational system along civic lines. That a reform of the universities was a principal object of the *Advancement* is clear from Bacon's concrete recommendations at the beginning of the second book."[25]

Bacon did two fundamental things in the *Advancement*. First, he identified the major defects in the existing learning system (particularly the universities), which he believed could be remedied only by the power of a king like James I. Second, he identified the one major defect that he believed he himself, a "private man," had remedied by the critical comprehensive survey of learning that he performed and reported on in Book 2.[26]

1605–1621: Bacon's Progress

As Bacon continued working to improve universities in particular and the traditional learning system in general, he changed his mind about what he had accomplished in the *Advancement*. "Even as he was writing" it, Leary observes, Bacon "began to sketch the outlines of a program for the renewal of natural science, which would culminate nearly two decades later in the plan for a 'Great Instauration.' The *Advancement* was an offering to the King and kingdom intended to redirect and revivify traditional learning in its traditional institutional setting, the university. By contrast, the 'Great Instauration' was an attempt to create a new kind of learning and to lay the foundations for a new learned community – Bacon's own commonwealth of learning devoted to the investigation of nature."[27]

In her introduction to the text of *The Great Instauration*, Rose-Mary Sargent notes that Bacon considered it his most important work, citing his earliest biographer, William Rawley, who wrote in 1657.[28] Although *instauration* is the English form of Latin words that mean *renewal* and *restoration*, Zagorin argues that in Bacon's "conception of his work as a great instauration, the motif of innovation is much more prominent than that of restoration."[29] Both Leary and Zagorin thus agree that *The Great Instauration* attempted to create a new kind of learning, raising this intriguing question: How did Bacon get from the *Advancement* of 1605 to *The Great Instauration* of 1620?

Leary emphasizes that the major project for "the Great Instauration" was "shaped decisively by Bacon's political experiences and ideas."[30] During the first decade of the reign of James I (1603–1612), Bacon advanced politically because he functioned as "the Crown's leading servant" in the House of Commons.[31] According to Leary: "All the major elements of what would become the *Great Instauration* were . . . present in Bacon's writings of this decade, though still embedded in scattered, tentative works which for the most part he left unpublished." These writings "were informed by a political sense and relied regularly on political language."[32]

Beginning in 1612, Bacon's political power and social status increased rapidly. He became attorney general in 1613 and lord chancellor in 1617.

A new title, Viscount St. Albans, marked his ascendancy in the king's inner circle. Although much of his time from 1612 to 1621 was devoted to self-indulgent, extravagant behavior, he spent some time on his scientific project and, in 1620, compiled the *Novum Organum (New Organon)*.[33]

In Sargent's opinion, the *Novum Organum* was "Bacon's most significant and original philosophical work."[34] It was also the only part of his extraordinary plan that Bacon completed. Zagorin notes that the *Novum Organum* was designed to function as the second of the six parts Bacon intended to include in *The Great Instauration*, which he chose to publish in an incomplete form, limiting this slender volume to a prelude and dedication to King James I, a sizable preface, an enumeration and sketch of each part, and an appendix. Bacon's sketch of his massive plan for *The Great Instauration*—which provides, in effect, a preface to the *Novum Organum*—was "the culmination of Bacon's efforts to achieve a decisive advance in man's knowledge of nature through the renewal and reconstruction of philosophy."[35] In Leary's view, *The Great Instauration* was intended to be "a program for conducting a collectively organized, rigidly disciplined inquiry into nature which would culminate in 'The New Philosophy, or Active Science,' . . . a massive research project, a grand effort to organize scientific inquiry in a new way . . . taking place under *the authority and guiding direction of a mastermind like himself*" (emphasis added).[36]

Early in 1621, at the height of Bacon's power, status, and intellectual achievement, disaster struck and radically changed his life and work. A new session of the Parliament had convened and taken up the question of judicial corruption in the House of Commons. Bacon stood accused of having accepted bribes while serving as the presiding judge of the Court of Chancery. Tried by the House of Lords, he confessed to wrongdoing and received penalties that disqualified him from holding office and marked the end of his political career.[37]

1621–1626: Assessing Bacon's Plans for a Science-Based Utopian Society

Bacon's exile from politics gave him ample time to concentrate on works he planned for the next stages of *The Great Instauration*.[38] Of Bacon's published works from this period, we regard the utopian *New Atlantis* as the most significant because it strongly supports our view of Bacon as probably the first European theorist of "scientific" organization and management.

To a considerable extent, this view derives from Leary's brilliant observation that "Bacon conceived the inquiry into nature as a single grand work, toward the accomplishment of which people must be organized and directed in a radically new way. . . . It is people who pose the most problematic challenge to the would-be reformer of science. It is people—even more than nature—who form the proper object of Bacon's attention, and it is to the reorganization of the social aspects of science that Bacon devoted his most concerted and interesting efforts. The problem of organization was hardly ancillary in Bacon's view, hardly a secondary matter of an essentially philosophical shift. Rather, it was the core issue of the intellectual reformation to which this deeply political man devoted himself."[39]

By far the most important institution in Bensalem, the imaginary island society Bacon created in *The New Atlantis* to demonstrate how his "Great Instauration" would advance scientific organization and benefit humanity when put into practice, was Salomon's House (also referred to as the College of the Six Days' Work). According to William Rawley, Bacon's secretary, chaplain, and first biographer, who published *The New Atlantis* posthumously in 1627, Bacon's primary reason for writing the utopian "fable" was to exhibit therein "a model or description of a college instituted for the interpreting of nature and the producing of great and marvellous works for the benefit of men, under the name of Salomon's House."[40]

Bacon hoped that his description of how Salomon's House was organized and managed and how it functioned would inspire readers to put his "model college" into universal practice in the real world. He of course never actually created anything remotely like the new community of scientists he envisioned in *The Great Instauration*. The imaginary Salomon's House, however, helps us understand Bacon's conception of *how* a great scientific foundation, designed to implement his ideal plan for the advancement of learning and natural science, would function as the most dynamic, productive, *benevolent* component of a well-administered, well-governed, well-run, highly hierarchical, utopian society.

Leary finds valuable evidence about Bacon's scientific ideas in the description of Salomon's House and his other writings on organized science. The biographer uses that evidence to contradict the many commentators who see "democratic, libertarian, egalitarian impulses" in Bacon's efforts to "organize scientific inquiry." On the contrary, Leary forcefully contends, Bacon urged "a tightly controlled, rigidly regimented, and deeply authoritarian organization for science."[41]

Leary depicts Bacon's historical role in the advancement of learning and scientific inquiry as both highly progressive and highly conservative. There is no denying that Bacon envisioned organized science as "a collective, collaborative enterprise . . . aimed positively at the improvement of the conditions of human life."[42] Why then was his conception of organized science essentially antidemocratic, antilibertarian, antiegalitarian? The answer, Leary shows, lies in the connection between Bacon's "political experiences and beliefs" as a "lifelong royalist" and his approach to organizing science: "For if we examine

Bacon's ideas about organization dispassionately and without prejudices as to his 'modernism' or 'progressivism,' we find no disjuncture between the ideas which underlay his political and his scientific schemes. On the contrary, there is a close correspondence."[43]

As Bacon's theories of "human nature, of social life, and of government" were "profoundly conservative," it would have been contradictory and illogical for him to adopt an approach to science founded on democratic principles that were anathema to his worldview:

> If he aimed positively at the improvement of the conditions of human life, his pursuit of this aim was conditioned by the fear of ungoverned change, particularly the kind of change that was likely to be produced by ordinary people in public forms of discussion. If he quarreled with the authority of the Ancients and at times employed an anti-authoritarian rhetoric against the tyranny of traditional learning, it was hardly his belief that people could do without authority in their intellectual lives or that intellectual liberty should be enshrined as a fundamental, constitutional principle in the commonwealth of learning. In the course of developing his views, Bacon expressly condemned intellectual "democratie." He was not a believer in the virtues of the masses or commonality, and one of his most insistently recurring themes in all his writing—intellectual no less than political—concerned the dangers which the "popular" and the "vulgar" posed for progress. He stood squarely for a view of science which emphasized its closed, nonpublic character, just as he consistently sought to insulate the core workings of government from public view and public participation. His vision of science was elitist in its external face and hierarchical in its internal organization.[44]

Throughout his pathbreaking but unfortunately neglected *Francis Bacon and the Politics of Science,* Leary skillfully analyzes Bacon as a complex, aristocratic, authoritarian, self-indulgent luminary who was also a philanthropic, charitable Christian, and who, despite his "fear and contempt for the mass of humanity,"[45] as Zagorin notes, passionately pursued knowledge to provide "a rich storehouse, for the glory of the Creator and the relief of man's estate."[46] Accepting Bacon's frequent assertion that he was genuinely motivated by *philanthropia,* Leary observes that the self-aggrandizing "Bacon believed that it was the responsibility of princes and statesmen [like himself] to act as benefactors of the people." Motivated by political and religious principles, this "*philanthropia* might go hand in hand with paternalistic authoritarianism."[47]

Paternalistic authoritarianism aptly conveys Bacon's conception of how Salomon's House would function in the imaginary society he sketched in *The New Atlantis* after his fall from power in 1621. This significantly incomplete fable failed to specify in any detail the legal and political institutions required by a happy, healthy, peaceful, utopian society like Bensalem. Leary observes, however, that "the partial portrait of the political and social life that we get in the *New Atlantis* is quite consistent with the main outlines of Bacon's political thought."[48]

As previously noted, Rawley's assertion that *The New Atlantis* was written to inspire readers to duplicate the Salomon House model and thereby help create a real world of utopian societies makes it reasonable to identify Bacon as probably the first European scientific organizational and managerial theorist. Like many great theorists, he never implemented his theories by creating anything remotely like the "new scientific community" he had long dreamed of and envisioned leading. But if we analyze critically his imaginary Salomon's House and his other writings on the organization and management of scientific research, we can reconstruct the broad outline of his theory of how a scientific community should be scientifically organized and managed.

Bacon argued that science would progress only if the state handsomely supported a single, highly authoritarian, highly rational organization in which people worked collectively and collaboratively, "with clear lines of control running from the top downward so as to rationalize and direct the entire enterprise."[49] Salomon's House was broadly depicted as an extraordinarily well-equipped scientific research foundation, rigidly governed by an elite group of thirty-six carefully selected Fellows and a small, unspecified number of very vaguely described Fathers or Elders, who might also be Fellows. Divided into nine categories, the Fellows carried out different but highly interrelated functions, linked together to constitute a complex, integrated, powerful system that advanced scientific knowledge and produced a wide variety of beneficial works for the rest of the population.[50]

Ranked below the governing elite of Fellows and Fathers were two other groups. One group consisted of "novices and apprentices" eligible to become Fellows, as some of them eventually did. Very distinctly ranked below the novices and apprentices were "a great number of servants and attendants, men and women," whose tasks were to carry out the "menial work of science." Leary speculates that the Fellows were "undoubtedly provided with servants to relieve them from working on tasks which were demeaning or which constituted, in Bacon's view, a poor use of their intelligence and skill."[51]

Leary emphasizes that the governing elite had the power to decide which of their inventions and discoveries should be published and which kept secret from the state: "Just as it controls the flow of new products into society at large, so does . . . [the elite] control the flow of information."[52] Bacon's assumptions about how a hierarchical scientific organization would be managed clearly revealed his authoritarian, even dictatorial, personality, principles, and convictions. One of his major contributions to the advancement of learning and scientific knowledge was his emphasis on the need for organizations consisting of people who worked together collectively, collaboratively, complexly, and *continuously over generations.* Genuinely productive collaboration, he forcefully argued, required expert management by "an organizing authority" who would "divide the work to be into parts and . . . oversee the completion and integration of those parts." For Bacon, productive collaboration meant "more than the mere joining of human energies. It required that the designer of a collaborative science think in civil terms, and be attuned to the propensities of people—their strengths and weaknesses—and to the history of learning's failures. It required that the designers think not merely in terms of truth, but also in terms of power and that they be prepared not merely to exhort but to command."[53]

Although *The New Atlantis* was regrettably incomplete and partial with respect to how power would be exercised in Salomon's House and Bensalem society, Leary concludes, based on other writings, that Bacon's ideal scientific community operated in splendid isolation from "the mass of vulgar humanity," an elitist organization that "was itself subject to an internal regimen in which the labors of scientific inquirers were not merely joined (as in a team), but also rigidly regulated—a regimen which narrowly directed the members of the community, which constrained them, and which prescribed what they might and might not legitimately do. The organization which Bacon envisioned aspired to be comprehensive in the sense that virtually all the human factors which might bear on the success of scientific inquiry were to be brought under the jurisdiction of the regimen with little left to chance or to the free play of human faculties."[54]

Bacon was convinced that increasing collective power required curtailing individual freedom. His "program for the discovery of true and useful knowledge required that human energies and efforts be harnessed, rationalized, directed, and controlled in a new way." He in effect invented what centuries later came to be known as "Fordism-Taylorism." Leary's description supports our assessment of Bacon as a scientific organizational and managerial theorist:

> Thus Bacon's program for a new natural science, so often conceived as signaling the advent of a new relationship between man and nature, also reflects a new attitude toward humanity. People are now seen as factors in the production of knowledge. They must be understood as such and deployed as crucial elements in a rational system for the discovery and refinement of natural knowledge. They become, in

other words, a kind of matériel to be used and, from the standpoint of the scientific planner or director, objects to be arranged, manipulated, and deployed, rather than fellow subjects to be counselled and advised.[55]

It seems appropriate to complete this chapter by posing and answering this vital question: What was Bacon's impact—positive or negative—on the advancement of learning and the conditions under which people live? For our purposes, two major contributions and one negative effect are clear.

Two Propositions: Humankind's Capacity to Advance Learning and "the Relief of Man's Estate" | The Role of Historical Development in the Advancement of Learning

Bacon's most significant contribution to the advancement of learning and the betterment of humanity was to develop and try to implement the proposition that biologically, sociologically, and psychologically, human beings possess an unlimited capacity to continuously advance learning and thereby continuously improve their well-being. To realize this proposition in progressive, real world practice, Bacon set in motion a long-term historical movement to overthrow what Zagorin calls the "old regime of knowledge" and replace it with a radically new regime. Bacon's extraordinarily innovative new regime emphasized what he viewed as the scientific organization of collective, collaborative, interactive groups of workers, a system that would make them capable of developing the knowledge and power needed to continuously improve all aspects of human life through science, art, politics, medicine, and more. Action, innovation, discovery—these terms, expressed in a seventeenth century idiom, would no doubt have been in Bacon's lexicon. In Zagorin's judgment, Bacon was "unparalleled among contemporary philosophers in his strong consciousness of modernity and its possibilities, his understanding of the meaning of progress and faith in its prospects, and his attempt to create a novel way of thinking that would be fruitful in revealing the hidden processes of nature."[56]

Bacon's contribution to the advancement of learning and human well-being in effect integrated two of his wide-ranging theories:

1. To be successful, any activity combining collective, collaborative, interactive groups of workers to achieve a specific goal, or set of goals, required scientific management and organization.
2. If human beings were hopeful, optimistic, and scientifically organized and managed, they would make continuous progress in realizing the learning, knowledge, and power required to bring about

"the relief of man's estate," which Bacon viewed as the basic goal of philosophy and science.

Bacon's second major contribution was the proposition that to understand, explain, and continue to advance any specific area of learning required intensive study of its historical development over time and space. Bacon's contribution was, according to Rose-Mary Sargent, a stark contrast to "the hasty generalizations that had been produced prior to Bacon's time."[57] William Whewell, a mid-nineteenth-century authority on the progress of science cited by Sargent, claimed that Bacon brought about an "entire *change of the Method* by which science was pursued" (emphasis in original).[58] Sargent underscores Bacon's proposition on the important role of historical development in studies of the advancement of learning: "In true Baconian fashion, Whewell maintained that the philosophy of science must be based on the history of science." Since Bacon, she notes, science has advanced by, in Whewell's words, "a gradation of truths, successively included in other truths."[59]

Similarly, Zagorin emphasizes the importance for Bacon of intensive study of historical developments in accounting for both specific advances and the advancement of learning in general. Significantly, Bacon's philosophy attended "to the history of science and to the conditions that promoted and retarded the advancement of the knowledge of nature"; his approach was "both historical and sociological." Bacon wrote historically when he charted developments in Greek philosophy from the pre-Socratics onward; he wrote sociologically when "he pointed to limitations in the Greeks' knowledge of nature and the globe," which he contrasted with "new prospects" for advancing knowledge made possible by "recent inventions and geographical discovery." Zagorin hails Bacon as "among the first thinkers to see philosophy and science as an integral part of the history of civilization and to recognize the significance of understanding the intellectual and social conditions of the development of knowledge."[60]

Bacon's Negative Impact on the Advancement of Learning

Properly conceived and properly applied, Bacon's general theory that organized groups, not individuals working alone, were the best means to advance human learning was a brilliant contribution to human knowledge and "the relief of man's estate." But depending on how they are conceived and used, groups can produce either positive or negative outcomes. Given Bacon's radically elitist, authoritarian, dictatorial personality and fundamentally contemptuous beliefs about human nature, his conception of how groups of workers should be organized and managed would, in practice, have had negative consequences for the advancement of learning and human welfare.

Leary argues that Bacon saw the corruption and unruliness of human nature as a serious problem for both organized science and society. First, government had to muzzle the negative propensities of human nature and bring the mass of humanity within its "vigilant" embrace. Second, it had to devise a "comprehensive, rational plan" for effectively organizing and managing productive workers. These tasks required coercion by the state in both the social and the scientific spheres. In Bacon's scheme, "the people" were to be excluded from active roles in political as well as organizational matters. Accordingly, he envisioned and advocated the organization of science as a zone of hierarchically controlled exclusivity.[61]

We now turn to Bacon's intellectual heir: Benjamin Franklin, whose contributions to knowledge included a revolutionary theory of education and an organization designed to realize in practice "the relief of man's estate."

2

Benjamin Franklin's Revolutionary Theory of Education

Nothing is of more importance to the public weal, than to form
and train up youth in wisdom and virtue. Wise and good men
are, in my opinion the *strength* of a state: much more so than
riches or arms, which, under the management of Ignorance and
Wickedness, often draw on destruction, instead of providing for
the safety of a people.
—BENJAMIN FRANKLIN TO SAMUEL JOHNSON
(23 August 1750)

To suggest that it [the College of Philadelphia, which subsequently became the University of Pennsylvania] anticipated the
most enlightened program evolved by the liberal university of
the late nineteenth century is to speak with caution; in fact,
it stands out like a beacon light in the long history of human
intelligence.
—CHARLES AND MARY BEARD,
The Rise of American Civilization (1930)

Benjamin Franklin viewed Francis Bacon as one of the great figures in
world intellectual history. In 1749 Franklin published in *Poor Richard's
Almanack* an article that commemorated the death in 1626 of "Sir
Francis Bacon, *great* in his prodigious genius, parts, and learning." Noting
that Bacon is "justly esteem'd the father of the modern experimental philosophy,"[1] Franklin then quoted this poetic tribute to the "great deliverer" who
denounced "jargon-teaching schools" and who powerfully inspired Franklin's
own orientation to the advancement of learning and knowledge:

> *Him for the studious shade*
> *Kind nature form'd, deep, comprehensive, clear,*
> *Exact, and elegant; in one rich soul,*
> PLATO, *the* STAGYRITE, *and* TULLY *join'd,*
> *The great deliverer he! Who from the gloom*

Of cloister'd monks, and jargon-teaching schools,
Led forth the true Philosophy, there long
Held in the magic chain of words and forms,
And definitions void: He led her forth,
Daughter of Heav'n! that slow ascending still,
Investigating sure the chain of things,
With radiant finger points to Heav'n again.[2]

An ardent Baconian, contemptuous from an early age of scholasticism and existing institutions of higher education, passionately devoted to the "modern experimental philosophy," Franklin continuously acted on this fundamental, far-reaching Baconian proposition: creative, effective organization is mandatory if knowledge is to function as power for good and help morally inspired, scientifically oriented individuals develop and implement practical solutions to strategic problems affecting human well-being. As one Franklin biographer admiringly observes: "No man in his day better understood, or more often and successfully practiced, the techniques of cooperative action than Franklin. He applied principles of mechanics to benevolence. By uniting many small private energies into a voluntary joint stock association, he created engines with power for infinite good in the American community."[3] That insight can appropriately be stated in more general terms: To satisfy his lifelong categorical imperative to "do good," Franklin became a master real-world problem solver—in our terms, a "master scientist of management." A remarkably creative organizational theorist, he developed and demonstrated an unusual capacity to systematically integrate theory and practice by searching for, and implementing, pragmatic means to realize socially significant human ends. Knowledge functions as wisdom and power to do good, he believed, only when human beings develop and use it to engage in action-oriented, collaborative, real-world problem solving designed to satisfy strategic human needs.

Inspired and informed by Bacon's emphasis on the importance of organized cooperative action to advance knowledge and do good for human beings, Franklin also adhered to Bacon's "admonition" that knowledge should not be pursued for private gain. On the contrary, he too was passionately convinced that it must be charitably motivated and pursued "for the benefit and use of life," as Bacon wrote in the preface to *The Great Instauration*.[4] Franklin refused to profit from any of his numerous inventions. Instead of patenting them, he made them freely available to anyone who wished to use them. As the historian Michael Zuckerman forcefully observes: "With all his inventions, he held undeviatingly to an abhorrence of monopolistic exploitation of innovations that might better the human condition."[5] In Franklin's words: "*As we enjoy great Advantages from the Inventions of others, we should be glad of an Opportunity to serve others by any Invention of ours, and this we should do freely and generously*" (emphasis in original).[6] Given his Baconian motivation for the pursuit of knowledge and his "insatiable curiosity" about human and natural phenomena, we can easily see why Franklin "told friends and family alike, he much preferred to have it said, 'He lived usefully' than 'He died rich.'"[7]

Bacon, as we note in Chapter 1, forcefully and frequently argued that effective collaborative organization was indispensable to produce knowledge. But for scientific inquiry to produce continuous human betterment, he emphasized, two other conditions must also be satisfied. First, knowledge must be pursued for charitable motives. Second, the scope of research must not be one-sided: It must comprehend the planned, dynamic, systemic, organizationally based, integrated production and use of knowledge for specified ends-in-view. Absent those two conditions, Bacon predicted, in effect, that the new mode of scientific inquiry would have an arrogantly overreaching character—Faustian, Frankensteinian, Strangelovian, in our terms.

Put another way, Bacon claimed that organized research entailed both the production and the use of knowledge. If production was isolated or separated from use, the results would not be beneficial. For learning and knowledge to function for good, effective organization must dynamically and systemically plan for the integrated production and use of learning and knowledge. Undertaken for amoral or immoral reasons, one-sided concentration on the production of new knowledge would have dreadful consequences—a Baconian insight and prophecy whose truth and power, alas, we see daily and horribly confirmed in 2017.[8]

Like Bacon, Franklin strongly believed that to advance the common good it was indispensable to create organizations capable of effectively integrating the production and use of learning and knowledge. From an early age he trained himself to (1) identify real-world problems that significantly affected the common good, (2) conceive the kinds of organizations that could take the course of action most likely to help solve these problems, and (3) develop and implement the strategies and tactics most likely both to create those organizations and to enable them to take the necessary courses of action. "This practical emphasis," James Campbell observes, was "central to all of his thinking to improve human well-being. . . . In general, his scientific work was in large part the imaginative attempt to use human rationality to advance the common good." For Campbell, Franklin is "the original American Pragmatist" because the "Pragmatic view that the discoveries of natural philosophy must be put to use in the practical affairs of people, that we must apply the knowledge we have gained in science to advance human well-being, is central to Franklin's way of thinking."[9]

To support this assessment, Campbell quotes the 1771 volume of the *Transactions of the American Philosophical Society*—the Baconian-inspired organization Franklin had founded in 1743 and was president of in 1771: "Knowledge is of little use, when confined to mere speculation. But when speculative truths are reduced to practice, when theories, grounded upon experiments, are applied to the common purposes of life; and when, by these, agriculture is improved, trade enlarged, the acts of living made more easy and comfortable, and, of course, the increase and happiness of mankind promoted; knowledge then becomes really useful."[10] Bacon was not the only source of Franklin's pragmatic philosophy, but directly and indirectly, he was the *primary* intellectual source of the pragmatic philosophy from which Franklin derived his theory of education.

Having studied history intensely and reflected thoughtfully on his own life experiences, Franklin had become convinced that "nothing is of more importance for the public weal, than to form and train up youth in wisdom and virtue."[11] That is, radically contrary to Karl Marx's theory that the economic subsystem functioned as the strategic subsystem of society, Franklin theorized that the schooling system was the strategic subsystem. In 1749, therefore, he proposed that the flourishing, dynamic, and cosmopolitan city of Philadelphia establish a radically innovative institution of higher education to "obtain the Advantages arising from an Increase of Knowledge."[12]

Unlike existing institutions of higher education in America and Europe, the college Franklin founded was a secular institution. Deliberately unaffiliated with any religious denomination, the College of Philadelphia (which subsequently became the University of Pennsylvania) was dedicated to the advancement of scientific learning and knowledge for the benefit of humanity. The historians Charles and Mary Beard glowingly characterized the institution as "a beacon light in the long history of human intelligence."[13]

Despite Franklin's brilliant originality—or, more precisely, *because* the educational system he envisioned was so brilliantly original—he found it impossible to establish the college as the radically innovative institution he outlined in his paper on the "Idea of the English School."[14] As Franklin conceived it, instruction in such a school "would be conducted not in Latin, but entirely in English. The use of the vernacular language was the crucial issue and the main departure from the traditional school in Franklin's proposals, and he fully recognized its importance. English, the common tongue, would set the basis and the underlying tone of the new school. The use of the vernacular would save an immense amount of time, Franklin argued, and for most students preparing for a trade or profession, time was indeed precious."[15]

Franklin never changed his mind on this point: "Late in his life [in 1789] Franklin returned to the attack on the ancient languages, perhaps because he found their position [in American higher education] still unshaken. Commenting in his usual pungent style, he noted that Greek and Latin were 'the quackery of literature.' Further, he wrote that they were the '*chapeau bras*' of learning, like the hat carried by an elegant European gentlemen [*sic*], a hat never put on the head for fear of disarranging the wig, but always carried quite uselessly under the arm."[16]

Franklin's general theory and system of education departed too radically from the traditional classical conception of higher education to be fully accepted by the elites whose support was mandatory to establish a college in Philadelphia. Ever the pragmatic realist, he yielded to their demands. Contrary to his theoretical propositions, Latin and Greek were the dominant languages of instruction at the College of Philadelphia. Inevitably, therefore, it functioned in practice as a much less radically innovative institution than the one he had envisioned and hoped to establish. In relative terms, however, it was a more progressive institution for the "good Education of Youth" than had yet been established anywhere else in the world.[17]

In this chapter we try to sketch partial but useful answers to three questions:

1. What were Franklin's goals for higher education?
2. How would these goals be realized in the new American society?
3. What methods did he think would best achieve these goals?

Franklin's Goals for Higher Education

Franklin's goals for higher education clearly derive from his theory of human nature. Contradicting Thomas Hobbes's atomistic theory, Franklin assumed that "Man" is naturally sociable and has a "strong natural Desire of being valu'd and esteem'd by the rest of his species," is "naturally benevolent as well as self-ish," can think and act rationally, and is naturally endowed with a "Desire of Happiness."[18] To achieve happiness, Franklin believed, it was necessary both to satisfy "natural wants" (i.e., food, clothing, shelter) and to be virtuous.[19] In their analysis of Franklin's views on human nature, virtue, and happiness, Elizabeth Flower and Murray G. Murphey quote Franklin's proposition that "without Virtue Man can have no Happiness in this World" and then observe: "There is no opposition for Franklin between benevolence to others and seeking happiness for oneself: both are parts of the same broad injunction to maximize the happiness of all God's creatures."[20] Franklin developed an integrated philosophy of life and education that we believe affirmed three systematically interrelated and strongly interactive principles: Do good to others; do well for oneself; be happy.

Given his theory of human nature and philosophy of life, it comes as no surprise that Franklin regarded Virtue, by which he meant service to others—in its largest sense, service to humanity—as the ultimate goal of education. He wrote firmly against the grain of scholasticism, the prevailing thought-world of the European universities of his age, echoing Bacon's forceful criticisms of those institutions 150 years earlier. In Franklin's view, the true purpose of higher education was to supply young people with the knowledge, skills, and dispositions to do good. The college he envisioned would have had an *American* curriculum; taught in English, it would be pragmatic and utilitarian, suffused with "useful" knowledge. A pragmatic, benevolent businessman, Franklin believed that Americans, properly educated by their colleges, would be able and disposed to do good even as they strived to do well.

Galvanized by Bacon's contempt for traditional curricula and antiquated universities suffocating "from the gloom of cloister'd monks, and jargon-teaching schools," and by his own longstanding contempt for American colonial colleges like Harvard, which anachronistically tried to imitate them, Franklin wanted to create a radically different kind of college for the "good Education of Youth."[21] As he conceived the ideal American college, its moral and intellectual components were highly intertwined. Moreover, its ends and means would be logically and practically integrated. John Locke, as well as Bacon, strongly influenced Franklin's educational ideas. In *Proposals Relating to the Education of Youth in Pensilvania*, Franklin emphasized Locke's prescription for education: "'Tis *VIRTUE*, then, direct *VIRTUE*, which is to be aim'd at in Education."[22] After describing his own radically innovative curriculum, Franklin concluded his *Proposals* on this high note (the emphasis is his).

> With the whole should be constantly inculcated and cultivated, that *Benignity of Mind*, which shows itself in *searching for* and *seizing* every Opportunity *to serve* and *to oblige;* and is the Foundation of what is called GOOD BREEDING; highly useful to the Possessor, and most agreeable to all.
>
> The Idea of what is *true Merit*, should also be often presented to Youth, explain'd and impress'd on their Minds, as consisting in an *Inclination* join'd with an *Ability* to serve Mankind, one's Country, Friends and Family; which *Ability* is (with the Blessing of God) to be acquir'd or greatly encreas'd by *true Learning;* and should indeed be the great *Aim* and *End*† of all Learning.[23]

Franklin's footnote, designated by the dagger superscript, catches the essence of his public philosophy and devotion to the common good:

> To have in View the *Glory* and *Service of God*, as some express themselves, is only the same Thing in other Words. For *Doing Good to Men* is the *only Service of God* in our Power; and to *imitate his Beneficence* is to *glorify him.*[24]

Viewed in historical perspective and in light of Franklin's ardent Baconianism, his proposal for the reformation of higher education clearly was designed to give organizational form to Bacon's fervent "admonition" that utilitarian inquiry, learning, and schooling must be morally inspired, guided, and driven. Convinced, however, that morally inspired and intellectually challenging education is best developed in secular rather than sectarian institutions, Franklin strongly opposed colleges founded and controlled by religious denominations determined to promote their particular beliefs, rituals, and conceptions of morality.[25]

All the existing colonial colleges were religiously founded and affiliated. Like the European colleges they anachronistically imitated, the colonial colleges were therefore subject to ecclesiastical control and restricted intellectual freedom and scientific inquiry. In radical contrast to them, the college Franklin envisioned would function, morally and intellectually, as an American institution that exemplified secular humanism and practiced Enlightenment ideals.[26] As a result, it would be free to develop the vastly more liberal and useful program of higher education required by the radically new kind of society developing in America.

A New Kind of Society Requires a New Kind of Education

Franklin's contempt for the existing colonial colleges stemmed in part from his conviction that they were radically dysfunctional for the new kind of society that was dynamically developing in the New World of America—a new kind of society that he had empirically observed, directly experienced, and personally benefited from in its archetypal community, Philadelphia. The classical curriculum of the colonial institutions essentially reproduced in America the traditional English curriculum designed to produce gentlemen of leisure and privilege capable of leading a highly stratified society. To Franklin, the colonial colleges were guilty of what we call the "mistransference fallacy." That is, they mindlessly transferred to America the classical college for gentlemen, which would be highly dysfunctional for the rising middle class produced by American conditions that worked against hereditary social stratification and fostered upward social mobility. To account for the radical differences between social mobility in America and social stratification in the Old World, Franklin developed a brilliantly original theory of population growth and stability.[27]

Succinctly summarized, Franklin's theory, as detailed in his "Observations Concerning the Increase of Mankind, Peopling of Countries, &c." (1751), focused on the societal consequences of varying relationships between the amount and price of land and the amount and price of labor. In European countries, land was scarce in relation to the number of people. As a result, the price of land was high, the price of labor was low, population grew slowly or was stable, and social stratification was rigid. In America, the land was vast in relation to the population. As a result, Franklin theorized and empirically observed, the price of land was low, the price of labor was high, the population multiplied rapidly, the rate of social mobility was high and growing, and "in another Century . . . the greatest number of *Englishmen* will be on . . . [the American] Side [of] the Water."[28] His basic theoretical proposition was that "People increase in Proportion to the Number of Marriages, and that is greater in Proportion to the Ease and Convenience of supporting a Family. When Families can be easily supported, more Persons marry, and earlier in Life."[29]

What conditions determine that families *cannot* be easily supported? Families cannot be easily supported if "all Lands . . . [are] occupied and improved to the Heighth; those who cannot get Land, must Labour for others that have it; when Labourers are plenty, their Wages will be low; by low Wages a Family is supported with Difficulty; this Difficulty deters many from Marriage, who therefore long continue Servants and single."[30] What conditions differentiate America from Europe and produce radical differences in population growth and social mobility?

> *Europe* is generally full settled with Husbandmen, Manufacturers, &c. and therefore cannot now much increase in People. . . . Land . . . [is plentiful] in *America,* and so cheap as that a labouring Man, that understands Husbandry, can in a short Time save Money enough to purchase a Piece of new Land sufficient for a Plantation, whereon he may subsist a Family; such are not afraid to marry; for if they even look far enough forward to consider how their Children when grown up are to be provided for, they see that more Land is to be had at Rates equally easy, all Circumstances considered.
>
> Hence Marriages in *America* are more general, and more generally early, than in *Europe* . . . [and] our People must at least be doubled every 20 Years.[31]

Given this rapid increase in its population, America, according to Franklin, would not soon experience the European conditions that produce hereditary social stratification and work against social mobility. "Notwithstanding this Increase, so vast is the Territory of *North-America,* that it will require many Ages to settle it fully; and till it is fully settled, Labour will never be cheap here, where no Man continues long a Labourer for others, but gets a Plantation of his own, no Man continues long a Journeyman to a Trade, but goes among those new Settlers, and sets up for himself, &c. Hence, Labour is no cheaper now, in *Pennsylvania,* than it was 30 Years ago, tho' so many Thousand labouring People have been imported."[32]

Franklin's brilliantly original theory of population growth and stability explains not only why social mobility was so much greater in America than in England but also why, as his own life demonstrated, ambitious and able men, no matter what their background, could make their way to fame and fortune here. And given the radical differences in American and English social mobility, Franklin logically concluded that the college he envisioned for ambitious young Americans should differ radically from the English classical colleges and their American imitators—colleges designed to produce upper-class gentlemen of leisure and privilege.[33] Given its secular nature, Enlightenment orientation, and, above all, location in a radically new kind of society, it logically followed that Franklin's college would use radically innovative methods and texts to cultivate in its students both their "Inclination" and their "Ability" to do "Good to Men."

Curriculum, Methods, and Texts

The college Franklin envisioned broke with the classical tradition and gave instruction entirely in the vernacular language. His radicalism is best appreciated if we note that all the existing colonial colleges required applicants for admission to be proficient in Latin and Greek. The historian of education Bruce Kimball offers a succinct summary of the classical curriculum and methodology:

> Apart from divinity, freshmen devoted nearly all their time to Greek grammar for "testament" and Latin grammar in orations, plus some arithmetic. Sophomores continued these studies while undertaking rhetoric, including perhaps some belles lettres in the vernacular, and picking up logic and advanced arithmetic or algebra. Juniors continued Latin, Greek and rhetoric and passed through algebra, geometry, and perhaps trigonometry or "fluxions," along with a course in natural philosophy. Seniors reviewed the previous three years, studied metaphysics, took the crowning course in moral philosophy from the president, and received more exposure to natural philosophy in the spring term if there was time. This generalized frame of studies was pursued through the long-standing practice of recitations and declamations, with the lecture format slowly creeping in.[34]

An American college's curriculum, methodology, and texts, Franklin theorized, should be appropriate for the education and development of *American* youth. For a college in Philadelphia to insist on instruction in Latin and Greek and a curriculum dominated by intensive study of classical texts in their original languages simply exemplified the disastrous tendency "in mankind [to] an unaccountable Prejudice in favour of ancient Customs and Habitudes, which inclines to a Continuance of them after the Circumstances, which formerly made them useful, cease to exist."[35] Franklin followed Bacon's lead and, in effect, repudiated Plato's highly speculative theory of the relationship between knowledge and wisdom.[36] As the authors of a magisterial history of American philosophy paraphrase Franklin's argument: "Knowledge is wisdom only if it is useful for the satisfaction of [human] needs: hence in all his schemes for the promotion and diffusion of knowledge, Franklin emphasized 'useful knowledge.'"[37]

Rather than succumb to "an unaccountable Prejudice" and historical inertia, Franklin wanted instruction to be given in English, based on texts in English, and supplemented by active and challenging exercises performed in English. That would create the necessary conditions for American students to learn how to adapt to their physical, social, and moral environments and develop the character, habits, and forms of expression they needed to pursue interrelated benevolent and practical goals and lead virtuous and happy lives.

Franklin's *Proposals* made History and English the primary subjects of the curriculum, to be taught in ways that helped students develop both their "Inclination" and their "Ability" to do good. That is, they should learn not only to want to do good but also how to do the particular good they want to do. Franklin's educational theory rested on the effective integration of ends and means: He explicitly specified both the goal he wanted to achieve and, in great detail, the means to achieve it.[38]

Students' inclination and ability to do good are best developed when they learn from concrete historical examples, not when "abstract Philosophical Lectures" are delivered to them.[39] "Indeed," Franklin argued, "the general natural Tendency of Reading good History, must be, to fix in the Minds of Youth deep Impressions of the Beauty and Usefulness of Virtue of all Kinds, Publick Spirit, Fortitude, &c."[40] To support this argument for using history to achieve those interrelated and interactive goals, Franklin quoted George Turnbull's treatise on *Liberal Education*: "History points out in Examples, as in a Glass, all the Passions of the human Heart, and all their various Workings in different Circumstances, all the Virtues and all the Vices human Nature is capable of; all the Snares, all the Temptations, all the Vicissitudes and Incidents of human Life; and gives Occasion for Explaining all the Rules of Prudence, Decency, Justice and Integrity, in private Oeconomy, and in short all the Laws of natural Reason."[41]

Among other benefits, Franklin asserted, students would learn from history "the wonderful Effects of ORATORY in governing, turning and leading great Bodies of Mankind, Armies, Cities, Nations." However, instead of relying exclusively on conventional historical texts, particularly those referring to ancient times, Franklin advocated the radical innovation of teaching the power and methods of oratory by using texts drawn from modern journalism. "Modern Political Oratory," he observed, "being chiefly performed by the Pen and Press, its Advantages over the Antient in some Respects are to be shown; as that its Effects are more extensive, more lasting, &c."[42]

Franklin's conception of how history should be taught and learned was broad. It should be taught in such a way that "almost all kinds of useful knowledge . . . [could be] introduc'd to Advantage, and with Pleasure to the Student." Among the subjects that could and should be studied historically, Franklin cited geography, chronology, ancient customs, morality, and commerce.[43] He proposed that students explore the history of commerce—in innovative ways that would help them better understand "Mechanical Philosophy," as well as how interrelated technological and economic changes produced significant societal changes and significantly improved the quality of human life:

> The History of Commerce, of the Invention of Arts, Rise of Manufactures, Progress of Trade, Change of its Seats, with the Reasons, Causes, &c. may also be made entertaining to Youth, and will be useful to all. And this, with the Accounts in other History of the prodigious Force and Effect of Engines and Machines used in War, will naturally introduce a Desire to be instructed in Mechanicks, and to be inform'd of the Principles of that Art by which weak Men perform such Wonders, Labour is sav'd, Manufactures expedited, &c. &c. This will be the Time to show them Prints of antient and modern Machines, to explain them, to let them be copied, and to give Lectures in Mechanical Philosophy.[44]

In addition to emphasizing the practical use of studying the history of commerce, Franklin emphasized the practical value of "Natural History" (an eighteenth-century term for science):

> With the History of Men, Times and Nations, should be read at proper Hours or Days, some of the best *Histories of Nature,* which would not only be delightful to Youth, and furnish them with Matter for their Letters, &c. as well as other History; but afterwards of great Use to them, whether they are Merchants, Handicrafts, or Divines; enabling the first the better to understand many Commodities, Drugs, &c. the second to improve his Trade or Handicraft by new Mixtures, Materials, &c. and the last to adorn his Discourses by beautiful Comparisons, and strengthen them by new Proofs of Divine Providence. The Conversation of all will be improved by it, as Occasions frequently occur of making Natural Observations, which are instructive, agreeable, and entertaining in almost all Companies. *Natural History* will

also afford Opportunities of introducing many Observations, relating to the Preservation of Health, which may be afterwards of great Use."[45]

Breaking even more radically with the classical curriculum and methodology, Franklin added that the students should, in effect, "learn by doing" (as John Dewey later termed the method). While students were "reading Natural History, might not a little Gardening, Planting, Grafting, Inoculating, &c. be taught and practiced; and now and then Excursions made to the neighboring Plantations of the best Farmers, their Methods observ'd and reason'd upon for the Information of Youth. The Improvement of Agriculture being useful to all, and Skill in it no Disparagement to any."[46]

Learning by doing also applied to the study of English and the development of writing skills. In his paper on the "Idea of the English School," Franklin noted that in addition to critically reading the "best English authors" and innovative texts such as contemporary magazine articles,[47] students should continuously practice "Writing Letters to each other on any common Occurrences, and on various Subjects, imaginary Business, &c. containing little Stories, Accounts of their late Reading, what Parts of Authors please them, and why. Letters of Congratulation, of Compliment, of Request, of Thanks, of Recommendation, of Admonition, of Consolation, of Expostulation, Excuse, &c. In these they should be taught to express themselves clearly, concisely, and naturally, without affected Words, or high-flown Phrases. All their Letters to pass through the Master's Hand, who is to point out the Faults, advise the Corrections, and commend what he finds right."[48]

Learning by doing was not restricted to letter writing. Students should also "write little Essays in Prose; and sometimes in Verse, not to make them Poets, but for this Reason, that nothing acquaints a Lad so speedily with Variety of Expressions, as the Necessity of finding such Words and Phrases as will suit with the Measure, Sound and Rhime of Verse, and at the same Time will express the Sentiment. These Essays should all pass under the Master's Eye, who will point out their Faults, and put the Writer on correcting them."[49]

Additional examples of Franklin's innovative methods and texts would only belabor the point. The college Franklin envisioned would have developed both a highly pragmatic, integrated, interactive set of goals and the means to achieve them, radically transforming American higher education. Instead of equipping a small number of upper-class students to become cultivated and socially prominent gentlemen in a highly stratified society, Franklin proposed to educate a large number of non-elite members of a socially mobile, rising middle class, who would possess both the "Inclination" and the "Ability" to "serve Mankind, one's Country, Friends and Family." As Edward Potts Cheyney regretfully observed in his *History of the University of Pennsylvania, 1740–1940*, the college Franklin envisioned would have provided "an education for citizenship" and led to "mercantile and civic success and usefulness." We say "regretfully observed" because Cheyney concluded his discussion on a somber, critical note: "It is unfortunate that it was never tried."[50]

The Burden of "Ancient Customs and Habitudes"

Viewed in historical perspective, we can see that Franklin's proposal for the New World reformation of higher education was designed to give organizational form to Bacon's fervent "admonition" that utilitarian inquiry, learning, and schooling should be morally inspired, guided, and driven. Both Bacon and Franklin asked, "What are the true ends of knowledge" (and learning), and why should they be sought? In Bacon's words, they should be sought "not either for the pleasure of the mind, or for contention, or for superiority to others, or for profit, or fame, or power, or any of these inferior things."[51] Positively stated in Franklin's eighteenth-century secular terms, they should be sought for "Doing Good to Men."

Unlike the appeals made for all the other colonial colleges, Franklin's proposal to establish a college in Philadelphia did not seek support on religious grounds. Nor did it base its appeal solely on the high-minded Baconian and Lockean grounds sketched above. On the contrary: Though less blatantly than promoters of other colonial colleges (e.g., the Brown brothers of Providence, Rhode Island), Franklin emphasized that his proposal would bring significant economic benefits to Philadelphia. Although he envisioned a college dedicated to what we would term "education for virtue," he argued that it would also produce education for profit (also our term).[52] Consciously or not, Franklin ignored the contradictions and tensions inherent in any educational institution designed to pursue such radically different aims.

Soon after the college began operation in 1751, Franklin left Philadelphia on a variety of missions that essentially kept him in Europe for more than thirty years. The men who controlled and managed the college during his long absence were strongly committed, in both theory and practice, to the traditional classical model. Nothing resembling Franklin's proposed Baconian reformation of higher education, therefore, was ever put into practice in Philadelphia—or anywhere else, to our knowledge.

Shortly before he died in 1790, Franklin angrily denounced the trustees of what by then had become, through a remarkably convoluted process, the University of Pennsylvania. Their disastrous "Deviations" from his original plan, he charged, their deceptions and bad faith, had produced an institution criticized severely by "the Publick" and suffering financially from the "great Loss of Revenue" brought about by their terrible "Mismanagement." Instead of conducting the institution along the lines of his innovative and utilitarian

English School, they had run a traditional college based on the outmoded Latin and Greek languages wholly unsuited to "such a country as ours."[53]

Why had the trustees followed this conservative, disastrous course? Franklin's answer to his own question invoked the general historical theory of intellectual and institutional inertia that Dewey would later invoke to explain his own failure to bring about progressive innovations in the American schooling and political systems. To repeat Franklin's own summary statement of the inertia theory (which he may well have gotten from Bacon): "There is in Mankind an unaccountable Prejudice in favour of ancient Customs and Habitudes, which inclines to a Continuance of them after the Circumstances, which formerly made them useful, cease to exist."[54]

A "Prejudice in favour of ancient Customs and Habitudes," in our judgment, continues to be an obstacle to the radical transformation of research universities into engaged, cosmopolitan institutions dedicated to the advancement of learning and knowledge for "the relief of man's estate." In Chicago at the turn of the twentieth century, Jane Addams at Hull House and William Rainey Harper as president of the University of Chicago worked tirelessly to overcome that prejudice. Addams developed an innovative and successful activist social settlement, and Harper envisioned and attempted to create a modern university that would help America realize and fulfill its intellectual and democratic promise.

3

William Rainey Harper
and Jane Addams

Progressive Era Organizational Innovation
and the American Research University

The real world is not to be found in books. That [real world] is peopled by men and women of living flesh and blood, and the great city can supply the human quality which the broad-minded man must not suffer himself to lack.

—SETH LOW, Inaugural Address,
Columbia University (1890)

As the college changed from teaching theology to teaching secular knowledge the test of its success should have shifted from the power to save men's souls to the power to adjust them in healthful relations to nature and their fellow men. But the college failed to do this, and made the test of its success the mere collecting and disseminating of knowledge, elevating the means into an end and falling in love with its own achievement.

—JANE ADDAMS,
"A Function of the Social Settlement" (1899)

A university which will adapt itself to urban influence, which will undertake to serve as an expression of urban civilization, and which is compelled to meet the demands of an urban environment, will in the end become something essentially different from a university located in a village or small city.

—WILLIAM RAINEY HARPER, "The Urban University,"
The Trend in Higher Education (1905)

William Rainey Harper, the first president of the University of Chicago (1890–1908), understood that the university he headed was inextricably part of and heavily dependent on the fortunes of the city of Chicago. The university, he insisted, was to be directly engaged in contributing to the city and ameliorating a myriad of urban problems. Harper's story is part of a larger social reform narrative of the Progressive Era that indispensably includes Jane Addams and the women of Hull House. The Chicago of Harper's new research university and of Addams's Hull House was no average American city; it was the city that Carl Sandburg powerfully described in his famous poem "Chicago":

> HOG *Butcher for the World,*
> *Tool Maker, Stacker of Wheat,*
> *Player with Railroads and the Nation's Freight Handler;*
> *Stormy, husky, brawling,*
> *City of Big Shoulders . . .*[1]

Fin de siècle Chicago was a burgeoning city of immigrants—41 percent of a total population of more than one million in 1890[2]—a city riven with political and economic corruption, labor violence, and grinding poverty. "On the faces of women and children I have seen the marks of wanton hunger," wrote Sandburg.[3] It was a city that called for Addams's activist social settlement and Harper's locally engaged urban university.

To better understand Harper's extraordinary contribution to learning, knowledge, and society, it is useful to place his work at the University of Chicago within the context of the American research university at the time of his presidency. This context also helps to illuminate the pioneering role Addams and Hull House played in the development of scientific social research designed to contribute to social reform.

The American Research University in the Progressive Era

The creation of the American research university in the late nineteenth and early twentieth centuries radically and irrevocably transformed higher education. Among other things, advancing democracy became the defining purpose of both public land-grant and private urban universities. Political scientist Charles Anderson brilliantly captures the "extraordinary recasting of historic predispositions"[4] that occurred during the early decades of the American research university:

> The classic understanding was that the life of philosophy, of self-conscious reflection, was the highest of human attainments, and reserved to the very few. Even in modern times, it has normally been assumed that the capacity for reflective intelligence was rather unevenly distributed. The work of the university was taken to be essentially aristocratic. It dealt with the higher questions. It prepared the qualified for

the *learned* professions. The university's role was rational speculation, and in the hierarchy of human interests this was thought to be quite remote from the concerns of everyday life.

With deliberate defiance, those who created the American university (particularly the public university, though the commitment soon spread throughout the system) simply stood this idea of reason on its head. Now it was assumed that the widespread exercise of self-conscious, critical reason was essential to *democracy*. The truly remarkable belief arose that this system of government would flourish best if citizens would generally adopt the habits of thought hitherto supposed appropriate mainly for scholars and scientists. We vastly expanded access to higher education. We presumed it a general good, like transport, or power, part of the infrastructure of the civilization.

Furthermore, it was assumed that not only the exalted subjects, but the humblest ones as well, were properly the subject of rational analysis. Thus, if we could improve philosophy, science, literature, and the arts through systematic critical analysis, we could do the same for agriculture, commerce, and home economics.[5] (Emphasis in original)

Anderson's description resonates with the words and actions of the founders and early leaders of the American research university. In 1876 Daniel Coit Gilman, in his inaugural address as the first president of Johns Hopkins, America's first modern research university, expressed the hope that universities would "make for less misery among the poor, less ignorance in the schools, less bigotry in the temple, less suffering in the hospital, less fraud in business, less folly in politics."[6] Belief in the democratic purposes of the research university echoed throughout higher education at the turn of the twentieth century. In 1908 Harvard's president Charles W. Eliot wrote: "At bottom most of the American institutions of higher education are filled with the democratic spirit of serviceableness. Teachers and students alike are profoundly moved by the desire to serve the democratic community. . . . This is a thoroughly democratic conception of their function."[7]

University presidents of the late nineteenth and early twentieth centuries worked to develop the American university into a major national institution capable of meeting the needs of a rapidly changing and increasingly complex society. Imbued with boundless optimism and a belief that knowledge could change the world for the better, these "captains of erudition" envisioned universities as leading the way toward a more effective, humane, and democratic society for Americans in general and residents of the city in particular. Progressive academics also viewed the city as their arena for study and action. They seized the opportunity to advance knowledge, teaching, and learning by working to improve the quality of life in American cities experiencing the traumatic effects of industrialization, immigration, and large-scale urbanization. This animating mission to advance knowledge "for the relief of man's estate" is readily identified in the histories of leading urban universities at the turn of the twentieth century, including Johns Hopkins, Columbia, and the University of Chicago.[8]

As president of Hopkins from 1875 to 1902, Gilman was the guiding force behind the Charity Organization Society (COS). Designed to provide a social-scientific approach to ameliorating poverty in Baltimore, the COS studied the causes of poverty, collected data, and worked to get at the root causes of destitution. Leading members of Gilman's faculty, including Herbert Baxter Adams and Richard Ely of the Department of History, Political Economy and Political Science, had close ties to Levering Hall, the campus branch of the Young Men's Christian Association, which was deeply engaged in work in the city's distressed neighborhoods. Students in Adams's and Ely's classes worked through Levering Hall "to use the city as a laboratory for economic study." John Glenn, chair of the executive committee of COS, remarked in 1888 that Hopkins was the first university where social welfare work was "almost a part of the curriculum."[9]

Hopkins was certainly not the only university to link social welfare work to the curriculum. Progressive Era academics viewed the city as an appropriate and valuable site for study and action. It was the center of significant societal transformation and of political corruption, poverty, crime, and cultural conflict, as well as a ready source of data and information. For Richard Mayo-Smith of Columbia, the city was "the natural laboratory of social science, just as hospitals are of medical science." It was, in short, the logical site for creative faculty and students to integrate theory and practice.[10]

Yet Progressive Era university presidents and academics, by and large, did not view local communities as reciprocal partners from whom they and their students could learn in the complex process of identifying and solving strategic community problems. University-community engagement was essentially a one-way enterprise motivated by elitism and *noblesse oblige*. University "experts" armed with scientific knowledge would identify community problems and authoritatively prescribe solutions, not work collaboratively with community members in a mutual relationship from which both groups might benefit and to which both groups would contribute knowledge, ideas, and insights. The expert's role was to study and assist, not to learn from and with, the community.[11]

There is no denying that William Rainey Harper largely shared this authoritative, elitist conception of the university's role. Nevertheless, we view him as a transformative president. He not only created one of the world's great research universities; he also recognized—and acted on the recognition—that a civically engaged and community-engaged urban university was essential to democracy. It was Seth Low, however, who, while president of Columbia University (1890–1901), first conceptualized and called for a *democratically engaged urban university.*

While falling far short of Harper and the University of Chicago in practice, Low provided a decidedly more democratic vision of Columbia's relationship with New York City and its communities. In his inaugural address, Low stated, "The city may be made to a considerable extent, a part of the university." Columbia was also to be part of the city, resulting in a democratic, mutually beneficial relationship between town and gown. In an article entitled "The University and the Workingman," Low wrote that the "workingmen of America . . . [should know] that at Columbia College . . . the disposition exists to teach the truth . . . without fear or favor, and we ask their aid to enable us to see the truth as it appears to them."[12] Low embraced New York City as the source of Columbia's greatness. He not only brought "the College into closer touch with the community" but also significantly improved Columbia by encouraging faculty and students to focus their intellectual work on helping New York solve its problems.[13]

A mediocre institution in the 1870s and 1880s, Columbia was widely viewed as a snobbish school for rich young men. Upon assuming the presidency, Low made his goal clear: "I am desirous," he told an alumnus, "to build Columbia into a great university, worthy of New York."[14] He took the occasion of his inaugural address to emphasize that Columbia was not simply *in* New York City but *of* New York City.[15] He echoed Bacon's proposition that the purpose of scholarship is service for the betterment of humanity:

> Consider for a moment the significance to the college of a great city about it. First of all, it means for every one of us that *there is no such thing as the world of letters as apart from the world of men.* There are such things, undoubtedly, as most unworldly scholars, men oftentimes "of whom the world is not worthy," but such scholars are never made except out of men who see humanity, as in a vision, ever beckoning from behind their books. The scholar without this vision is a pedant. He mistakes learning for an end in itself, instead of seeing that it is only a weapon in a wise man's hands. (Emphasis added)[16]

Low went beyond posing and answering the question "knowledge for what?" He called on students to become engaged directly with the city and its communities. Engagement with and study and action in New York City, according to Low, would produce educated, prepared, and moral students, as well as significant contributions to knowledge:

The real world is not to be found in books. That [real world] is peopled by men and women of living flesh and blood, and the great city
can supply the human quality which the broad-minded man must not
suffer himself to lack. There is a variety of life in this city, a vitality
about it, and, withal, a sense of power, which, to my thought, are of
inestimable value to the student whose desire it is to become a well-
rounded man. . . . There is but one New York on all this continent,
and, for the purposes of technical and professional training, her location in New York supplements the work of Columbia with advantages
not elsewhere to be had. So, also, I believe the great city will lend itself
readily to the encouragement of profound research. As there is no
solitude like that of a crowd, so there is no inspiration like it.[17]

In effect repudiating Plato's Groves of Academe and the physical and intellectual separation of town and gown, Low identified a mutually beneficial,
interactive relationship between Columbia and the city as crucial to intellectual and institutional advancement. He even invoked Bacon's standard of
progress as the test of inquiry and research—specifically, Columbia's ability
"to influence the life of New York."[18]

Low's presidency was in general a success. As one authority has noted, "By
1901, Seth Low had taken a small, dissension ridden college and made it into
a great university. He had taken a financially undernourished institution and
infused it with great quantities of fresh money, and, by building Columbia a
new home [on Morningside Heights], he had made certain that the university
would remain in the City of New York."[19] Low's vision of a cosmopolitan, democratic, civic university, however, was significantly ahead of its time. He was
unable to galvanize faculty sentiment to organize anything like the University
of Chicago's outreach activities. He himself participated in University Settlement, on New York's Lower East Side, and encouraged Columbia faculty to lecture in working-class venues like Cooper Union, but otherwise his rhetoric fell
on deaf ears. The relative brevity of his tenure, especially in contrast with the
imperious forty-three-year reign of his successor, Nicholas Murray Butler, and
the continued dominance of Plato's aristocratic, scholastic, elitist educational
theory in American colleges and universities also limited Low's influence.

Jane Addams's Hull House: Organizational Innovation, Knowledge Production, and Social Change

Of all universities, Harper's University of Chicago, in practice, had the closest
ties to its locality. Work emanating from Hull House, the social settlement
founded by Jane Addams and Ellen Gates Starr on Chicago's West Side in

1889, was enormously significant in forming ties between the university and its city. Adopting a multifaceted institutional approach to the social problems of the immigrant groups in the Nineteenth Ward, Hull House residents offered activities along four lines designated by Addams as the social, educational, humanitarian, and civic. In addition to its various residents' programs, Hull House was a site for labor union activities, a forum for social, political, and economic reform, and a center for social science research. Regarding its research function, Addams noted, "The settlements antedated by three years the first sociology departments in universities and by ten years the establishment of the first foundations for social research."[20]

Addams emphasized the benefits that accrued to the activist social worker from engagement with the community and its problems. "'There is nothing after disease, indigence and a sense of guilt, so fatal to health and to life itself as the want of a proper outlet for active faculties,'" she wrote. Yet "a fast-growing number of cultivated young people . . . have no recognized outlet for their active faculties. They hear constantly of the great social maladjustment, but no way is provided for them to change it, and their uselessness hangs upon them heavily."[21] Women particularly felt the lack of constructive social outlets for their reform impulses, constricted as they were by Victorian gender roles. Settlement work provided them with a satisfactory professional outlet that was not incommensurate with established gender roles and practices, particularly the idea of the "women's sphere."[22] Addams acknowledged this when she remarked that "many women today are failing properly to discharge their duties to their own families and households simply because they fail to see that as society grows more complicated, it is necessary that woman shall extend her sense of responsibility to many things outside of her home, if only in order to preserve the home in its entirety."[23]

For activist-oriented young women and men of Addams's generation, settlement work was, in her apt phrase, a "subjective necessity." In 1889 Starr told a friend that "Jane's idea, which she puts very much to the front and on no account will give up, is that [the settlement] is more for the people who do it than for the other class."[24] The inspiration and model for "Jane's idea" was Toynbee Hall, an East London settlement house founded in 1884 and organized by Oxbridge graduates for the benefit of the poor and working classes of St. Jude's Parish. Addams herself later wrote, "I hope it will never be forgotten in Chicago, at least where Hull House feels somewhat responsible for the Toynbee Hall idea, that Toynbee Hall was first projected as an aid and outlet to educated young men. The benefit to East Londoners was then regarded as almost secondary, and the benefit has always been held as strictly mutual."[25]

In 1895 Addams and the residents of Hull House—notably Florence Kelley, Agnes Holbrook, and Julia Lathrop—published *Hull-House Maps and Papers,* a sociological investigation of the neighborhood immediately to the east of Hull House; in Addams's words, it was a record of "certain phases of neighborhood life with which the writers have become most familiar."[26] Inspired by Charles Booth's *Labour and Life of the People in London,* the Hull House residents compiled detailed maps of demographic and social characteristics and produced richly descriptive accounts of life and work in a poor immigrant neighborhood.[27] Theirs was not dispassionate scholarship, as evidenced by Kelley's poignant advocacy for sweatshop laborers, whose "reward of work at their trade is grinding poverty, ending only in death or escape to some more hopeful occupation."[28]

It is no overstatement to call the creation of Hull House as an activist-academic center of learning and social change an organizational landmark in the production of knowledge. In effect, Hull House represents the real-world implementation of Bacon's imaginary Salomon's House, a model college for organizing and managing scientific research (see Chapter 1). Hull House, of course, went far beyond Bacon's concept, creating a residential community that integrated living, learning, knowledge production, civic involvement, and local neighborhood improvement. Moreover, Addams's Hull House functioned as an actual demonstration of the benefits of significant, sustained engagement with the problems of a city and its communities. It is reasonable to assume that it served as the "proof of concept" and inspiration for Harper's creation of a truly urban university organized and developed through planned interaction with its environment.[29]

In its early years, the University of Chicago demonstrated that by doing good, a research university could do very well. It is not surprising that male sociologists at the University of Chicago were closely associated with Hull House, acknowledging that "it was Addams and Hull House who were the leader and leading institution in Chicago in the 1890s, not the University of Chicago." Indeed, as the historian Mary Jo Deegan forcefully argues, *Hull-House Maps and Papers* "established the major substantive interests and methodological technique of Chicago Sociology that would define the School for the next forty years."[30]

The Chicago School of Sociology was created in this nexus of "serving society by advancing intellectual inquiry."[31] In the early years of the Chicago School, no invidious distinctions were made between the applied, activist sociology pursued by Addams and the Hull House residents and the academic research of the first generation of University of Chicago sociologists. The two groups had a close working relationship, grounded in personal friendships, mutual respect, and shared social philosophy. Four men of the early Chicago School—Albion Small, Charles Henderson, Charles Zeublin, and George Vincent—were ministers or ministers *manqué,* intellectual Social Gospellers with strong civic commitments. (The exceptions, with limited theological proclivities, were George Herbert Mead and William I. Thomas.) Like the women of Hull House, the Chicago sociologists were "social activists and social scientists."[32] Activist social research Chicago-style encompassed scholarly documentation of a social problem and lobbying of politicians and local community groups to obtain action.[33]

Addams herself strongly believed that Hull House, not the University of Chicago (or universities in general), represented the organizational vehicle that would most effectively advance learning, knowledge, and civic and community life. Committed to maintaining her and the settlement house's independence, she declined Harper's offer to have Hull House absorbed by the university. In 1895, in a strongly worded letter to Harper, Addams unequivocally rejected his proposal, emphasizing the special contribution and unique value of the settlement house:

> Of course, we must feel that any absorption of the identity of Hull-House by a larger and stronger body could not be other than an irreparable misfortune, even although it gave it a certain very valuable assurance of permanency. Its individuality is the result of the work of a group of people, who have had all the perplexities and uncertainties of pioneers. This group is living in the 19th Ward, not as students, but as citizens, and their methods of work must differ from that of an institution established elsewhere, and following well defined lines. An absorption would be most unfair to them, as well as to their friends and supporters, who believe that the usefulness of the effort is measured by its own interior power of interpretation and adjustment.[34]

Addams, indeed, was sharply critical of higher education's abstract, academic approach and growing disdain for application. In a 1899 paper delivered to the American Academy of Political and Social Science, she argued that the settlement house, with its "attempt to test the value of human knowledge by action" and "effort to apply knowledge to life," was far superior to the university, which had lost its way through the "mere collecting and disseminating of knowledge" for its own sake:[35]

> Having thus the support of two philosophers [John Dewey and William James, whom Addams quoted in a previous paragraph], let us assume that the dominating interest in knowledge has become its use, the conditions under which, and ways in which it may be most effectively employed in human conduct; and that at last certain people have consciously formed themselves into groups for the express purpose of effective application. These groups which are called settlements have naturally sought the spots where the dearth of this applied knowledge was most obvious, the depressed quarters of great cities.

They gravitate to these spots, not with the object of finding clinical material, not to found "sociological laboratories," not, indeed, with the analytical motive at all, but rather in a reaction from that motive, with a desire to use synthetically and directly whatever knowledge they, as a group, may possess, to test its validity and to discover the conditions under which this knowledge may be employed.[36]

Later in her paper, Addams's argument developed a striking resonance with the Bacon-Franklin critique of higher learning and knowledge production. She observed that the purpose of the early "Anglo-Saxon" colleges was the training of "religious teachers" who would "prepare the mass of the people for life beyond the grave." For Addams, such an education held the application of knowledge as an end in view: "Knowledge dealt largely in theology, but it was ultimately applied, and the test of the successful graduate, after all, was not his learning, but his power to save souls." With the ascendancy of secular knowledge in the colleges, she insisted, "The test of its success should have shifted from the power to save men's souls to the power to adjust them in healthful relations to nature and their fellow men. But the college failed to do this, and made the test of its success the mere collecting and disseminating of knowledge, elevating the means into an end and falling in love with its own achievement."[37]

William Rainey Harper and the University of Chicago: The Urban University as the Strategic Institution for Improving Communities, Schools, and Society

William Rainey Harper did not share Addams's critique—at least when it came to his own university. His strategy from the outset was to connect the University of Chicago to the city in order to help solve its complex, integrated problems and develop a real-world laboratory for producing knowledge, community improvement, and institutional advancement. Darnell Rucker, in his illuminating study of *The Chicago Pragmatists*, wrote:

The University of Chicago quickly became an important part of the social ferment in Chicago. The University of Chicago Settlement [House] took its place in the stockyards district in 1894 to work along with Hull House. President Harper served on the Chicago Board of Education [and chaired its commission on school reorganization] and a large number of his faculty were actively engaged in work with the elementary and secondary schools of Chicago and other sections of Illinois. The faculty also provided members and chairmen for a wide range of organizations and commissions concerned with philanthropy, improved sanitation, slum clearances, cultural developments, waterways, labor legislation, strike settlements, and a host of other activities. Such practical endeavors were encouraged as fitting for a university, providing a broad field for testing ideas and theories. In fact Harper defended the emphasis upon pure science in the university by pointing out that "sooner or later in an environment like that of Chicago the practical side would be sufficiently cared for." Therefore the university was immediately concerned with intellectual inquiry into all sorts of problems, while the city around it provided a vast laboratory for testing solutions.[38]

Even before his appointment in 1890 as the first president of the University of Chicago (which formally did not begin operation until 1892), Harper was a notable innovator in the teaching and organization of religious studies. A passionately dedicated and creative scholar, he had become a leading biblical authority at an early age. According to Harper's biographer, James P. Wind, "Scholars in the emerging profession of Old Testament Studies looked to Harper as their dean." Harper not only studied the Old Testament; his "fundamental vision" for the University of Chicago was inspired by it.[39] Wind writes:

> In the Hebrew Scriptures Harper found the raw material that provided the ground of his personal beliefs, the field of his professional competence and the paradigm for reshaping education in America. Within those cherished texts, Harper discerned a God at work in history lifting humanity toward a still to be realized "higher life." The most fundamental idea of all for him was that God moves some to suffer vicariously for others. Israel suffered for the scattered nations; Jesus suffered for a fallen humanity; the biblical scholars struggled to provide new meaning for suffering moderns; and the university, in its grappling with the great problems of the ages, was called to suffer for society in order that all its members might ascend to higher life. Ultimately, Harper's vision was messianic. He traced the messianic idea from its prophetic origins up to its application in his day; indeed he could claim without batting an exegetical eye—that the university was "Messiah."[40]

Inspired by this vision, Harper's seminally important theoretical contribution was to identify the university as the strategic institution for creating a truly democratic society: an institution with the singular, "holy" purpose of being the "prophet of democracy."[41] No other university president so passionately and farsightedly envisioned the university's democratic potential and purpose. Profoundly religious and deeply dedicated to the progressive Social Gospel, Harper conceptualized the university as the holy place designed to fulfill democracy's creed—"the brotherhood, and consequently the equality of man"[42]—through "service for mankind wherever mankind is, whether within scholastic walls or without those walls and in the world at large."[43]

In his 1899 essay "The University and Democracy," Harper presented a radical, uniquely American idea of the university in powerful, moving language:

> The university, I contend, is this prophet of democracy—the agency established by heaven itself to proclaim the principles of democracy. It is in the university that the best opportunity is afforded to investigate the movements of the past and to present the facts and principles involved before the public. It is the university that, as the center of thought, is to maintain for democracy the unity so essential for its success. *The university is the prophetic school out of which come the teachers who are to lead democracy in the true path.* It is the university that must guide democracy into the new fields of arts and literature and science. It is the university that fights the battles of democracy, its war-cry being: "Come, let us reason together." It is the university that, in these latter days, goes forth with buoyant spirit to comfort and give help to those who are downcast, *taking up its dwelling in the very midst of squalor and distress.* It is the university that, with impartial judgment, condemns in democracy the spirit of corruption which now and again lifts up the head, and brings scandal upon democracy's fair name. . . . The university, I maintain, is the prophetic interpreter of democracy; the prophet of her past, in all its vicissitudes; the prophet of her present, in all its complexity; the prophet of her future, in all its possibilities. (Emphasis added)[44]

For Harper, the new urban university, in particular, would be the strategic agent to help America realize and fulfill its democratic promise. Daniel Coit Gilman of Johns Hopkins and Seth Low of Columbia enthusiastically seized the opportunity to build their institutions by working to improve the quality of life in American cities, but Harper went much further than his presidential colleagues when he predicted that an institutional transformation—a positive mutation—would result if universities engaged in planned interaction with their urban environments. At Nicholas Murray Butler's inauguration as president of Columbia University in 1902, Harper prophetically hailed those intellectual and institutional advances: "A university which will adapt itself to urban influence, which will undertake to serve as an expression of urban civilization, and which is compelled to meet the demands of an urban environment, will in the end become something essentially different from a university located in a village or small city."[45]

In the same address, Harper, in effect, invoked John Dewey's fundamental premise that major advances in knowledge tend to occur when human beings consciously work to solve the central problems confronting their society. "The urban universities found today in three or four of the largest cities in this country . . . and in [Europe]," Harper stated, "form a class by themselves, inasmuch as they are compelled to deal with problems which are not involved in the work of universities located in smaller cities. . . . Just as the great cities of the country represent the national life in its fullness and in its variety, so the urban universities are in the truest sense . . . national universities." To conclude his address, he proclaimed that of all the great institutions in New York City, Columbia University was "the greatest."[46] In Chicago, Harper certainly believed, his university held that preeminent position. Harper's messianic thesis viewed the university as the prime mover of modern democratic societies.

As these quotations demonstrate, long before Clark Kerr hailed the post–World War II American "multiversity" as the most important institutional innovation of the mid-twentieth century,[47] Harper advanced the theory that the new urban university was the strategic organizational innovation of modern society. Logically, therefore, he placed great importance on his university's engagement with the severe problems confronting its dynamically growing city, particularly its public school system. By helping to solve the city's problems, Harper hoped to gain enthusiastic support for his new university from Chicago's wealthy elite, especially those members who shared his interest in improving the public schools. What might be called Harper's institutional pragmatism, therefore, was highly compatible with, indeed powerfully reinforced, his theoretical conviction that collaborative, action-oriented, real-world problem solving was the best strategy to advance knowledge and learning.

Harper's theory of democracy in industrial societies saw the schooling system functioning as the leading societal subsystem, and its continuing development and effective integration from the elementary school to the university as essential for democratic progress. Harper worked tirelessly to make his university in that major city function as the center of an integrated web of midwestern schools, academies, and colleges dedicated to fulfilling democracy's "mission to the world."[48]

We have noted that for all his commitment to democracy, Harper believed that expert guidance was essential to administering a democratic society. His vision, in other words, was decidedly *not* one of participatory democracy. The historian Daniel Lee Meyer explains Harper's position:

Despite the egalitarian thrust of his democratic idealism, Harper recognized the important role to be played by an educated and university trained elite. "The University is of the people, and for the people," said Harper, sounding the democratic anthem; but he also stressed that a democratic society could be administered only if it was prepared to accept "the guidance of those who have been prepared to lead," and quoted approvingly Gladstone's remark that "The nation draws a great, perhaps the greatest, part of its light from the minority placed above." The elite to be drawn from the ranks of the university would guide the public in deciding difficult questions of policy and serve as a pool from which would come "leaders in the different callings in whom the people may have full confidence," the "university men" who would in time "occupy high places throughout the earth."[49]

One of Harper's "university men" who would occupy a very high place in the first half of the twentieth century was John Dewey, the prophet of participatory democracy, who by 1894 chaired two departments at Chicago: Philosophy and Pedagogy. Even before the university began formal operations in October 1892, Harper had "expressed some interest in establishing a school of pedagogy," primarily to attract students to the new university and gain support from wealthy Chicagoans interested in improving the city's public schools. He was at first unimpressed with the utility of courses in pedagogy, but creating the Department of Pedagogy helped him recruit Julia E. Bulkley as the university's first dean of women. Harper was impressed with Bulkley's organizational abilities, but "she insisted that her responsibilities at the university include work in education." Acceding to her demands, he appointed her to the rank of associate professor of pedagogy, gave her a leave of absence until 1895 to travel to Europe and secure a Ph.D., and staffed the Department of Pedagogy with a teaching fellow from the Department of Philosophy.[50]

Dewey was not Harper's first choice for head of the Philosophy Department. Dewey owed his appointment to James H. Tufts, an assistant professor in that department, who had been a colleague of Dewey's in Michigan. Aware of the vacancy, Tufts wrote a letter to Harper strongly recommending Dewey on several grounds. None were related to pedagogy or schools, nor were any of the "more important publications of Professor Dewey" that Tufts listed to support his recommendation.[51]

To our knowledge, no document exists that helps explain why Harper appointed Dewey as head of the Department of Pedagogy (which he had created in 1892) or the Department of Philosophy. (Pedagogy and Philosophy continued to be separate departments headed by Dewey for several years.) Harper may have wanted to justify acceding to Dewey's demand for a salary of five thousand dollars, rather than the four thousand dollars originally offered. Bulkley was still on leave in Europe. Moreover, by 1894 Harper's views on pedagogy had changed dramatically. He was now actively engaged in the accelerating efforts to improve the Chicago public school system and wanted to strengthen his university's Department of Pedagogy. Appointing a respected full professor of philosophy to head it might achieve that goal and appeal to the city's elite as well. Dewey's appointment as head of the Department of Pedagogy is best understood as resulting from a series of events related to public education in Chicago that had transformed Harper's interests in education. So complete was the transformation that when a university trustee criticized him for sponsoring a journal focused on pedagogy in precollegiate schools, Harper proclaimed, "As a university we are interested above all things else in pedagogy."[52]

Harper's conversion logically derived from two propositions central to his messianic vision for the University of Chicago in particular and American universities in general:

1. "Education is the basis of all democratic progress. The problems of education are, therefore, the problems of democracy."[53]
2. More than any other institution, the university determines the character of the schooling system: "Through the school system, the character of which, in spite of itself, the university determines and in a large measure controls . . . through the school system every family in this entire broad land of ours is brought into touch with the university; for from it proceed the teachers or the teachers' teachers."[54]

Given these two propositions and the role Harper assigned the American university as the "to-be-expected deliverer"[55] of American democracy, he theorized that the major responsibility of universities is the performance of the schooling system as a whole. If the American schooling system does not powerfully accelerate "democratic progress," then American universities are performing poorly—no matter whatever else they are doing successfully. "By their democratic fruits shall ye know them" is the pragmatic Baconian performance test that Harper, in effect, prescribed for the American university system.

By the time Dewey arrived in Chicago from the University of Michigan in July 1894, Harper was playing a prominent role in a campaign by leading citizens and powerful civic groups to radically change public education in the city.[56] Given Dewey's limited interest in education and work in that area while he was in provincial Ann Arbor, it seems clear to us that it was Harper's intense commitment to school reform that influenced Dewey's ideas about education and society once he was, in Robert Westbrook's description, "thrust . . . into the maelstrom of the prototypical metropolis of industrializing America."[57]

During his ten years at Chicago, Dewey's work was powerfully influenced, both directly and indirectly, by Harper's vision, program, and wide-ranging activities. Harper's stress on pedagogy and education helped Dewey see that the schooling system was the strategic agency to help institute the society based on participatory democracy that he had envisioned in his path-breaking essay "The Ethics of Democracy" (1888). It was only after Dewey came to Chicago that he essentially adopted Plato's educational strategy as the best approach to the Good Participatory Democratic Society. Chicago was also where Dewey, through Addams's influence, concluded that schools functioning as social centers were the best means to realize that society in practice.

4

John Dewey and
the Community School Idea

The pressing thing, the significant thing, is really to make the
school a social centre; that is a matter of practice, not of theory.
Just what to do in order to make the schoolhouse a centre of
full and adequate social service to bring it completely into the
current of social life—such are the matters, I am sure, which
really deserve the attention of the public and that occupy your
own minds.

—JOHN DEWEY, "The School as Social Centre" (1902)

In Chapter 1 we noted Dewey's eloquent paean in *Reconstruction in Philosophy* to Bacon, "the great forerunner of the spirit of modern life," for
whom progress was the pragmatic real-world test of "genuine knowledge."
Bacon's emphasis on "active experimentation" and "logic of discovery," as well
the benefits to be obtained by "the organization of co-operative research," profoundly influenced Dewey's variant of pragmatism, which he called "experi-
mentalism."[1]

Yet for all the inspiration Dewey drew from Bacon, Plato was the philosopher he most liked to read, even though their worldviews differed radically—Plato's aristocratic and contemplative, Dewey's democratic and activist.
Despite their differences, Dewey's immersion in the dynamic Chicago schooling environment led him to see the value of the ideas Plato had developed in
The Republic concerning relationships between education and society.[2] Citing
Immanuel Kant's proposition that "the greatest and most difficult problem to
which man can devote himself is the problem of education," the philosopher
Steven M. Cahn observes that he knows

of two major philosophers who exemplified this principle in their philosophical work: One was Dewey, the other was Plato. He too found
it difficult to discuss any important philosophical problem without
reference to the appropriateness of various subjects of study, methods
of teaching, or strategies of learning. But while Dewey's philosophy of
education rested on his belief in democracy and the power of scientific

method, Plato's philosophy of education rested on his belief in aristoc-
racy and the power of pure reason. Plato proposed a planned society,
Dewey a society engaged in continuous planning. Plato considered
dialectical speculation to be the means toward the attainment of truth;
Dewey maintained that knowledge is only acquired through intelligent
action.... Suffice it to say that John Dewey is the only thinker ever to
construct a philosophy of education comparable in scope and depth
to that of Plato.[3]

Like the ancient Greek philosopher, Dewey theorized that education and society were dynamically interactive and interdependent. It followed, therefore,
that if human beings want to develop and maintain a particular type of society or social order, they must develop and maintain the particular type of
educational system most conducive to it—without an effective democratic
schooling system, no democratic society.

It is important to emphasize another radical difference between Plato and
Dewey. To implement his aristocratic philosophy of education and society,
Plato created the Academy—in a sense, the first university—whose elitist,
idealist philosophy of education continues to dominate Western schooling
systems to this day. Surprisingly, Dewey never saw what Plato—and William
Rainey Harper—saw so clearly: Universities are invariably the most strategic
component of a society's schooling system. Dewey's failure to see this had disastrous consequences. His work on education pays remarkably little attention
to the role of universities, and therefore he never developed the comprehensive
strategy necessary to realize in practice the democratic system of "school and
society" that he so passionately desired and so passionately preached.

Having noted this significant omission in Dewey's theory—to which we
will return—we now take up his project: to construct a comprehensive, democratic, practical-theoretical approach that would free Western thought and
the institutions of Western societies from Plato's "dead hand," an approach
that would, in our term, "de-Platonize" their social, political, and educational
systems.[4] The instrumental means *and* end-in-view of Dewey's comprehensive project was participatory democracy, a term he did not coin but whose
meaning he specified along with the general conditions that would be necessary for its development.[5]

Participatory Democracy in Schooling
Systems and Societies

Probably the clearest statement of Dewey's fundamental proposition that a
participatory democratic society must be based on a participatory democratic
schooling system is found in his 1897 essay "Ethical Principles Underlying

Education." The essay addressed a strategic problem that had to be solved for Dewey's vision of participatory democracy to be realized in practice—namely, what *practical means* could be developed and implemented to achieve his utopian theoretical end? More generally, what conditions had to be satisfied for all individuals to be capable of participating actively, effectively, and wholeheartedly in the authoritative decision-making processes of their community and society, and thereby realize their fullest personal development? Dewey's answer to this question was that a public schooling system would have to be developed that would provide a student with "training in science, in art, in history; command of the fundamental methods of inquiry and the fundamental tools of intercourse and communication . . . a trained and sound body, skillful eye and hand, habits of industry, perseverance, and above all, habits of serviceableness." Moreover, for the student to be an active, effective member of a "democratic and progressive society," he "must be educated for leadership as well as for obedience. He must have power of self-direction and power of directing others, power of administration, ability to assume positions of responsibility." And since society is now—and in the future certainly will be—changing rapidly,

> it is an absolute impossibility to educate the . . . [student] for any fixed station in life. . . . [Thus] the ethical responsibility of the school on the social side must be interpreted in the broadest and freest spirit, . . . which will give him such possession of himself that he may take charge of himself; may not only adapt himself to the changes which are going on but have power to shape and direct those changes. . . . Apart from the thought of participation in social life the school has no end nor aim. . . . The fundamental conclusion is that the school must be itself made into a vital social institution to a very much greater extent than obtains at present. . . . Excepting in so far as the school is an embryonic yet typical community life, moral training must be . . . [severely deficient]. Interest in the community welfare, an interest which is intellectual and practical, as well as emotional—an interest, that is to say, in perceiving whatever makes for social order and progress, and for carrying these principles into execution—is the ultimate ethical habit to which all the special school habits must be related.[6]

By 1897, when Dewey published "Ethical Principles Underlying Education," he was deeply engaged in developing an elementary school at the University of Chicago. Though it was designed to aid the work of the Department of Pedagogy and was therefore partly subsidized by the university, it was essentially a private school founded by Dewey and almost completely controlled by him. Officially named the Laboratory School of the University of Chicago, it soon acquired the sobriquet "the Dewey School." Dewey had conceived it as a scientific laboratory to develop educational theories and empirical propositions that would radiate out and revolutionize the entire American schooling system.[7]

Dewey's Laboratory School and His Scientistic Fallacy

Dewey discussed his educational ideas most fully in *The School and Society* (1899), a collection of essays drawn from the experience of the Dewey School. In this book, which catapulted him into the role of world-famous educator, and in subsequent writings, Dewey sought to lead a crusade to transform, modernize, and democratize the American schooling system. In the process, he developed a general theory of instrumental intelligence derived from the proposition that intelligence is not a fixed quality. Intelligence, like speech, is an *innate capacity* that human beings possess by virtue of their unique biological nature as human organisms. People can develop their innate capacity for intelligence by using it *instrumentally* to solve the multitude of strategic problems that inevitably confront them in their daily lives from birth until death—and by reflecting on their experiences and thereby increasing their capacity for *future* intelligent thought and action. Intelligence does not develop simply as a result of problem-solving action and experience; it develops best as a result of *reflective, strategic,* real-world problem-solving action and experience. Education is a powerful means human beings have evolved to develop their innate biological capacity to solve problems by thinking and acting purposefully, effectively, and reflectively. Dewey further emphasized that action-oriented, collaborative, real-world problem-solving is the most powerful means to raise the level of instrumental intelligence in individuals, groups, communities, societies, and humanity in general. To provide the education that would develop and advance this kind of problem solving, good modern schools were necessary. But the existing American schools were not good modern schools. Dominated almost entirely by the medieval conception of learning, traditional schools reflected their intellectual origins in Plato's theory of education for a "good" aristocratic social order.

Dewey viewed existing American schools as stultifying places dominated by the philosophy and methods of the "old education." For various reasons and in various ways, they were structured to suppress children's natural curiosity, eagerness to learn, and dynamic activism. Summarizing his indictment, Dewey charged that the typical features of the "old education" are "its passivity of attitude, its mechanical massing of children, its uniformity of curriculum and method. It may be summed up by stating that the centre of gravity is outside the child. It is in the teacher, the text-book, anywhere and everywhere you please except in the immediate instinct and activities of the child himself."[8] In short, he charged that traditional American schools were unnatural institutions that confined, repressed, and failed children rather than directing and educating them healthily and liberally.

To replace traditional schools based on the "old education," Dewey advocated a radically "new education" that would combine the best qualities of the "apprentice-like, household-and-community problem-solving, informal natural learning system of preindustrial society" (our lengthy term for Dewey's concept) with the stimulating, liberating, and enlightening qualities of formal public schools organized according to the new functional psychology and instrumentalist theory of knowledge that he was developing.[9] To test and develop his theoretical ideas, he founded the Laboratory School of the University of Chicago and directed it from 1896 to 1904.

The Laboratory School curriculum was sequentially organized around the history of American economic development. Proceeding from the early grades, children recapitulated in school aspects of the history of occupations that Americans had practiced in community and society from colonial days to the present. That is, consonant with Dewey's commitment to active rather than passive learning, as children advanced from grade to grade, they not only studied but "actually practiced" (in a very limited way, of course) the main occupations of successive generations of Americans, including weaving, sewing, cooking, and metallurgy. The children worked experimentally and cooperatively as they discovered why wool preceded cotton in the history of cloth manufacturing; they examined the effects of scalding, simmering, and boiling water on eggs; and they built a miniature smelting furnace, among other construction activities.[10] The purpose, Dewey emphasized, was not manual training: it was to enable children attending school to benefit from the functional equivalent of the active roles children played in the household and community life of preindustrial society. The goal was to give them, in his famous phrase, a "first-hand contact with actualities."[11] Yet the Laboratory School, despite Dewey's brilliant insights and best intentions, was flawed by a fundamental contradiction. To explain this contradiction, it is critical to recognize that the operations of the Laboratory School were profoundly shaped by the experimental psychological laboratory that Wilhelm Wundt had established at the University of Leipzig and by Wundt's philosophical and psychological theories.

Wundt founded psychology as a separate discipline and in 1879 created the first laboratory in the world dedicated to experimental psychology. His theories and methodology powerfully influenced the development of Dewey's "functional psychology and his instrumentalist version of pragmatism."[12] Once we recognize this influence, we can see more clearly that Dewey's Laboratory School was quite literally conceived as a scientific laboratory to test and develop educational theories, and we can better appreciate why its students could not benefit from the real-world problem solving that Dewey brilliantly theorized was the best way to engage their intense, sustained interest and develop their capacity for reflective critical inquiry and collaborative practical action. The Laboratory School exemplified *scientism*—"an exaggerated trust in the efficacy of the methods of natural science applied to all areas of investigation (as in philosophy, the social sciences and the humanities)"— not science.[13] Dewey used "un-Deweyan" means to try to achieve his instrumentalist, democratic, humanist goals for American public schools.

Rather than presenting a detailed critique of Dewey's program to transform American public schools, we need only note that his Laboratory School did not (and by its scientistic, decontextualized nature could not) solve the problems he posed: how to help children learn by "do[ing] things with a real motive behind and a real outcome ahead"; how to connect what children did in school with what they did outside school; how to combine the benefits of the preindustrial learning system with the benefits that could be derived from a modern, cosmopolitan, activity-based, formal schooling system; and how to minimize each system's particular disadvantages and optimize its advantages.[14]

The Laboratory School of the University of Chicago was just that: an unnatural, artificial *university laboratory* isolated from American life as it was lived or had been lived. Instead of functioning as a natural laboratory that experimentally studied the real, complex links between school and community, the school was effectively isolated from the community and society in which its pupils lived. In contrast, the informal learning system of preindustrial society was deeply rooted in, and functioned as an integral part of, the local geographic community in which children lived and their families made their livings.

Unlike the real occupations of children in preindustrial communities, from which they gained first-hand, direct experience of the world, confronting real problems that they were forced to try to solve, "with a real motive behind and a real outcome ahead," students in the Laboratory School practiced make-believe, simulated occupations and solved simulated problems unconnected to contemporary household or community problems. As Dewey acutely and strongly emphasized, in the preindustrial informal learning system, children learned by real-world, consequential doing as helpers and apprentices to adults in activities like tanning and leatherworking, barn raising, blacksmithing, hog scalding, and furniture making. But in the isolated, artificial Laboratory School that his scientism led him to develop, children learned by inconsequential doing of well-structured problems whose solutions were well known, presented no real challenge, and required no real imagination or initiative. The Laboratory School was—and could only be—a simulated pseudo-community, not the real "miniature community" or "embryonic society" Dewey imagined it to be.[15] It did not practically connect school and community; it created a radical disjunction between them.

Given its scientistic nature, unusually great resources, extraordinarily high teacher-to-student ratio, and insulation from *fin de siècle* Chicago and the intense conflicts fragmenting the American societal and schooling systems at the time, the Laboratory School was remarkably unrepresentative of American public schools as they were or as they *could be* in the foreseeable future. There was little to no reason, therefore, to believe that lessons learned from the Laboratory School could be transferred to traditional public schools and "ordinary" teachers without a great deal of sophisticated, painstaking analysis, translation, and adaptation. Even if the Laboratory School worked well for its own students, it was far from obvious that the model it developed would work well for the great majority of students in American public schools.[16]

As Robert Westbrook has observed, most Laboratory School "students were from professional families, many of them the children of Dewey's colleagues." To practice "Deweyan pedagogy" effectively in the school's simulated world, teachers had "to be highly skilled professionals, thoroughly knowledgeable in the subject matter they were teaching, trained in child psychology, and skilled in the techniques of providing the stimulus necessary to make the subject matter part of the child's growing experience." The fact that the world-famous Laboratory School of the University of Chicago, directed by the world-famous Dewey, could attract those "highly skilled professionals" did not mean that traditional public schools would be able to.[17]

Dewey's crusade to transform the American public school failed, among other reasons, because his scientism so distorted his practice that the *specific solution* he proposed was scholastic, academic, impractical, and unrealistic. We emphasize *specific solution* because we strongly agree with his *general* theories, propositions, and orientation and are convinced that, appropriately applied, they can be highly practical. They can radically transform contemporary American public schools for the better and, in the process, help solve the Dewey Problem—that is, develop the means to construct a participatory democratic society in America.

One of Dewey's best general ideas was "the school as social centre," inspired by Addams and the women of Hull House. With this idea, his theorizing took a practical turn toward a restructuring of urban schooling that would, unlike the Laboratory School, take account of real-world social conditions and the threats to American democracy engendered by rapidly changing social and economic conditions.

Addams and Hull House: Dewey's "School as Social Centre"

William Rainey Harper powerfully influenced Dewey's work on education during his ten years at the University of Chicago (see Chapter 3), but in many ways Dewey benefited even more significantly from his warm friendship and close association with Addams and the other Hull House settlement workers who were struggling to improve the quality of life for the poverty-stricken immigrant residents of their Chicago neighborhood.[18] Their work—and the powerful theories they derived from it—led Dewey to see both the critical role that local communities played in American society and ways in which public schools could function as strategic agents to develop participatory democratic communities. Those communities, in turn, would be the organizational foundation of the "organic" participatory democratic society he had envisioned in his democratic manifesto, "The Ethics of Democracy" (1888).[19]

Addams in Chicago, Lillian Wald in New York City, and other deeply motivated, socially concerned, brilliantly creative settlement house workers pioneered the transfer of social, health, cultural, and recreational services to the public schools of major U.S. cities at the turn of the twentieth century. Theoretically guided, community-based, and community-engaged, these feminist settlement leaders observed that although there were very few settlement houses, there were many public schools. "Every neighborhood public school a neighborhood settlement house" sums up the vision that impelled settlement leaders to function as strategically important school reformers during the late nineteenth and twentieth centuries. Inspired by their innovative ideas and impressed by their practical community activities, in 1902 Dewey presented a brilliantly prophetic, highly influential address, "The School as Social Centre," at a National Educational Association conference.[20]

Viewed in historical perspective, Dewey's address clearly anticipated some of the key ideas and principles of the variously named "community school" movements that rose and fell in the United States during the twentieth century and are rising again now. Thanks in considerable measure to his close association with Addams and Hull House, by 1902 Dewey experienced Chicago differently than he had in 1894 when he first conceived and began to organize what became the Laboratory School. That may explain why the concrete, practical content of his address to the National Educational Association differed so radically from the abstract philosophical and theoretical concerns that had motivated him to organize the school.

By 1902 Dewey recognized that enormous "industrial and commercial changes and adjustments" were producing a radically new type of society—one in which the "old education" was increasingly anachronistic. In this radically new society, "social, economic and intellectual conditions are changing at a rate undreamed of in past history. Now, unless the agencies of instruction are kept running more or less parallel with these changes, a considerable body of men [i.e., people] is bound to find itself without the training which will enable it to adapt itself to what is going on." In this radically new society, community life was increasingly riven by racial, class, and religious conflict, and becoming "defective and distorted."[21]

Through his interactions with Addams and others at Hull House, Dewey saw that only a radically new conception of schooling could provide a way out of these dilemmas, as well as hope for the future of American democracy. The American schooling system and urban schools in particular would have to assume a much broader societal role than the one traditionally assigned to them under the terms of the "old education," which was to ramrod "intellectual instruction" into children. Dewey recognized that the settlement idea offered an appropriate model for this radical reconstruction, acknowledging Hull House as "the working model upon which I am pretty continuously drawing."[22] Rebuilt in the spirit of the settlement house, the school would be "a center of life for all ages and classes . . . a thoroughly socialized affair in contact at all points with the flow of community life"; it would educate *all* members of the community to participate effectively in "all the relationships of all sorts that are involved in membership in a community."[23]

Evening social, educational, and recreational programs would draw adults into "the school as social centre." Here they would have opportunities to mix and interact "under wholesome influences and under conditions which will promote their getting acquainted with the best side of each other." The school as social center would provide and direct "reasonable forms of amusement and recreation. The social club, the gymnasium, the amateur theatrical representation, the concert, the stereopticon lecture—these are the agencies the force of which social settlements have long known." Specialized classes would be offered "in music, drawing, clay-modeling, joinery, metal-working, and so on," even "scientific laboratories . . . for those who are particularly interested in problems of mechanics or electricity; and so the list might be continued." Here Dewey presciently emphasized the need for "continuous instruction," which we now call "lifelong learning," and the school's responsibility to "provide at least part of that training which is necessary to keep the individual properly adjusted to a rapidly changing environment."[24]

In Dewey's conception, the neighborhood school would function, in effect, as a "social clearing house" where face-to-face communication would be the stock in trade, "where ideas and beliefs may be exchanged, not merely in the arena of formal discussion—for argument alone breeds misunderstanding and fixes prejudice—but in ways where ideas are incarnated in human form and clothed with the winning grace of personal life. Classes for study may be numerous, but all are regarded as modes of bringing people [and 'their ideas and beliefs'] together, of doing away with barriers of caste, or class, or race, or type of experience that keep people from real communion with each other."[25] School social centers would be alive with "social intercourse," a term by which Dewey meant the collaborative sharing of goods of the type necessary for full personal development of all members of the community: "the intangible things of art, science, and other modes of social intercourse." These are not finite. Because they are unlimited, neither individuals nor communities need to compete in zero-sum games to secure them. On the contrary, "social intercourse" focused on the sharing of such goods could both enrich and strengthen the community.[26] By 1902 Dewey viewed the neighborhood school as uniquely well positioned to function as the central institution of the local community because—in principle, though not yet in practice—it was uniquely well positioned to bring about a socialism of goods relating to "the intelligence" and "the spirit."[27] Much of the history of twentieth-century community school movements can be viewed as a series of failed attempts to identify and develop the concrete approaches and activities needed to realize in practice what Dewey believed community schools could do in principle.

The Schooling System as the Strategic Subsystem of Modern Societies

Having paid Dewey the homage of criticizing him when we thought it appropriate, we now praise him for the strategic contributions "The School as Social Centre" made to the analysis of the internal functioning of modern societal systems and, in particular, to community school movements. Perhaps his greatest contribution was his farsighted observation that during the twentieth century, the schooling system would function as the strategic subsystem of the increasingly complex industrial and "postindustrial" societies produced by the post-1800 economic and communication revolutions. To use the term now in vogue, Dewey predicted that the school-based operations of "civil society" would become more important than the traditional functions performed by the state in solving "the difficult problems of life."[28] Just as he saw citizenship expanding to take on functions that were beyond the capacity of the state in an advanced capitalist society, he saw an expanded role for the school in preparing citizens to assume those functions.

Extending Dewey's observations into the twenty-first century, we can say that it is not the judicial, legislative, and administrative state, but rather the complex schooling system of American society, from early childhood centers to elite research universities, that (1) functions as the *strategic subsystem* of the society, (2) has performed that function poorly in the past and continues to do so, *at all levels,* (3) must radically improve its performance, at all levels, if we hope to solve the problems of American life, and (4) can be radically reformed only if questions about its performance (in the past, present, and likely future) are given the highest priority by action-oriented researchers and administrators dedicated to advancing knowledge for "the relief of man's estate," which Bacon specified as the goal of science.

This does not imply that in 1902 Dewey said exactly what we have just stated. Because we stand on his shoulders and are blessed by 20/20 hindsight, we believe that the course of history justifies our extension of what he actually did say in that year. We have such a high regard for "The School as Social Centre," as well as such a high estimation of its influence on our neo-Deweyan strategy to achieve a participatory democratic schooling system and society, that we feel it is not far-fetched to say that what the *Communist Manifesto* was for Marx, "The School as Social Centre" was for Dewey.

It is crucial to recognize that Dewey had little or nothing to say about two critically important functions of the community school: (1) as a community institution actively engaged in the solution of community problems, and (2) as a community institution that educates children, intellectually and morally, by engaging them *appropriately* and *significantly* in real-world community problem solving—as children were educated in the informal, natural learning system of preindustrial society. Dewey ignored both possible functions, even though they were logically entailed in his general theory of "learning by doing."

Dewey's analysis of the complex social consequences of late-nineteenth- and twentieth-century "industrial and commercial changes and adjustments" was farsighted and creative.[29] He did not use the specific terms "advanced industrial society" and "world economy," but the phenomena that those terms designate are emphasized in his analysis. His argument, freely recast, was that the development of advanced industrial societies in an increasingly worldwide economy produced an unprecedented set of complex societal problems—so unprecedented and so complex as to require radical reconstruction of social and political theory.

Existing social and political theories could not provide solutions for the multitude of problems suddenly manifesting themselves. They were inadequate because they had been inspired by very different types of problems in very different types of societies. Dewey claimed that neither the operations of the private-enterprise "free-market" system developed in the nineteenth century nor the operation of governmental systems as they had traditionally functioned over the centuries could solve the new and myriad problems produced by the new type of advanced industrial society. "The School as Social Centre" was a pioneering, insightful attempt to reconstruct and update social and economic theory to deal more effectively with the unprecedented set of problems confronting members of advanced industrial societies in the twentieth century.

If neither the operations of the "free market" nor the traditional operations of government could cope with those problems, which institution—or combination of institutions—could? Dewey's answer essentially pointed to the local community.

How, specifically, could the community carry out those unprecedented responsibilities? Primarily, Dewey answered, *through the neighborhood school,* organized and functioning as a social center "for all classes of whatever age."[30] In essence, inspired by the work of Hull House, Dewey's pioneering reconstruction of social and political theory called for the neighborhood school, a publicly owned site, to act as a publicly controlled and organized catalyst to bring people together and develop local coalitions of neighbors to solve a multitude of suddenly emerging problems.

Viewed in historical perspective, Dewey's 1902 address clearly anticipated some of the key ideas of the democratic community school movements of the twentieth century. His ideas about communities and community schools can be logically extended and developed to suggest a practical solution to the Dewey Problem: What is to be done beyond theoretical advocacy to transform American society and other developed societies into participatory democracies capable of helping to transform the world into a "Great Community"? Our proposed solution, in its simplest form, is based on the idea that community schools, appropriately developed and powerfully assisted by institutions of higher education and other community organizations, can help create cohesive "organic communities" that enable all community members to participate "in the formation of the common will," feel that they are full members of a "commonwealth," and really have a "share in society."

Unfortunately for the development of participatory democracy and the advancement of knowledge, that possible solution to the Dewey Problem represents only our own logical extension and development of the powerful ideas Dewey prophetically sketched in "The School as Social Centre." After 1902 he himself did almost nothing to extend and develop his ideas along those lines.

After Dewey: Social Centers, Community Centers, and Community Schools

The idea that Dewey described in theory first took a real-world form in Rochester, New York, where, from 1907 to 1910, the progressive administrator Edward J. Ward operated social centers in a total of eighteen schools. Rochester's social centers provided evening recreation programs, self-governing neighborhood clubhouses where citizens from all walks of life debated democratically selected, politically charged issues, and art galleries, health offices, and employment bureaus. Yet Rochester's social centers were short-lived. The city's mayor—a political boss—and conservative business leaders vigorously opposed the participatory democratic features of the civic clubs, assailed the social centers as socialist and atheist, and leveraged the firing of Ward and his associates.[31]

Undaunted, Ward left Rochester to organize social centers in the hinterlands of Wisconsin for the University of Wisconsin's extension division. The First National Conference on Social Center Development convened in the fall of 1911 on the progressive Wisconsin campus. Attended by delegates "from

New York to California, from Texas to North Dakota," this conference spurred a national social center movement, with seventy-one cities in twenty-one states boasting social centers by 1913, and seventeen states enacting legislation for the "wider use of schools" by 1914. New York City had the greatest concentration of social centers. Cooper Union, a privately funded education center for New York's working class, was the primary catalyst. Working closely with the board of education, the People's Institute of Cooper Union, which provided a venue for public lectures and democratic forums, set out to replicate Ward's Rochester model in two public schools. So popular were the social centers modeled by the People's Institute that New York's board of education took over its work; by 1918, the city had eighty social centers (now called community centers) in operation.[32]

On the eve of America's entry into World War I, in New York City and elsewhere, trained social workers, working under the aegis of the National Community Center Association, took control of the community centers. During World War I, these organizations were transformed, becoming local subsidiaries of the National Defense Council. Red Cross relief, Liberty Loan drives, soldier's aid work, and other war-mobilization activities displaced neighborhood issues and social reform as the foci of community center organizing. Between the world wars, the community center movement, now far distanced from Ward's Rochester model, merged with the U.S. playground and recreation movement of the 1930s. New York City's community centers became recreation hubs, serving a yearly aggregate of eight million adults by 1939.[33]

In the 1930s, the Addams-Dewey-Ward tradition of reform-minded social centers saw a limited revival. As Michael Johanek and John Puckett argue:

> While the community centers turned away from the civic and social meliorist agendas of the [pre–World War I] social center movement, a small group of determined social progressives in the 1930s struggled to maintain the reform tradition of community-centered schooling. By mid-decade a community school movement was aborning. Disparate community-centered educational projects, in some cases fully functioning community schools, sprang up in response to the Depression, more often than not in unrelated ways. In a sense this was a social movement in search of itself—that is, it required the efforts of progressive educators to find a common ground and to coalesce projects that already existed in far-flung and often isolated areas into a national movement.[34]

It is not our purpose to explain the rise and fall of this fledgling movement; suffice it to say that fully functioning community schools failed to take hold except in a few rural and urban localities. Yet two of the 1930s commu-

nity school experiments are significant. One was organized in the hardscrab-
ble coalfields of central Appalachia by Dewey's disciple Elsie Ripley Clapp; the
other was founded in East Harlem by the Italian American educator Leonard
Covello.[35]

We turn first to Elsie Clapp's contributions to community schools. From
1934 to 1936, Clapp directed the community school experiment at Arthurdale, West Virginia, where the Franklin D. Roosevelt administration created
a "federal subsistence homestead" to relocate and uplift impoverished coal-
mining families living and dying along Scott's Run, a fetid stream in a central Appalachian coalfield that had gone bust. With New Deal funding, a new
community, Arthurdale, arose on a wind-swept plateau in Preston County,
replete with 165 Cape Cod–style houses, a town-center complex, a cooperative
store, and a community school, which was to serve as the catalytic hub for the
community's development. Eleanor Roosevelt, Arthurdale's primary sponsor
and advocate, appointed Clapp, a noted progressive educator, rural education
expert, and former teaching assistant to Dewey, to organize the community
school. Arthurdale would involve an adventurous extension of Dewey's theories of education, learning, and participatory democracy.[36]

Clapp built on and extended the theory Dewey espoused in *The School and
Society* and "The School as Social Centre." Unlike Dewey's Laboratory School,
the Arthurdale School focused its curriculum on occupations that were engaged in building the Arthurdale community. In this sense, "Clapp's strategic
conceptual (and instrumental) advance was both to construct her new school
as a community problem-solving institution and, progressing beyond Dewey's
Chicago theory, to illustrate concretely the principle of 'community as text' as
the basis of curriculum reconstruction."[37] The curriculum of Arthurdale's "socially functioning school" (Clapp's term) interfaced with real-world community development processes such as road building, house construction, barn
raising, agricultural operations, well digging, and glassmaking.[38]

As it began its second year, the Arthurdale School, operating with large
private grants and progressive-minded teachers who were recruited by Clapp,
opened several shiny new school buildings— a nursery school, an elementary
school, a high school, a greenhouse, and a multipurpose gymnasium—across
the road from the town center. The complex's main building housed a community primary-care clinic and doctor's office, with space for a monthly dental clinic. Yet Arthurdale's federal overseers and the philanthropists recruited
by Eleanor Roosevelt concluded that their continuous support of the community school would create a dependency on the part of the homesteaders;
they decided to transfer control of the school to the Preston County board
of education—a move that put the onus of sustaining the school on West
Virginia authorities. By the fall of 1936, Clapp's progressive curriculum was
in disarray, undermined by the abandonment of her sponsors. Unsurprising-

ly, the county school board soon replaced Clapp's hand-picked progressive educators with traditional teachers and jettisoned the community school idea.[39]

Clapp's former professor and career mentor Dewey, in a four-page foreword, praised her 1939 book *Community Schools in Action* for clearly portraying what good community schools do and how they function.[40] Yet he omitted any reference to the peculiar social circumstances surrounding the Arthurdale experiment—namely, the racial segregation of the federal subsistence homestead and its community school, which was consistent with West Virginia's Jim Crow statutes.[41] Why would the nation's foremost theorist of American democracy do this? Quite simply, Dewey chose not to distract his readers from the virtues of community schools, the nonvirtuous, racist, antidemocratic behaviors of particular communities notwithstanding. And implicitly recanting the theory of his groundbreaking essay "The School as Social Centre," published some forty years earlier, Dewey now declared that community-centered schooling was appropriate only for rural communities. "For I am convinced it is a mistake to believe," he said, "that the most needed advances in school organization and activities are going to take place in cities—especially in large cities. From the viewpoint of genuine community education, country districts provide the greatest opportunity as well as exhibit the most crying need—the most vocal even if not in fact the deepest."[42]

Ironically, in light of Dewey's paean to rurality, Leonard Covello implemented the community school idea on a large scale in the same decade in New York City. Covello was the founding principal of the aptly named Benjamin Franklin High School in East Harlem, which became the largest and longest-standing (1934–1956) community school of the twentieth century. Covello was the century's leading practitioner of the community school idea.

Covello immigrated with his family from southern Italy to East Harlem in the mid-1890s and experienced the anti-immigrant biases prevalent in the New York City public schools he attended. The negative aspects of his schooling experience and his growing appreciation of Italian language and culture spurred him to embark on a career in teaching after his graduation from Columbia University in 1911. From his base as the chair of the Italian department at New York City's DeWitt Clinton High School, he led a successful campaign in the 1920s to achieve parity for Italian with French, German, and Latin in the city high schools. His part-time Ph.D. studies in educational sociology, and his experience as a "teacher researcher" under the tutelage of the New York University sociologist Frederick W. Thrasher, led him to the community school idea and an instrumental role in founding Benjamin Franklin High School, a single-sex (male), comprehensive school that functioned as a de novo community school. He served as principal from the school's opening in 1934 until his retirement in 1956.[43]

From 1934 to 1942 the school, which served a multiethnic constituency (the plurality was Italian), was housed in an aging elementary school building on East 108th Street between First and Second Avenues. Assisted by the federal Works Progress Administration (WPA), Covello and his staff constructed a vigorous community center program that included citizen action projects, storefront social and recreational clubs, community and ethnic-group research bureaus, citizenship programs, a WPA adult school, ethnic programs and festivals, and the *East Harlem News,* a school-based community newspaper.[44]

Closely allied with Mayor Fiorello LaGuardia and Congressman Vito Marcantonio's Harlem Legislative Conference, Franklin High School's Community Advisory Council (CAC) helped obtain the East River Houses, the district's first federally subsidized housing project. Involving teachers, community members, and students, the school-community committees were the CAC's task forces, responsible for social problem-solving initiatives and advocacy campaigns in the domains of health and sanitation, housing, safety, beautification, and citizenship. Although Covello, in collaboration with Rachel Davis-Dubois, helped pioneer multicultural education, he never attempted a systematic restructuring of the high school curriculum. Curricular units on intercultural relations and housing, for example, had an ad hoc quality: socially relevant thematic units were never sustained elements of coursework. On the curriculum side, Franklin High School remained in most respects a traditional academic high school; Covello and his colleagues failed to exploit the community linkages that might have transformed the curriculum for youth alienated by the pedagogy of traditional schooling.[45]

The school-based campaign for the East River Houses illustrates how the community high school worked successfully in a limited sphere as a catalyst for social reform. In 1937 Congress passed the Wagner-Steagall Act, which allocated $800 million to the newly created Federal Housing Authority for public housing loans to municipalities. The prospect of obtaining a federal subsidy for East Harlem stimulated a campaign for low-income housing that radiated from the new high school outward to the community. Working in conjunction with the East Harlem Housing Committee, formed by the East Harlem Legislative Conference, Franklin High School students worked as ambassadors for housing reform in their home neighborhoods, while the school's English, Spanish, social studies, and art departments supported the housing campaign through various curricular activities. The upshot of the campaign—demonstrating the power of a fully functioning urban community school to catalyze community development—was the federal government's agreement to subsidize the East River Houses, which opened in 1941 on East River Drive between 102nd and 105th Streets.[46] (That high-rise public housing in East Harlem ultimately failed in no way detracts from the active citizenship and optimism this campaign inspired at Franklin High School in the 1930s.)

In 1942, following an East Harlem campaign that paralleled the housing campaign, New York City's board of education opened a splendid new building to house Franklin High School—an elegantly appointed Georgian-style structure located on East River Drive next to Jefferson Park.[47] After WPA support was terminated, however, the high school lacked the resources to sustain many of its community programs. The war years and events of the late 1940s, a period of social upheaval in which East Harlem's population base shifted from plurality Italian to majority Puerto Rican with attendant ethnic conflict, also took a heavy toll on the community school. These social forces amplified a major structural flaw in Franklin High School's design and operation: it was East Harlem's *only* community school, and it strived to encompass that entire area. The city's commitment to Covello's project diminished. With the onset of the Cold War, progressive education, stereotyped as susceptible to Communist ideology, was anathematized nationwide; by the 1950s, Franklin had become in most respects an ordinary high school. After Covello retired in 1956, the community school idea was eclipsed by other agendas.[48]

What happened to the community school idea after Elsie Clapp and Leonard Covello? In the decades following World War II, the idea was overshadowed by, and often conflated with, an approach known as "community education," whose emphasis was on recreation and, secondarily, adult education. "'Community education' was coined as an omnibus term for community schools and community-based educational programs that operated outside schools," according to Johanek and Puckett. "While 'community ed' created a rhetoric and national discourse about community schools and related educational programs, it failed to inspire anything like Covello's citizen-centered community school. . . . The memory of that adventurous social experiment faded and then vanished in the community education literature of subsequent decades."[49]

New Models of Community Schools and the Coalition for Community Schools

A client-centered approach of a different order was salient in a variant of the community school idea that gained impetus in the mid-1980s and included some five hundred school-based health and social service programs in operation by the mid-1990s. Schools that housed these programs were soon being called "full-service community schools" or "safe passage schools." The specialized health and social services themselves responded to "the new morbidities of substance abuse, unprotected sex, stress, school failure, and increasing levels of violence" and were "largely funded through a creative packaging of state and federal categorical funds."[50]

Other new models of community schools were emerging in the late 1980s and early 1990s. Four of this book's authors (Lee Benson, Ira Harkavy, Francis

Johnston, and John Puckett), along with other colleagues at the University of Pennsylvania, designed a historically and theoretically grounded, neo-Deweyan strategy called "university-assisted community schools" (UACS) and developed it through work with the West Philadelphia Improvement Corps (WEPIC). (The Penn–West Philadelphia coalition is described in Chapter 7.) This approach draws theoretically from a number of sources, including Dewey's "School as Social Centre" and his seminal 1927 book *The Public and Its Problems,* with its emphasis on the importance of face-to-face local communities for democracy, as well as Harper's brilliant insight that the university, particularly the urban university, functioned as the strategic organization for advancing societal development and democracy.

The UACS strategy also draws lessons from the two Depression-era community schools we have discussed. The Clapp and Covello narratives clearly indicate that charismatic leadership of community schools must be institutionalized. Put another way, a cohesive leadership structure must be developed that ensures continuity of community schools when the founders move on. In the UACS model, the university's sustained institutional support—effected in partnership with businesses, churches, hospitals, social agencies, and cultural organizations—provides a functional substitute for charismatic leadership, resolving, in theory at least, the problem of institutional continuity illustrated by Clapp and Covello. As these examples show, sustained institutional support is a key element—perhaps the essential one—in overcoming resource obstacles. In Covello's case, the resource problem was underscored by the withdrawal of the WPA, which had staffed important components of Franklin High School's community school operations. What functional substitute for the WPA is available to inner-city community schools of the twenty-first century? We argue in later chapters that the university is playing this role—one that strengthens rather than detracts from its academic performance.

Soon after the creation of university-assisted community schools in West Philadelphia, two community school models were developed in New York City. In 1992 the Children's Aid Society opened its groundbreaking community school, I.S. 218, which provided a range of social and health services and was organized into thematically focused learning communities. Also in the 1990s, the Beacon program of the Youth Development Institute of the Fund for the City of New York returned to the "lighted school house" approach, keeping schools open into the evening for students and the broader community.[51]

By 1997, the three models described above, along with the United Way's Bridges to Success, were supported by the DeWitt Wallace–Reader's Digest Fund's "extended-service schools" initiative to adapt their models nationally.[52] In the same year, leaders of the burgeoning new community schools movement, including the Children's Aid Society's chief operating officer Pete Moses, Harkavy, the influential independent researcher Joy Dryfoos, and others, recognized the need for a central and coordinating agenda. Early meetings and discussions led to the formation of the Emerging Coalition for Community Schools, which was housed at the Institute for Educational Leadership (IEL) in Washington, DC; a member of the IEL staff, Martin Blank, who focused on school and community collaboration, became the director of the Emerging Coalition, and Harkavy was named chair.[53] The Emerging Coalition had one hundred partners by 1999 and formally became the fully emerged Coalition for Community Schools in recognition of its changed status.[54]

Today the Coalition has over two hundred partners, which include national, state, and local organizations in K–12 and higher education, youth development, community planning and development, family support, health and human services, and government and philanthropy, as well as national, state, and local community school networks. A broadly representative steering committee oversees the organization. A number of the community school models with national networks—Beacon National Network, Children's Aid Society, Communities in Schools, 21st Century Schools, Edward Zigler Center in Child Development and Social Policy (Yale University), and the Netter Center for Community Partnerships at the University of Pennsylvania—have permanent membership on the Coalition's steering committee. The Coalition views the community school as a strategy rather than a suite of programs.[55] Specific activities are locally determined in response to school and community needs and resources. The Coalition emphasizes that

> a community school is both a place and a set of partnerships between the school and other community resources. Its integrated focus on academics, health and social services, youth and community development and community engagement leads to improved student learning, stronger families and healthier communities. Community schools offer a personalized curriculum that emphasizes real-world learning and community problem-solving. Schools become centers of the community and are open to everyone—all day, every day, evenings and weekends.[56]

Given its emphasis on the local determination of community school programs as well as the various stages of implementation at individual school sites, the Coalition has functioned as a "big tent," helping sites that identify as community schools to advance their practice. Over five thousand community schools, nationally and internationally, have been identified by the Coalition.[57] With a small staff in Washington, DC, the Coalition extends its reach through its partner organizations and a series of networks that have developed over time. These networks include leaders of community school initiatives in their localities (over ninety communities have major community school efforts, and sixty-one are part of the Community Schools Leaders Network) and a community school coordinators' network.[58] Learning networks have also been developed for school superintendents who are implementing the community school strategy districtwide in collaboration with the American Association of School Administrators, as well as for United Way leaders from across the country who are organizing and supporting local community schools. And most relevant to the focus of this book, the University-Assisted Community Schools Network was formed in 2015 by the Coalition in collaboration with the Netter Center and Rutgers University–Camden, in response to the growing numbers of institutions of higher education engaged with such schools.[59]

UACS, like community schools in general, help educate, engage, activate, and serve all members of the community in which the school is located. The model focuses on the school as the core institution—"the hub"—for community engagement and democratic development. School-day curricula and afterschool programs are connected and focus on solving locally identified, real-world, community problems. For neighborhood schools to function as genuine community centers, they need additional human resources and support. UACS engage universities as lead partners, providing broadly based, comprehensive, sustained support for community schools. This partnership between a higher education institution and a local school and its community is designed to improve both the quality of life in the community and the quality of learning from prekindergarten through graduate or professional school.

In the next chapter, we describe the development of a movement for democratic civic engagement in higher education that, among other things, has emphasized the powerful benefits that result when colleges and universities partner with their local communities.

5

The Higher Education Democratic Civic and Community Engagement Movement

Realizing Bacon's and Franklin's Ideals

> At bottom most of the American institutions of higher edu-
> cation are filled with the democratic spirit of serviceableness.
> Teachers and students alike are profoundly moved by the desire
> to serve the democratic community. . . . This is a thoroughly
> democratic conception of their function.
>
> —CHARLES W. ELIOT,
> *University Administration* (1908)

> I have this growing conviction that what's . . . needed is not just
> more programs, but a larger purpose.
>
> —ERNEST L. BOYER,
> "The Scholarship of Engagement" (1996)

Colleges and universities, as Derek Bok and others have emphasized,
have become the central societal institutions in the modern world.[1]
The path to power and success for the vast majority of leaders in science, health care, business, law—indeed, in nearly every area of American
life—passes through colleges and universities. They have become the primary engines of growth for an increasingly knowledge-based global economy.[2]
Colleges and universities have also come to play a key role in their local environments as anchor institutions.[3] They possess enormous resources (especially human resources), develop and transmit new knowledge, educate for
careers and advancement, function as centers of artistic and cultural creativ-
ity, and have a significant influence on the norms, values, and practices of the
preK–12 schooling system. They are catalysts and hubs for local and regional
economies as employers, real estate developers, clients for area vendors, and
incubators for business and technology. In cities that have experienced a decrease in capital investments and the departure of industrial jobs, institutions
of higher learning often serve as critical sources of employment and stabil-

ity. In the past several decades, enlightened self-interest has prompted many colleges and universities to respond to external pressures from government, foundations, and public opinion by partnering in local community economic development efforts to ameliorate such significant problems as poverty, crime, violence, and physical deterioration. Such activities also manifest a renewed commitment to the civic and democratic purposes of higher education.[4]

The scope of these efforts has led some scholars to liken them to a social movement. Social movements tend to be sustained by a clear understanding of what they hope to achieve and the obstacles they have to surmount to realize their aims. For example, the Civil Rights Movement not only worked for racial understanding and equality but also actively opposed bigotry and the laws, customs, and practices that upheld segregation and racial injustice. In a similar vein, the movement for democratic civic and community engagement in higher education promotes civic agency and participatory democracy as aims that should be integral to the university, while mounting a sustained critique of the idea of the university as an ivory tower. It opposes the passive pedagogy still all too prevalent in college and university classrooms, where faculty experts make "deposits" of knowledge in the minds of students through lectures—what Paulo Freire referred to as the "banking approach" to education[5]—and advances active and experiential forms of learning. In Baconian fashion, the movement also rejects pursuing knowledge for its own sake in favor of knowledge "for the relief of man's estate."

The higher education democratic civic and community engagement movement emphasizes that collaboration inside and outside the academy is necessary for producing knowledge that solves real-world problems and results in positive changes in the human condition. In this way it counters the tendency of colleges and universities to imitate cloisters apart from the real world. This movement has also worked to link institutions of higher education with their local communities through sustained and mutually beneficial higher education–community partnerships that not only provide learning for students and faculty but also empower and improve the community at large. The movement advocates a vision of the university as a democratically engaged institution—a part of the community, rather than a gated and privileged enclave within it or, as one of us (Harkavy) puts it, "shores of affluence, self-importance, and horticultural beauty at the edge of seas of squalor, violence, and despair."[6]

A number of strategies have been used by institutions of higher education to advance these ideals. These include integrating community-based activities into courses to enable students to grapple with complex real-world problems (that is, service learning), reorienting scholarly activities to address significant societal and community concerns (for example, community-based research

and action research), developing sustained and reciprocal university-community partnerships, and preparing students to live in an increasingly diverse
democracy and an increasingly interconnected world.

As the movement for democratic civic and community engagement in
higher education gains wider legitimacy, tensions persist regarding its aims.
Should the movement seek to disrupt and challenge prevailing academic
norms or amend them? Is it sufficient to teach students to develop competen-
cy in a discipline and to understand the workings of a democracy, or, in the
words of bell hooks, should we also teach them to transgress—to challenge
the status quo and change the world?[7] As we turn to the roots and evolution
of the movement, four questions guide our analysis:

1. What accounts for the long decline of university civic engagement
   after a flowering in the Progressive Era?
2. What explains the reversal of this seventy-year trend and the renewed interest in higher education's civic and democratic commitments?
3. What were the developments and approaches that led to the present
   movement?
4. How does the development of a democratic, community-engaged,
   civic university radically advance learning and knowledge?

The Short Rise and Long Decline of University Civic Engagement in the Twentieth Century

A civic purpose is evident in the founding documents of nearly every college
and university in the United States. Many speak about preparing students to
serve society as a whole and specific communities.[8] Franklin, envisioning the
institution that would become the University of Pennsylvania (see Chapter 2),
wrote of developing in students "an *Inclination* join'd with an *Ability* to serve
Mankind, one's Country, Friends and Family; which *Ability* . . . should indeed
be the great *Aim* and *End* of all Learning" (emphasis in original).[9] Franklin's
call to service is echoed in the founding documents of hundreds of private
colleges established after the American Revolution, as well as in the speeches of
many college presidents.[10] A similar blend of pragmatism and idealism found
expression in the subsequent century in the Morrill Act of 1862, which established land-grant colleges and universities whose purpose was to advance
the mechanical and agricultural sciences, expand access to higher education,
and cultivate citizenship. Using language typically found in documents from
these institutions, the trustees of the Ohio Agricultural and Mechanical College
(now The Ohio State University) in 1873 stated that they intended to educate

students not just as "farmers or mechanics, but as men, fitted by education and attainments for the greater usefulness and higher duties of citizenship."[11] Later, the "Wisconsin Idea" would broaden the concept of civic engagement from preparing graduates for service to their communities to developing institutions intended to solve significant, practical problems that affected citizens across the state.

Charles McCarthy, a graduate of the University of Wisconsin and the first legislative reference librarian in the United States, coined the phrase the "Wisconsin Idea" in 1912 to describe a concept that had been in practice for a number of years. In 1903 Charles Van Hise, president of the University of Wisconsin, joined forces with his former classmate, Governor Robert La Follette, to realize the vision of making "the boundaries of the university . . . the boundaries of the state."[12] When asked what accounted for the great progressive reforms that spread across the Midwest in the first two decades of the twentieth century, McCarthy replied that it was a union "of soil and seminar."[13] His answer captured the essence of the Wisconsin Idea—focusing academic resources on improving agricultural productivity and the quality of farm life, with benefits to all citizens of the state.

A focus on "city and seminar" infused the rhetoric and actions of the urban captains of erudition such as William Rainey Harper of the University of Chicago (see Chapter 3). Yet the universities these transformative presidents led did not institutionalize their urban agendas going forward in the twentieth century; in fact, their institutions disengaged from the American city and its problems. The retreat from ameliorative-reformist social science at the University of Chicago in particular prefigured the long decline of higher education's commitment to civic and moral purposes in the seventy years after World War I and the end of the Progressive Era.[14]

World War I greatly accelerated this development. The brutality and horror of that conflict ended the buoyant optimism and faith in human progress and societal improvement that had marked the Progressive Era. American academics were not immune to the general disillusionment. Social scientists "began to talk of the need for a harder science, a science of facts and numbers that could moderate or dispel the pervasive irrational conflicts of political life."[15] This "harder science" demanded moral and ethical neutrality from academic researchers, who embraced the new "objectivist" norms of their disciplines. "Sociology as a science is not interested in making the world a better place in which to live, in encouraging beliefs, in spreading information, in dispensing news, in setting forth impressions of life, in leading the multitudes or in guiding the ship of state," Chicago sociologist William F. Ogburn declared in his 1929 presidential address to the American Sociological Society. "Science is interested directly in one thing only, to wit, discovering new knowledge."[16] The major philanthropies that funded the social sciences endorsed this conservative perspective. In 1920 the Carnegie Corporation announced that it would no longer sponsor research that was linked to reform. In 1924 the Laura Spelman Rockefeller Memorial made a similar declaration.[17] Once-dominant progressive social and political theories, now attacked as naively unrealistic and societally dysfunctional, lost much of their power to influence opinion, policy, and action. Formerly progressive American social scientists jumped on board the scientistic and allegedly "value-free" bandwagon.[18]

Independent disciplinary communities crystallized on campuses nationwide. Between the wars, major universities formed analogous departments, and a faculty member's source of identification and allegiance became not the university but his or her discipline. The growth of discipline-based identification and a discipline-based reward system weakened the university as a collective entity and simultaneously led to the transfer of institutional power from local to national and foreign policy issues. The latter completely dominated research agendas during World War II and the early Cold War era, while the campus and its surrounding community mattered less and less.[19]

From the 1920s forward, for most students college life centered on intercollegiate athletics, fraternities and sororities, and other forms of "campus fun." Even after 1929, as Page Smith's angry indictment of American higher education reminds us, "the universities showed little inclination to respond to the onset of the Great Depression. If one were to judge from the typical university curriculum, there was little, if any, recognition that the nation was entering the greatest crisis since the Civil War. On the university campus it was business as usual."[20]

The decade after World War II also saw little change. In the 1950s "the collegiate way" reflected the conservative values and dispositions of the so-called bobby sox generation, and college life continued to revolve around athletics and Greek life.[21] The typical Cold War university curriculum did not expose students to the social issues of the day or encourage their involvement in public affairs. As the historian Jonathan Zimmerman has noted, "Things probably got even worse in the postwar era," as massive infusions of Cold War research dollars, from federal and private sources, accelerated the disengagement of many university professors from teaching undergraduates.[22]

After the mid-1960s, as is well known, a generation of student activists born in the decade after World War II organized for large-scale social change, their activism fueled by the moral urgency of civil rights, outrage over the Vietnam War, and great optimism for the nation's future. Their unifying goals were social justice, participatory democracy, racial equality, and peace.

Yet this optimism began to crash in 1968, an *annus horribilis* that saw the onset of corrosive disillusionment within the "Movement," beginning with the assassinations of Martin Luther King Jr. and Robert F. Kennedy in April and June, and intensified by the Warsaw Pact's crushing of the Prague Spring in August and, close on the heels of that event, brutal suppression of demonstrators at the Democratic National Convention by the Chicago police. The fatal shooting of demonstrators by members of the Ohio National Guard at Kent State and Jackson State Universities in May 1970 also had a chilling effect. By this point Movement politics were irreversibly fragmented. Members of the Weatherman organization, the most unhinged and violent of several extremist groups composed of former members of Students for a Democratic Society (SDS), would soon go underground and engage in bomb-making zealotry.[23]

In the early 1970s, as identity-group agendas replaced Movement politics on U.S. campuses, college students were burned out by protest and disillusioned with politics of any kind—and the draft had ended. Focused on advancing their individual social mobility in a decade fraught with economic uncertainty, college students for the most part stood aloof from societal issues and progressive change. As Robert Rhoads puts it, "Student social and political issues fell into a kind of slumber as the pursuit of more individualistic goals took precedence for the vast majority."[24] The American Freshman survey of the Higher Education Research Institute charted a decadal shift in college students' reported values. For example, the goal of "having a meaningful philosophy of life" declined from 85.8 percent of all freshmen in 1967 to 60.3 percent in 1979; "keeping up to date with political affairs" declined from 60.3 percent in 1966 to 41.0 percent in 1975. "Being well off financially" had declined from 42.2 percent in 1966 to 36.2 percent in 1972; it then leapt to 58.5 percent by 1979.[25] In contrast with the 1960s, mainstream activism was more apolitical, episodic, and self-referential, with demonstrators mobilizing en masse to protest such "me-oriented campus issues" as tuition increases and cuts in extracurricular programs.[26]

A marker of the conservatism of post-1960s college campuses was the resurgent popularity of fraternities. In contradistinction to the late 1960s, when the climate of opinion was hostile to fraternities, Greek life experienced a boisterous revival by the mid 1980s—marked by the disturbing phenomenon of widespread fraternity gang rape, among other pathological and antisocial behaviors.[27] At roughly the same time, however, a countertrend that would lead by degrees to a civic revival in American higher education was forming.

Public and Community Service

The seeds of the movement were campus-based public- and community-service programs. One early initiative got its start in January 1984 when a recent Harvard graduate, Wayne Meisel, undertook a "walk for action" from Colby

College in Waterville, Maine, to Washington, DC. Meisel's wanderings in the winter and spring of 1984 took him to sixty-seven campuses. "I'd just arrive and ask someone if I could sleep on his floor," he recalled. "And over the next couple of days I'd track down the chaplain or the newspaper editor or the president and discuss community-service programs. And over and over again the person I talked to would get excited." Meisel advocated "a lifelong commitment to community service . . . [to] promote sensitive, thoughtful and effective citizenship and leadership."[28]

Meisel steered clear of political activity in his recruitment work. Recollecting his years at Harvard, he explained: "I saw a group of politically active knee-jerk liberals on the one hand and on the other hand there was a group of people who just wanted to head off to Wall Street to make money. I wanted to try to reach that big group of students in the middle, between the knee-jerks and the jerks."[29] On campus after campus, Meisel invited students to take leadership roles in campus outreach activities, and his message resonated. By the time his walk ended in late May 1984, he had formed the base for a national network that he and a former Harvard classmate would organize as the Campus Outreach Opportunity League (COOL).[30] By 1989 staff members were working with student leaders at more than 450 institutions and hosting an annual meeting that drew thousands of these students.

During the period of COOL's development, Frank Newman, the president of the Education Commission of the States, wrote an influential report entitled *Higher Education and the American Resurgence* (1985), in which he argued, "If there is a crisis in education in the United States today, it is less that test scores have declined than it is that we have failed to provide the education for citizenship that is still the most significant responsibility of the nation's schools and colleges."[31] The report caught the attention of the presidents of Stanford, Georgetown, and Brown Universities. Together they formed Campus Compact as a coalition of college and university presidents personally committed to promoting civic engagement. To their surprise, in the first year 110 college and university presidents joined their effort. At the first meeting of the coalition on 16 January 1986, Newman argued that its purpose was to teach students to "see the larger issues as a citizen. [That] is the first task of the institution and . . . how to achieve that has to be at the head of the list."[32]

To achieve that aim, Campus Compact chose to advance what the group termed "public service"—that is, volunteerism—serving in a soup kitchen, cleaning up trash in a local park, or tutoring children at local schools. A transcript of that first meeting offers a window into the mindset at the time. One president raised the issue of academic credit: "I'd like to ask a question—and this is probably dangerous—how many in the room either give or think it would be alright to give some form of academic credit for service? [Some hands go up.] How many would be opposed? [Some hands go up.] And the rest are just in the middle waiting for leadership. It looks like a real minority."[33] In fact, very few faculty members nationwide were experimenting with integrating community-based activities into their classes or seminars to enhance learning outcomes: that is, service learning. It is therefore not surprising that some of the presidents at the first meeting questioned the propriety of giving academic credit for service. Although they saw service activities as worthy, they could imagine them only as extracurricular activities.[34] Unfortunately, many ventures in volunteerism were short-term, and few offered students meaningful opportunities to reflect on the problems they were trying to address. These programs fell short of providing the "education for citizenship" that Newman had advocated.

Service and the Curriculum

Campus Compact's decision to advance volunteerism as the acceptable standard of civic engagement worried two of the coalition's leaders, Donald Kennedy, president of Stanford, and David Warren, president of Ohio Wesleyan. Proponents of service learning, they commissioned Timothy Stanton, a staff member at Stanford who worked on issues of civic engagement, to write *Integrating Public Service with Academic Study: The Faculty Role*, which the Education Commission of the States published in 1990. Stanton's report had a significant influence on the national debate on the relationship of community service to the university curriculum. It also signaled a decisive shift from community service to service learning in higher education outreach programs—and the beginnings of a national movement.[35]

Ernest Boyer contributed to this growing civic discourse through his 1990 book *Scholarship Reconsidered*, which offered a broadened conception of faculty work. Although he recognized the value of the "scholarship of discovery"—traditional forms of research that produce disciplinary peer-reviewed articles— he regarded its dominance as highly problematic. "Beyond the campus, America's social and economic crises are growing— troubled schools, budget deficits, pollution, urban decay, and neglected children," Boyer powerfully argued. "Can we define scholarship in ways that respond more adequately to the urgent new realities both within the academy and beyond?"[36] He advocated recognizing and rewarding the application of scholarly expertise "to pressing civic, social, economic, and moral problems"—what eventually came to be called the scholarship of engagement.[37] "What is needed [for higher education] is not just more programs," he wrote, "but a larger purpose, a larger sense of mission, a larger clarity of direction in the nation's life."[38]

Boyer's message was taken up by the American Association for Higher Education (AAHE), which in 1991 inaugurated an annual Forum on Faculty Roles and Rewards that henceforth would draw together administrators and faculty members from hundreds of colleges in order to reconceptualize the work of the professoriate. A number of the individual state compacts that were part of Campus Compact also launched initiatives throughout the 1990s aimed at promoting both service learning and community-based research. Moreover, many institutions would advance their own change efforts around Boyer's ideas. In a 2001 survey of 729 chief academic officers conducted by KerryAnn O'Meara and R. Eugene Rice, two-thirds (68 percent) indicated that their institution had engaged in efforts "to encourage and reward a broader definition of scholarship," and a third (32 percent) said that the ideas in Boyer's *Scholarship Reconsidered* were a "major influence" in the decision to do so.[39]

With support from the Johnson Foundation, a group of individuals advancing these ideas met in 1989 at the Wingspread Conference Center in Racine, Wisconsin. Their thinking was codified in the *Principles of Good Practice for Combining Service and Learning,* whose preamble linked the practice of service learning with "active citizenship and participation in community life." Those principles argue that service learning

- is an effective (and legitimate) teaching and learning strategy;
- allows students to grasp the complexity of real-world problems and develop skills in collective problem solving;
- deemphasizes personal charitable acts (community service) and instead helps students understand the root causes of social problems;
- ought to be conducted in a spirit of reciprocal partnership with the community.[40]

In 1991 Susan Stroud, Campus Compact's director, secured a major grant from the Ford Foundation to promote service learning through a new initiative, Integrating Service with Academic Study (ISAS). ISAS funded 130 service learning workshops nationwide.[41] It also generated a renewed sense of purpose for Campus Compact's leadership. "I almost felt like one of the apostles taking this gospel out and trying to convert [people]," ISAS's director, Sandra Enos, recalled.[42]

Service learning's fortunes rose dramatically in 1993, when President Bill Clinton established the Corporation for National and Community Service. The Learn and Serve America Higher Education (LSAHE) program within the corporation became a major funding source for service learning initiatives, which the corporation actively promoted. A 1999 RAND report indicated that LSAHE had awarded $10 million to approximately one hundred institutions of higher education from 1995 to 1997; given the program's emphasis on subgranting, funds were distributed to some five hundred campuses.[43]

The first half of the 1990s also saw the inaugural issue of the *Michigan Journal of Community Service Learning*, "a national, peer-reviewed journal for college and university faculty and administrators, with an editorial board of faculty from many academic disciplines and professional fields at the University of Michigan and other U.S. higher education institutions,"[44] which increased the academic legitimacy of service learning. (At this writing the journal is in its twenty-third year of publication.)

What accounts for the rise and expansion of the democratic, engaged, civic university in the early 1990s? The fall of the Berlin Wall and the end of the Cold War provided catalytic conditions for significant change.[45] Long-ignored internal problems could no longer be neglected. Over forty-five years of looking outward had exacted terrible costs, as unresolved domestic problems developed into highly visible crises. No crisis was more visible and damaging than the crisis of the American city.

Although the end of the Cold War was, in our judgment, a precondition for the emergence of the new type of university a century after Harper first envisioned it, the development of the democratic, engaged, civic university can be most credibly explained as a defensive response to the increasingly obvious, increasingly embarrassing, increasingly immoral contradiction between the status, wealth, and power of American higher education—particularly its elite, research university component—and the pathological state of American cities. To adapt Oliver Goldsmith's late eighteenth-century lament, "The Deserted Village": While American research universities flourished in the late twentieth century as never before, "ill-fared the American city, to hastening ills a prey."[46] After the Cold War ended, the contradiction became indefensible. The manifest contradiction between the power and the performance of American higher education sparked the emergence of the *actually* (not simply rhetorically) engaged university and the growing acceptance of the proposition that power based on a great capacity for integrated production and use of knowledge should mean responsible performance. Accelerating external and internal pressures (including pressures generated by the civic engagement movement) forced research universities to recognize, reluctantly, that they must—and could—be moral and intellectual institutions simultaneously engaged in advancing universal knowledge and improving the well-being of their geographic communities: that is, the local ecological systems that affect their own health and functioning. We believe that after 1989 the combination of external pressure and enlightened self-interest spurred American research universities to recognize that they could—indeed, must—function simultaneously as universal and local institutions of higher education, not only *in* but also *for* their local communities. While this change was occurring, however, a division emerged that would slow the development of engaged civic universities.

The Service Learning Movement Divides

Early advocates of service learning tended to see it as a means of transforming students and the academy in the interest of promoting a just society.[47] Later adopters more often saw it as a practical and effective means of conveying disciplinary learning.[48] Nowhere was this division more evident than in the Invisible College, an initiative directed at faculty and founded by John Wallace, a professor of philosophy at the University of Minnesota. The name paid homage to the seventeenth-century organization that preceded the Royal Society of London for Improving Natural Knowledge. Wallace envisioned the group, composed of faculty and staff from across the country with significant experience in community-based teaching, learning, and research, as a medium for highlighting and disseminating the most current and promising practices in the field. A significant ideological rift was soon evident, however. As one participant noted:

> It didn't take long to see that there were two very, very different visions of what the Invisible College should be. One vision was that this organization could provide the concrete resources that would legitimize faculty concerned with community-based work. . . . [Then there was] a group that saw the Invisible College as almost like a confraternity of people who share a certain spiritual vision of higher education as a moral-ethical force.[49]

One of the most thoughtful advocates of the former position, Edward Zlotkowski, wrote in 1995:

> Until very recently the service learning movement has had an "ideological" bias; i.e., it has tended to prioritize moral and/or civic questions related to the service experience. Such a focus reflects well on the movement's past but will not guarantee its future. . . . Only by paying careful attention to the needs of individual disciplines and by allying itself with other academic interest groups will the service learning movement succeed in becoming an established feature of American higher education.[50]

Zlotkowski subsequently led a project funded by the Atlantic Philanthropies and sponsored by AAHE and Campus Compact that produced twenty-one monographs on the uses of service learning in a range of academic disciplines. These works tended to emphasize the illumination of disciplinary concepts, not the use of disciplinary expertise to address and alleviate problems facing communities or advance civic and democratic competencies.[51]

The leadership of Campus Compact recognized the disparate values and beliefs motivating members of the movement. In a 1996 memorandum to the organization's leadership, ISAS director Sandra Enos referred to Everett Rogers's seminal theory on the diffusion of innovations. "We can generally suggest that the first wave [of service learning adopters] is motivated by community concerns, sometimes tied to social and civic responsibility and social transformation," she wrote, "while the second wave is motivated by a strong perceived pedagogical value."[52] The impetus for civic engagement activities began to change. Service learning, rather than fostering the civic and democratic development of students and means for building partnerships with the community, began to be seen on many campuses primarily as a way of promoting disciplinary understanding. Service learning placements increasingly looked much like traditional internships, where the primary goal was connecting academic theory to practice, rather than providing students with the opportunity to work alongside people in the community, reflect on that experience, and help contribute to positive change. Strategically, the greater emphasis on the pedagogical benefits of service learning no doubt contributed to the tremendous growth of Campus Compact, which increased its membership from 235 campuses in 1990 to almost 520 in 1995; membership stood at 689 in 1999–2000—and more than 900 in 2002.[53]

While adapting to prevalent academic norms broadened the membership, the discipline-focused framing was problematic. Pioneers who had envisaged the transformation of higher education through service learning and were deeply committed to promoting social justice now felt alienated from the movement. One service learning pioneer, Nadinne Cruz, the associate director of Stanford University's Haas Center for Public Service, was deeply disappointed to find herself in the position of having to defend social justice as a desired outcome of service learning at a meeting of the National Society for Experiential Education.[54] Others with a similar orientation increasingly saw service learning being promoted not as a strategy for transformation but merely as a better way to convey traditional disciplinary content. In a real sense, the service learning movement had reached a crisis of purpose. At this critical juncture, a more comprehensive conceptualization began to emerge, one that would foreshadow the development of what we have termed the higher education democratic civic and community engagement movement.

Toward Democratic Civic and Community Engagement

In the late 1990s, the notion of reclaiming the democratic civic purposes of the movement gained momentum. In 1997 the position of ISAS director was vacant. John Saltmarsh, a historian who had spearheaded an innovative service learning program at Northeastern University, was encouraged to apply for the position. Despite his high regard for the initiative, Saltmarsh balked at the opportunity, although he agreed to speak with Campus Compact's leadership: "I went down and I pretty much said to them, 'Let's stop talking about service learning. It's not that it's not important. But let's talk about reforming American higher education. That's what the Compact should be doing. That's what ISAS should be doing.'"[55] Campus Compact's executive director, Elizabeth Hollander, had been thinking along similar lines,[56] and she prevailed on Saltmarsh to help advance this effort.

That year the National Commission on Civic Renewal, co-chaired by former U.S. secretary of education William J. Bennett and former senator Sam Nunn, issued a report that noted a decline in civic participation and indicated "stirrings" of "a new movement." Conspicuously absent was any mention of higher education.[57] This slight galvanized college and university associations. Hollander began meeting with other association heads about promoting higher education's civic role. These discussions led to two meetings of university administrators, faculty members, and foundation and association representatives at the Wingspread Conference Center in Racine, Wisconsin, in December 1998 and July 1999. The upshot was the *Wingspread Declaration on Renewing the Civic Mission of the American Research University*, authored by Harry Boyte, a senior fellow at the University of Minnesota's Humphrey School of Public Affairs, and Elizabeth Hollander. Invoking the words of Charles W. Eliot, Harvard's president from 1869 to 1909, the declaration asked how students, faculty, staff, and administrators, as well as colleges and universities themselves, might be "filled with the democratic spirit."[58] In July 1999, Campus Compact and the American Council on Education convened fifty-one university presidents at the Aspen Institute to set an agenda for promoting civic engagement. They issued the *Presidents' Declaration on the Civic Responsibility of Higher Education*, which was drafted by Thomas Ehrlich, a senior scholar at the Carnegie Corporation for the Advancement of Teaching, a former Penn provost and former president of Indiana University, and Elizabeth Hollander; the declaration was eventually signed by 585 community college, college, and university presidents. The document underscored the fact that for many higher education leaders, community engagement or service learning efforts had fallen short:

> We are encouraged that more and more students are volunteering and participating in public and community service, and we have all encouraged them to do so through curricular and co-curricular activity. However, this service is not leading students to embrace the duties of active citizenship and civic participation.[59]

The document called for a radical restructuring of higher education engagement around the formation of civic knowledge, skills, and dispositions. It gave voice to a growing sentiment that the movement had to do more than instill a sense of social responsibility—it had to empower young people to act.[60]

In 1999 a third widely circulated document on civic engagement in higher education appeared. *Returning to Our Roots: The Engaged Institution* was developed by the Kellogg Commission on the Future of State and Land-Grant Universities, a group composed of twenty-four land-grant presidents as well as foundation and corporate representatives. Noting "a growing emphasis on accountability and productivity from trustees, legislators, and donors," the document defined engaged colleges and universities as "institutions that have redesigned their teaching, research, and extension and service functions to become even more sympathetically and productively involved with their communities, however community may be defined." The document called for a recommitment to the historic land-grant ideal of service to the state, and it articulated seven "guiding characteristics": (1) responsiveness to communities, regions, and states, (2) respect for partners, (3) academic neutrality, (4) accessibility to "outsiders," (5) integration or interdisciplinary work, (6) coordination of institutional efforts, and (7) the commitment of resources to these ends.[61]

Though similar to the *Wingspread Declaration* in its call for community involvement, in other ways this conceptualization of "engagement" was very different. *Returning to Our Roots* held up "value neutrality" as a core principle, in stark contrast to the declaration's admonition that faculty members and administrators ought to embrace their role as moral agents. The call in *Returning to Our Roots* to serve the locality and the state is a familiar one, conforming to ideals found in the mission statements of most public four-year institutions.[62] Except for its emphasis on reciprocal community partnerships, the "engaged university" is in many respects indistinguishable from the traditional university. The vision is sensible (and politically prudent), but it is undeniably a more conventional one than the vision of a *democratic,* civically engaged university. The declaration and *Returning to Our Roots* point to similar methods (for example, community-based learning, service learning, the application of scholarly and community expertise in the mutual resolution of pressing problems), but their ends are quite different. *Returning to Our Roots* calls for a recasting of ongoing, traditional activities in a new civic light; the declaration asks institutions to commit to a transformation whose goal is to strengthen our democracy.[63]

In the first decade of the twenty-first century, some civic engagement proponents raised hard questions about the willingness of the academy to commit to an engagement agenda.[64] Of particular concern was the tendency of colleges and universities to steer away from encouraging democratic engagement, which involves helping students to understand and *use* the levers of change in a democracy to promote civic agency and citizen action.[65]

Two reports and several organizational developments mirrored their concern. In 2002 the Task Force on Public Engagement of the American Association of State Colleges and Universities (AASCU) published *Stepping Forward as Stewards of Place,* which described the ways in which state colleges and universities might "answer the call to join with public and private partners in their communities and regions to take advantage of opportunities and confront challenges." In a similar vein, in 2003 AASCU launched the American Democracy Project, which engaged 143 institutions in deliberation on civic and political matters, both in courses and in a variety of co-curricular venues. In 2005, Campus Compact convened representatives from thirteen research universities and established The Research University Civic Engagement Network (TRUCEN) to examine opportunities and challenges. The Democracy Commitment, modeled on the American Democracy Project, was developed in 2011 by leaders from community colleges as a "national initiative to engage community college students in civic learning and democratic practice." And in 2012 the Association of American Colleges and Universities (AAC&U) played a major role in compiling the widely disseminated *A Crucible Moment: College Learning and Democracy's Future,* which calls on universities to reclaim their democratic purposes by incorporating civic inquiry and civic problem solving into the curriculum.[66]

Despite the progress these efforts represent, on many campuses the predominant form of civic engagement consists of volunteerism or community service. In our judgment, a key challenge that remains is incorporating civic engagement into the core work of the academy—teaching, learning, and research.[67] There is certainly value in having students work in their local communities: It enables them to witness what is occurring there and tends to foster in participants a sense of responsibility to those communities.[68] However, systematic instructional efforts to help students understand the complex factors that perpetuate the status quo are all too often missing,[69] as is "a well-designed service-learning program to engender participatory or activist commitments integral to a strong civic identity."[70]

Some of the most promising initiatives today are built on deep, ongoing partnerships between colleges and universities and their local communities. These partnerships also involve the development of significant, serious, sustained efforts that draw together faculty, students, and community members to address community-identified real-world problems. They provide rich opportunities for students to develop the skills they need to be effective democratic-minded citizens. They give rise to research activities that link the expertise within the university with the expertise outside its walls—that is, the expertise embodied in community members who understand the local context in which problems are situated. Sustained partnerships of this kind not only foster the civic development of students; they also strengthen democracy at the local level. It is worth noting that on these campuses, a serious commitment to such partnerships has led to changes in the colleges and universities themselves—altering assumptions about how we should teach and whose knowledge counts, and encouraging new and broader understandings about what faculty work is important and what kind of research matters. A powerful commitment to the democratic ideal moves institutions from a commitment to promoting civic education among its students to a commitment to advancing democratic civic engagement by means of university-community partnerships.[71]

Democratic engagement is at the core of the Anchor Institutions Task Force (AITF). In 2009 the Task Force on Anchor Institutions, an ad hoc national panel, advised the U.S. Department of Housing and Urban Development (HUD) on how the agency could "strategically leverage anchor institutions, particularly institutions of higher education and medical centers ('eds and meds'), to improve their local communities and help solve significant urban problems." Soon after the task force submitted its report, "Anchor Institutions as Partners in Building Successful Communities and Local Economies," it became a permanent, formal organization, the AITF, with the mission of forging democratic civic partnerships involving anchor institutions. The AITF, which has grown to include approximately 700 individual members, is guided by the core values of collaboration and partnership, equity and social justice, democracy and democratic practice, and commitment to place and community.[72] It seems reasonable to speculate that the AITF's impressive growth is attributable, in no small way, to its unequivocal commitment to democratic engagement, locally, nationally, and globally. (For further discussion, see Chapter 8.)

The Path Ahead

The higher education democratic civic and community engagement movement has come a long way. Only two decades ago, community-based teaching and research lingered on the periphery of the academy. Individuals were laying important groundwork, but they often labored in obscurity and endured more than a little skepticism.[73] In a meeting with college and university presidents in 1986, Frank Newman, then president of the Education Commission of the States, observed that during visits to numerous campuses to discuss his book *Higher Education and the American Resurgence*, he found faculty members to be "remarkably resistant" to the idea that "they had a responsibility for more of their students' education than simply the development of the students' knowledge about their own discipline."[74]

A survey of faculty attitudes conducted in March 1988 revealed great puzzlement over how community-based activities might be meaningfully linked with coursework. The report's author, Tim Stanton, concluded, "Faculty have been noticeably absent from these activities."[75] In the subsequent 1990–1991 annual survey of Campus Compact members (there were 235 members at the time), only 16 percent of students were involved in service efforts (nearly all involving volunteerism and much of that episodic); 15 percent of member institutions had offices to support civic engagement activities; and 59 percent of presidents characterized their faculty's involvement in this work as "little" or "not at all."[76] If we consider 2014 data from Campus Compact (with 434 of a total of 1,080 member institutions responding), we find that 39 percent of undergraduate and graduate students participate in service and service learning courses annually, for an average of 3.5 hours per week; approximately 97 percent of member institutions have an office or center supporting this work, with 35 percent reporting that academic service learning is the primary purpose of this office; and 65 percent of campuses reward service learning and community-based research in promotion and tenure decisions.[77] This is an impressive shift.

Like all social movements, this one has continuously adapted in order to achieve its aims and secure broader legitimacy. For example, the originating civic vision for Campus Compact was initially displaced by the goal of simply encouraging "public service," or volunteerism. Although service learning was initially advanced as a strategy for cultivating civic knowledge and producing social change, for a time in the mid-1990s these aims were eclipsed by an initiative to promote service learning as an effective means of conveying disciplinary knowledge. Despite this countertrend, the democratic impulse that gave rise to this movement has shown remarkable staying power. The heart of the movement continues to echo Franklin's ideal of instilling in young people an inclination to serve joined with an ability to serve and to work pragmatically toward creating a better society.

Dewey argued that knowledge is best created when human beings work collaboratively to solve specific, strategic, real-world problems. "Thinking," he wrote, "begins in . . . a *forked-road* situation, a situation that is ambiguous, that presents a dilemma, that poses alternatives" (emphasis in original).[78] This was in opposition to the passive pedagogy still all too prevalent in college and university classrooms—what Dewey called "teaching by pouring in, learning by a passive absorption."[79] As colleges and universities work collaboratively with members of their local communities on universal problems (such as poverty, health inequities, substandard housing, and inadequate, unequal education) that are manifested locally, they will be better able to advance learning, research, teaching, and service. And in so doing, they will accomplish what we view as their founding and primary mission: helping to realize the democratic promise of American life for all Americans.[80]

In Part II we provide a case study of the development and work of the Netter Center for Community Partnerships and its contributions to Penn's more-than-thirty-year effort to become a better neighbor and help realize in practice its founding civic mission as defined by Franklin in 1749.

II

The Netter Center

Higher Education and Civic and Community Engagement

6

The Netter Center for
Community Partnerships

Intellectual and Practical Roots

The main results of the inquiry . . . are therefore presented to
the public, not as complete or without error, but as possessing
on the whole enough reliable matter to serve as the scientific
basis of further study, and of practical reform.

—W.E.B. Du Bois, *The Philadelphia Negro* (1899)

There is nothing as practical as a good theory.
—Kurt Lewin, "Psychology and the Process of Group Living,"
Journal of Social Psychology (1943)

In 1749 Benjamin Franklin, an ardent Baconian, proposed a thoroughly
radical, uniquely American curriculum for the College of Philadelphia,
which became the University of Pennsylvania in 1791 (see Chapter 2). As
we also discussed, Franklin strongly opposed the classical curriculum prevalent in eighteenth-century sectarian colonial colleges, which essentially reproduced the European universities Bacon had criticized. Designed to prepare
a leisured gentry class for leadership in a highly stratified society, the classical curriculum, as Franklin saw it, was radically dysfunctional in colonial
America, an evolving society that, as his own experience demonstrated, was
open and dynamic, with abundant opportunities for social mobility. In the
historian Edward Potts Cheyney's summary of Franklin's conception, which
we repeat here: "His ideas are pretty clear. He would have had an education
utilitarian rather than cultural, entirely in the English language, though following the best models in that language, devoting much attention to training
in thought and expression. It would include mathematics, geography, history,
logic, and natural and moral philosophy. It should be an education for citizenship and should lead to mercantile and civic success and usefulness. It is
unfortunate that it was never tried."[1]

Franklin, a realist and pragmatist, grudgingly acceded to a compromise
with the "Latinist" majority on the board of trustees. That compromise pro-

duced two courses of study in the fledgling college: a traditional classical course and an English school along the lines Franklin had proposed. To his deep and lasting chagrin, the classical course never gave way to his idea of an English school, proving, in his view, the inertial power of "a Prejudice in favour of ancient Customs and Habitudes." Writing in 1789, Franklin, the last living original trustee, ruefully acknowledged the "long defeat" of his main ideas.[2] Yet Cheyney's gloomy assessment that Franklin's conception "was never tried" merits some fine-tuning. One of his key ideas was tried more than a century after his death by the Wharton School, where "an education for citizenship" flourished for a time in the Progressive Era.

Around 1980 Lee Benson and Ira Harkavy became acquainted with Steven Sass, who was writing a centennial history of the Wharton School.[3] Through Sass and his work, they learned of the civic activism of the early Wharton School, which powerfully and directly shaped their strategy of academically based community service. A paper published by the Wharton School sociologist Leo Rowe in 1904 was a decisive influence.[4] Rowe's pivotal paper is properly viewed against the backdrop of the Wharton School's formative decades in the Progressive Era.

The Wharton School in the Progressive Era

In 1872, to escape Philadelphia's burgeoning industrial core,[5] the University of Pennsylvania relocated its small campus from 9th and Chestnut Streets across the Schuylkill River to 34th and Walnut Streets, in the partially settled, leafy suburb of West Philadelphia.[6] The university brought with it a host of "ancient Customs and Habitudes." One anachronistic, even "stultifying," custom was direct governance by committees of the trustees, without a president. Since Franklin's time, Penn's chief administrative officer was the provost, who was charged to execute even the most trivial directives issued by the trustee committees—a recipe for bogging down the administration in minutiae. This arrangement—unprecedented in American higher education—would remain in place until 1930, when Penn finally appointed its first president.[7] Fortunately for the university, this inefficient governance structure did not impede the work of two forceful provosts, William Pepper and Charles Curtis Harrison, who oversaw the first great expansion of the West Philadelphia campus (1881–1913) and the creation of new schools and departments. Among those new academic units was the Wharton School. Wharton's rise as "a genuine seat of learning and free research in all the social disciplines"[8] is associated with the provostships of Pepper and Harrison and, more particularly, with the early school's farsighted intellectual leaders, Edmund James and Simon Nelson Patten.[9]

Endowed in 1881 at the beginning of Pepper's tenure as provost, the Wharton School of Finance and Commerce took its name from its benefactor, the Industrial Age ironmaster Joseph Wharton. The economist and social progressive Edmund James headed the Wharton School from 1886 to 1895. James's aim was to mold the school as a research organization that would use social science methods to solve the problems of corporate industrialization. This aim was dangerously political for its time and place. That James practiced what he preached—namely, the value of policy-oriented, reformist social science—is evident in his own social science investigations.

A case in point is James's 1886 report to the Philadelphia Social Science Association, entitled *The Relation of the Modern Municipality to the Gas Supply, with Special Reference to the Gas Question in Philadelphia*. Published by the American Economic Association, this seventy-six-page monograph drew widespread acclaim and provided the evidence municipal reformers needed to compel the city to stop leasing the municipal gas works to private operators—the notorious "Gas Ring." Under James's tutelage, Wharton undergraduates conducted scholarly research on the city's administrative departments for their baccalaureate theses. Their findings appeared as a collection of essays entitled *The City Government of Philadelphia* (1893).

An activist-scholar and organizer extraordinaire, James played a major role in establishing the Municipal Reform League of Philadelphia and the National Municipal League. He also founded the American Academy of Social and Political Science and its journal, *The Annals*, which is still published by the University of Pennsylvania. Yet James provoked Provost Charles Harrison, who resented the autonomy Pepper had accorded James and the latter's considerable salary of six thousand dollars a year. Such was Harrison's ire that on his first day as provost, he compelled James, a future president of both Northwestern University and the University of Illinois, to resign his professorship.

Simon Nelson Patten, one of the foremost scholars of the early twentieth century, succeeded James as head of the Wharton School. Like James, Patten emphasized publicly engaged scholarship and a focus on social revitalization. He and his faculty protégés not only instituted a program of practical, reformist sociology; they also established a school of "social work"—a term Patten is credited with having coined. Wharton graduate students, widely known as "Patten's men," exposed, through their social investigations, rate-gouging in utility and transit companies, child labor in the coal and textile industries, and inefficiency in the food-distribution system. They were, as Patten aptly put it, "on the firing line of civilization."[10]

A paper by Leo S. Rowe, a professor of political science at Wharton from 1896 to 1917, was of particular interest to Benson and Harkavy. Rowe had adapted Patten's "investigation method" for his undergraduate classes in municipal government. Here was an intellectual pioneer who understood the promise of young adults and their ability to contribute meaningfully to scholarship and social reform. In 1904 Rowe presented his program at the annual meeting of the National Municipal League. He had designed an instructional plan in terms strikingly similar to Franklin's paean to service in his 1749 *Proposals*: "Bringing the student into direct contact with the actual operation of political institutions" would be "the most effective means of *developing an ability and arousing a willingness to do service to the community*" (emphasis added). Such "direct contact with the affairs of the city" was "not only feasible . . . but productive of excellent results." Describing the Wharton program for undergraduates and its educational benefits, Rowe hoped to inspire social scientists at other universities to create similar programs. "The zeal, ingenuity, persistence and attention to detail with which the college student will take up a work of special inquiry," he said, "is one of the most inspiring as well as the most hopeful indications of the civic effects of these special investigations."[11]

Among the most important studies published by Patten's Wharton School was W.E.B. Du Bois's sociological survey *The Philadelphia Negro*. This pioneering volume originated in 1896, when Susan P. Wharton, a co-founder of Philadelphia's College Settlement House, persuaded Provost Harrison to authorize a study of post-depression (1893–1896) social conditions among African Americans in Philadelphia's Seventh Ward. To conduct the survey, Patten's protégé Samuel McCune Lindsay, a Wharton School sociologist, hired Du Bois, who was the first African American to receive a Ph.D. from Harvard University and, at the time, a professor at Ohio's Wilberforce College. Du Bois and his wife took up residence in the impoverished Seventh Ward neighborhood, near College Settlement. He and his College Settlement assistant, Isabel Eaton, tirelessly canvassed the central Seventh Ward, site of the city's oldest African American community, interviewing more than five thousand residents, and completing the study in just fifteen months. Published in 1899 to some critical acclaim, though otherwise little noted by academics at the time, *The Philadelphia Negro* forcefully explained black crime as a structural effect of whites' unremitting racism; in particular, Du Bois exposed the catastrophic effects of racial discrimination on black employment opportunities and access to single-family housing.[12]

Today *The Philadelphia Negro* claims pride of place alongside *Hull-House Maps and Papers* (1895) and the *Pittsburgh Survey* (1907–1909) as a benchmark of Progressive Era ameliorative-reformist social science. The sociologists Elijah Anderson and Douglas Massey argue that Du Bois "anticipated in every way the program of theory and research that later became known as the 'Chicago school.'"[13] Such recognition of his now-classic community study largely eluded Du Bois throughout the remainder of his life.

From 1900 to World War I, the Wharton School was arguably the premier center of American social science. Yet the window of reform opened by the Progressive *zeitgeist* had already begun to close. A conservative board of trustees newly infused with wealthy industrialists was to wreak havoc on Patten's program of social reform. They foreshadowed the coming purge with their appointment of Edgar Fahs Smith, a chemistry professor, to succeed Charles Harrison as provost in 1913. "An intimate of the city's notorious Republican machine," Smith reputedly confronted several Wharton instructors with this accusatory question: "Gentlemen, what business have academic people to be meddling in political questions? Suppose, for illustration, that I, as a chemist, should discover that some big slaughtering company were putting formalin in its sausage; now surely that would be none of my business."[14]

For the Penn trustees the fact that Wharton professors made outrages like formalin-tainted sausage their business was a problem. In the years before World War I, a reactionary tide swept the James-Patten Wharton School. The political stance of Patten's protégé Scott Nearing, a vehement critic of the use of child labor, was particularly onerous to the wealthy businessmen on Penn's board. The proximate cause of the attack on Wharton's progressives may have occurred when Nearing ridiculed Edward Townsend Stotesbury, a partner of J. P. Morgan and a Penn trustee, in a class attended by Stotesbury's stepson. In any case, the trustees fired Nearing without a hearing in the spring of 1915, and the following year they denied Patten a courtesy traditionally accorded a professor of extending his contract beyond the retirement age. In his centennial history of the Wharton School, Sass scathingly marks the treatment of Nearing and Patten as a turning point in the school's history: "In the aftermath of the Nearing affair and the disgrace of Patten, a stench lay over the university. The scandal prevented the Wharton School from attracting any first-rate, critical mind to replace Patten, and it raised serious questions about the future of the institution. In 1917, the school lost its intellectual, a man who lived for ideas. Thereafter, it had to make do with professionals who lived off ideas."[15]

Separated from Wharton's curriculum after World War I, the active citizenship development associated with the school's academic program defaulted to the fringes of campus life, where service activities were organized by small groups of liberal students and campus religious associations. Following a national trend, Penn students subscribed to the collegiate way: the pleasures of dormitory life, fraternities, and self-referential social activities; prideful denigration of scholarship and one's professors; and often delinquent, sometimes deadly, campus rituals.[16] Another half-century would pass before a group of university members, in the face of Philadelphia's post–World War

II urban crisis and the frayed community relations resulting from Penn's role in urban renewal, would reclaim the progressive banner of the James-Patten Wharton School.

In the remainder of this chapter, we look at emergent neo-progressivism at Penn in the mid-1980s and the community-minded organizational innovations that preceded the Netter Center for Community Partnerships. Here, our answers to the following questions form a backdrop for the Netter Center's development since 1992 (see Chapter 7). What was the university's response to urban decline in the 1960s and 1970s? What were the consequences of its actions or inaction? What was the magnitude of the urban crisis impinging on Penn in the 1980s? What positive steps did the university, under President Sheldon Hackney, take to mitigate this crisis? We now turn to the inextricable link between Penn and its immediate geographic community of West Philadelphia.

West Philadelphia: Social Forces and Contexts, 1960–1990

In the middle decades of the twentieth century, Philadelphia, like New York and Chicago, looked to its universities to play key roles in the city's urban renewal plans: the University of Pennsylvania, Drexel Institute of Technology, and Temple University. These universities, in turn, enlisted the city's help to achieve their expansionist goals. By 1970, redevelopment properties owned or controlled by the University of Pennsylvania made up the lion's share of land earmarked by the Redevelopment Authority of Philadelphia for urban renewal in an eighty-block area of West Philadelphia designated as the University Redevelopment Area. Penn built its modern campus through the instrumentality of Redevelopment Authority Units 1B, 2, and 4—the planning units dedicated to Penn in the University Redevelopment Area. Here Penn exercised a legal writ for academic, residential, and commercial expansion, supported by millions of federal dollars released under Section 112 of the 1959 Housing Act.[17]

Penn had no such writ in the Market Street corridor, an area two blocks north of the campus designated by Philadelphia's City Council and the City Planning Commission as "blighted," where Penn desired a sphere of influence—a "compatible neighborhood," in urban renewal parlance. Mindful of Penn's interests, the Redevelopment Authority announced in 1960 the creation of Unit 3, an eighty-two-acre urban renewal zone. The properties were to be redeveloped under the auspices of the West Philadelphia Corporation, an institutional coalition that included the University of Pennsylvania as the senior partner and Drexel Institute of Technology (now Drexel University), Philadelphia College of Pharmacy and Science (now University of the Sciences in Philadelphia), Presbyterian Hospital (now Penn Presbyterian Medical Center), and Osteopathic Medical School (now Philadelphia College of Osteopathic Medicine) as the junior partners.[18]

The planners envisaged a science center as a catalyst for the economic, cultural, and scholarly flowering of "University City," the name they gave to the neighborhoods that bounded the West Philadelphia Corporation's member institutions. As recruitment magnets for the University City Science Center and the scientists and scholars they hoped to attract, the West Philadelphia Corporation dedicated dollars and human capital across University City to school-improvement initiatives, demonstration houses and residential planning, housing conservation and condominium developments, a guaranteed mortgage plan for Penn faculty and staff, historical preservation, arts and culture, beautification, recreation, and retail and restaurant development in the Walnut Street corridor.[19]

The Science Center was to rise one block deep along both sides of Market Street between 34th and 38th Streets and on the south side of Market between 39th and 40th Streets. The existing university-related research parks that might have served as models were located in spacious bucolic surroundings; the University City Science Center was to be distinctively urban, and the planners hoped to lure the research units of major technology industries, such as General Electric and IBM, to West Philadelphia. They denied charges that they had conspired to construct a buffer zone between Penn and working-poor blacks in Mantua and Belmont, neighborhoods north of Unit 3. Yet there was no denying that the professionals the Science Center hoped to recruit would be overwhelmingly white, simply by virtue of the racial demographics of higher education and the learned professions in the 1960s. Unit 3 redevelopment, with the University City Science Center at its core, effectively created a barrier between Penn and its neighbors to the north.[20]

As demolitions instigated displacement of working-poor blacks in the Market Street corridor, a neighborhood known locally as the Black Bottom, racial politics flared. Of the 2,653 people displaced in Unit 3, roughly 2,070 (78 percent) were black; the Science Center and the projected Science Center–affiliated University City High School caused just over half of the Unit 3 displacements. Protests by displaced residents and their West Philadelphia allies, including student demonstrators at Penn, fell on deaf ears at the Redevelopment Authority and the West Philadelphia Corporation, which managed the affair with hubris and insensitivity to the probable consequences of the removals, one of which was to be long-lasting damage to Penn's community relations.[21]

By the mid-1960s, at least in some quarters of the Penn campus, students and faculty had awoken to changing times with a newfound sense of civic purpose. An activist minority engaged in community service, participated in environmental protests ("Save Open Spaces") and antiwar demonstrations (typically sit-ins), advanced curriculum reforms, and ended *in loco parentis* practices. They opposed the university's complicity in military research at the Science Center and, by implication, its support for the Vietnam War; they also decried the displacement of working-poor blacks in Redevelopment Authority Unit 3, the paucity of low-income housing in West Philadelphia, and the absence of democracy in all of these developments.[22]

In February 1969 a student protest at a Science Center construction site escalated into a six-day sit-in at College Hall, which was supported by area-wide college and university students and local black activists. This highly publicized, nonviolent sit-in, controlled in the end by moderate student activists led by Ira Harkavy (then a Penn undergraduate), concluded with an agreement between the "community of demonstrators" and the Penn trustees. The trustees agreed to establish a "Quadripartite Commission" of students, faculty, administrators, and black leaders from West Philadelphia. This was to be a nonprofit watchdog that would guarantee equity in the university's future land dealings west and north of the campus. (In actuality, the Quadripartite Commission was by this time beside the point—Penn's involvement in urban renewal was over as of 1968, when the last house disappeared from the Black Bottom.) When they created the Quadripartite Commission, the trustees promised, albeit ambiguously, to establish a $10 million community development fund to build affordable housing in West Philadelphia's poorer neighborhoods. The fund never materialized. After two years, the Quadripartite Commission broke apart over irreconcilable interpretations of the trustees' vaguely phrased intentions. In any case, by most measures a reform-oriented, decidedly nonradical campus, "with trustees and campus administrators who were conciliatory and willing to negotiate with demonstrators," Penn avoided the violent eruptions that roiled other major universities in the late 1960s.[23]

With the Science Center issue largely settled, Penn activists in the spring of 1970 turned their attention to Richard Nixon's secret war in Cambodia. Thereafter, campus politics began to fragment: toward identity group mobilization on the one hand and civic/political apathy on the other, with the latter persuasion claiming the large majority. The attitudes of Penn undergraduates, in the main, reflected the central tendency of civic quiescence and careerism that marked the 1970s generation of American college students.[24]

Alienation and drift characterized Penn's community relations in the 1970s. Penn students were fearful of venturing into West Philadelphia, which was increasingly a high-crime, drug-plagued district. (Penn was by no means unique in this respect; urban universities nationwide were threatened by the collapse of neighboring communities.) Distracted by a five-year budgetary crisis and frequent student and labor protests, Penn's president, Martin Meyerson, a world-renowned urban planner by profession, was unable to respond positively to the urban crisis. Lacking community allies and the time and resources needed to develop a proactive approach, Meyerson exercised his only option: he battened down the hatches. He expanded Penn's security apparatus, adding campus police (by 1979 the Public Safety Department had forty-nine full-time uniformed police), high-intensity lights, blue-light emergency phones, dormitory guards, and an escort service.[25]

Setting Penn's Course Aright

Drug-related crime, school failure, joblessness, widespread anomie, marauding youth gangs, homelessness, and other social maladies—this was the situation that confronted Sheldon Hackney, a historian of the U.S. South, former provost of Princeton University, and president of Tulane University since 1975, when he succeeded Meyerson as Penn's president in 1981. John Puckett and Mark Lloyd, in their history of Penn in the postwar era, describe Hackney as a "conciliator" who strove to restore relations with the community and support a neo-Progressive proactive strategy inaugurated by activist faculty members to help solve West Philadelphia's numerous social problems. Hackney made several significant contributions. As ex-officio chairman of the West Philadelphia Corporation, he restructured the corporation as the West Philadelphia Partnership. This was more than a symbolic change: The new Partnership, unlike its predecessor, accorded equal voting rights on the board of directors to West Philadelphia's neighborhood associations. Another contribution was Penn's "Buy West Philadelphia" program. By 1993, the year Hackney left office, the policy had directed $10 million ($18 million in 2015 dollars) in contracts to West Philadelphia vendors, roughly a fifty-fold increase since 1985. The greatest local impact stemmed, in our judgment, from Hackney's support for programs that provided direct assistance to the beleaguered public schools of West Philadelphia. The most comprehensive of these was the West Philadelphia Improvement Corps (WEPIC), which originated in an undergraduate seminar taught by Benson and Harkavy in 1985. The growth and expansion of WEPIC would ultimately lead to the founding in 1992 of the Netter Center for Community Partnerships (see Chapter 7 for WEPIC's development and the organizational changes at Penn that led to the creation of the Netter Center).[26] As we turn to the historical and theoretical grounding of the center, it is good to bear in mind the social psychologist Kurt Lewin's famous dictum that "there is nothing as practical as a good theory."[27] Where did the practical theory that underpins the approach adopted by the Netter Center originate?

Benson and Harkavy (both historians by training) cast a wide net for ideas: Bacon's writings and Franklin's *Proposals Relating to the Education of Youth in Pensilvania,* as well as Franklin's major biographers and essayists. They turned to Dewey's theories of democracy and education and, through Dewey, the works of Addams and Harper. They also looked to earlier comprehensive efforts to use schools as centers and catalysts for community revitalization. After reading Elsie Clapp's 1939 *Community Schools in Action* and *The Community School,* a volume published by the National Society for the Study of Education in 1953, they began to think deeply about how the community school idea described in these books, and in Dewey's 1902 "The School as Social Centre," might be effectively updated and applied in the West Philadelphia schools—and what resources urban community schools would require. In 1991 they called on John Puckett to undertake a preliminary survey of the history of schools as social centers, community centers, and community schools (see Chapter 4), which Puckett completed with a postdoctoral fellowship from the Spencer Foundation in 1992. Reading the literature in the fields of urban studies and the history of higher education, Benson and Harkavy found other sources of inspiration and ideas (for example, Low's vision for Columbia University), as well as studies that enabled them to identify the myriad obstacles they would confront while trying to create effective linkages between academics and practitioners.

Significantly, Benson and Harkavy discovered the reform-minded faculty of the early Wharton School, largely through Sass's excellent account in *The Pragmatic Imagination: A History of the Wharton School, 1881–1981,* which was published in 1982, and biographies of Edmund James and Simon Nelson Patten.[28] The Progressive Era Wharton School was a source of both inspiration and a practical strategy. Above all, they took to heart Rowe's 1904 paper on the Wharton curriculum. More than any other source, this paper shaped their conception of academically based community service.

As we have seen, Penn's involvement in West Philadelphia before the 1980s with respect to Redevelopment Authority Unit 3, the Black Bottom removals, and the creation of the University City Science Center, had decidedly harmful effects. Developing an effective response to the urban crisis was all the more daunting and complex in light of the profound distrust with which the university was regarded by African Americans in West Philadelphia. In Chapter 7, we focus on the development of what we later designate as "the Penn model." Elements of this model (if not the whole) would, we believed, be useful to other urban universities as they confronted their own versions of the urban crisis. That model is today embedded, we believe, in the Netter Center for Community Partnerships.

7

Penn and West Philadelphia

From Conflict to Collaboration

The picture that emerges is one of a relationship in which the
University and the City are important to one another. We stand
on common ground, our futures very much intertwined.

—*PENN AND PHILADELPHIA*,
University of Pennsylvania Annual Report (1987–1988)

At Penn, local engagement is one of the core tenets of the Penn
Compact—Penn's Strategic Vision for moving from excellence
to eminence—and is an integral part of the University's mission.

—*ENGAGING LOCALLY*,
University of Pennsylvania Financial Report (2008–2009)

In 1983 the Office of Community-Oriented Policy Studies (OCOPS)
was founded in Penn's School of Arts and Sciences. (OCOPS became
the Penn Program for Public Service [PPPS] in 1988. PPPS was the immediate predecessor of the Center for Community Partnerships, which was
named the Netter Center for Community Partnerships in 2007.) Ira Harkavy,
formerly the student leader of the 1969 College Hall sit-in, directed OCOPS
and co-taught an undergraduate seminar on university-community relations
with Lee Benson and Sheldon Hackney. In the spring of 1985, four students
in the Benson-Harkavy-Hackney seminar focused their research on creating
a youth corps, the West Philadelphia Improvement Corps (WEPIC), which
combined the resources of community organizations under the West Philadelphia Partnership. The student proposal received funding from the UPS
Foundation to implement WEPIC over the summer in five West Philadelphia neighborhoods. The infamous MOVE fire that occurred on 13 May in
West Philadelphia's Cobbs Creek neighborhood led Benson and Harkavy and
community leaders to focus WEPIC's activity exclusively in the area affected by the fire.[1] With funds from Philadelphia's summer youth employment
program, WEPIC hired high school students from Cobbs Creek to work on
school- and neighborhood-beautification projects in their community.

The first project site was the Bryant Elementary School, located within four blocks of the MOVE fire. On the strength of its enthusiastic reception from city, public school, and local leaders, WEPIC was able over the next several years to attract an assortment of state, federal, and local grants, hire full-time staff, and expand to six schools, including the John P. Turner Middle School and West Philadelphia High School. At these sites WEPIC sponsored evening and weekend cultural, educational, vocational, and recreational workshops and programs for students, their families, and local residents. The myriad activities ranged from African American storytelling to ceramics and calligraphy to basketball and swimming. At the middle school, WEPIC offered co-curricular programs in landscaping and horticulture during the school year (projects included a school garden and a gazebo), as well as a six-week summer program in community health care. As part of the latter program, Turner students, assisted by Penn medical students, took the blood pressures of community members and received instruction in health care screening. At the high school, WEPIC enlisted skilled artisans to teach co-curricular programs in pipe-organ restoration (to restore a Curtis organ in the eighty-year-old high school's auditorium), carpentry, and housing renovation. The Penn–West Philadelphia joint initiative that emerged from these programs linked Penn faculty, staff, and students with teachers, school administrators, local politicians, and neighborhood cultural affairs leaders in creating university-assisted community schools (UACS) in West Philadelphia (see below).

Benson and Harkavy also looked to the University City Science Center to help create a school-based economic development strategy for West Philadelphia—a strategy that would build on and complement the WEPIC approach. The Science Center was the only freestanding institution in the Delaware Valley whose mission expressly included entrepreneurship and economic growth. Having failed to attract any major technology corporations to University City, the Science Center had turned in the 1980s to small-business incubation as its main focus. Benson and Harkavy sought out the Science Center's president, Randall Whaley, to explore the development of a plan to leverage a partnership between the Science Center's incubator and the Hackney-led West Philadelphia Partnership, whose mission was economic and community development. Whaley endorsed the strategy in a 1987 concept paper directed to Pennsylvania Secretary of Labor and Industry Harris Wofford, but after Whaley's death two years later, the Science Center expressed no further interest in this approach to improving the area's economy.

There was no shortage of entrepreneurial talent in West Philadelphia. Latent economic opportunities that might have been exploited by this partnership with the Science Center included WEPIC-sponsored activities such as housing rehabilitation, pipe organ repair, and landscaping and horticulture.[2]

Adding insult to the injury of the Black Bottom removals (see Chapter 6), "the Science Center had marginal economic impact in West Philadelphia, as most of its jobs were tailored to individuals with 'a great deal of education or training.'"[3] The Netter Center for Community Partnerships, in contrast, has from its inception focused on West Philadelphia residents with lower socio-economic status and educational attainment.

Two Strategies for University-Community Partnerships

Many centers at Penn are fully dependent on external resources. The Netter Center for Community Partnerships, however, has since its founding been institutionalized within the university's formal administrative structure. Its director and administrative staff are funded by Penn's Office of the President and the School of Arts and Sciences, with direct reporting lines to both these offices, as well as a dotted-line report to the Provost's Office.[4] The center's lon-gevity—twenty-five years at this writing—is properly attributed to its fidelity to the university's academic mission; in fact, academically based community service courses offered by the university's faculty in multiple schools and de-partments are a hallmark.

The creation of the center was based on the assumption that one highly effective and efficient way for Penn to serve its institutional self-interest and simultaneously carry out its academic mission was to focus research and teach-ing on universal problems—problems of schooling, health care, and economic development, for example—that were manifested locally in West Philadelphia and the rest of the city. By focusing strongly and strategically on universal problems and effectively integrating general theory and concrete practice, as Franklin had advocated in the eighteenth century, Penn would improve sym-biotically both the quality of life in its urban ecological community and its research and teaching.

As it was optimistically envisioned, the Center for Community Partner-ships would constitute a far-reaching innovation within the university. To help overcome the remarkably competitive institutional fragmentation that had developed after 1945 as Penn evolved and became a large research uni-versity,[5] the center would identify, mobilize, and integrate Penn's vast resourc-es in order to help transform West Philadelphia, particularly by improving its public schools.

During Hackney's presidency, the center advanced two key strategies that continue to underpin its work. The first strategy is *academically based community service* (ABCS): community service rooted in and intrinsically connected to research, teaching, and learning. The second, *university-assist-ed community schools* (UACS), provides an organizing framework for ABCS courses and center-mediated grants to West Philadelphia schools. A definition of community schooling that inspired Benson, Harkavy, and Puckett's early discussions appeared in 1953 in a volume published by the National Society for the Study of Education entitled *The Community School:*

> A community school is a school which has concerns beyond the training of literate, "right-minded," and economically efficient citizens who reflect the values and processes of a particular social, economic, and political setting. In addition to these basic educational tasks, it is *directly concerned with improving all aspects of living in the community* in all the broad meaning of that concept, in the local, state, regional, national, or international community. To attain that end, the community school is *consciously used* by the people of the community. Its curriculum reflects planning to meet the discovered needs of the community with changes in emphasis as circumstances indicate. Its buildings and physical facilities are at once a center for both youth and adults who together are actively engaged in analyzing problems suggested by the needs of the community and in formulating and exploring solutions to those problems. Finally, the community school is concerned that the people put solutions into operation to the end that living is improved and enriched for the individual and the community. [Emphasis in original][6]

Based on their evolving understanding of the community school idea, Harkavy and Puckett presented a neo-Deweyan rationale for UACS as institutions that "involve, educate, serve, and activate *all* members of the community":

> The key assumption is that schools can be *the* strategic institutions for creating healthy urban communities. They can function as environment-changing institutions—but only as they become centers of broad-based partnerships involving a variety of community organizations and institutions, including universities and colleges. Because they belong to all members of the community, public schools are particularly suited to be the catalytic hubs around which local partnerships are generated and formed. In this partnership role, schools can function as community institutions *par excellence,* providing a decentralized, community-based response to socially significant problems.
>
> The curriculum of the community school is to be community-centered and action-oriented. By *community-centered,* we mean that the academic agenda is wedded to community history, culture, and socially significant problems. These broad thematic areas provide immediate contexts for reading, writing, reflection, and discussion related to

the study of academic subject matter. As part of their academic studies, students are involved in ongoing, community-based project work.
This strategy builds on the assumption that students' interest in having
their work come to fruition as highly visible products will suffuse the
educational process with a desire to master *and* to apply the academic
knowledge necessary to complete high-quality products. . . . In all its
facets the curriculum expressly incorporates the motivational power of
students' immediate, real-world, out-of-school experiences. In short,
learning is experiential and "hands-on," related in every phase to community issues and concerns.[7]

The Netter Center's activities are different from those associated with the
dominant form of service learning, which tends to focus on the learning of
the college student as the primary goal. ABCS is a problem-solving variant
of service learning with an emphasis on both student and community outcomes. Harkavy, Puckett, and Francis Johnston participated in the debates at
the Campus Compact Institute on Integrating Service with Academic Study,
held at Stanford University in the summer of 1991, which strongly differenti-
ated service learning from other forms of student community service. Their
proposal to create the Center for Community Partnerships, drafted at the
1991 Institute, benefited from these debates, even as its authors made clear
the distinctiveness of ABCS as a service learning approach (see Chapter 5).

Robert G. Bringle and his associates argue that service learning assumes
many forms, "reflecting the different assumptions, ideologies, norms, and
identities of different personal, organizational, and cultural contexts." Yet they
find that "despite variations, there is a broad consensus that service learning involves the integration of academic material, relevant service activities,
and critical reflection and is built on reciprocal partnerships that engage students, faculty/staff, and community members to achieve academic, civic, and
personal learning objectives as well as to advance public purposes." In this
vein, they describe service learning as "a course or competency-based, credit-
bearing educational experience in which students . . . participate in mutually
identified service activities that benefit the community and . . . reflect on
the service activity in such a way as to gain further understanding of course
content, a broader appreciation of the discipline, and an enhanced sense of
personal values and civic responsibility."[8]

ABCS is similar to conventional service learning with respect to these
criteria: the Penn courses are credit-bearing, they involve reflection, and the
service activities are "mutually identified." Yet it is the strategic focus on the
local manifestation of a universal problem (such as the perennial crisis of
West Philadelphia's public schools) that differentiates the Netter Center's conception of service learning from other approaches. Having a strategic focus

means bringing assorted disciplinary lenses and resources to the study and possible solution of localized real-world problems that by their nature are multidisciplinary in scope, necessitating a multifaceted approach. It also means seeking to solve those problems collaboratively with community members, with potential solutions often taking a programmatic form. ABCS not only is community-driven but also, at its best, involves research with undergraduate and graduate students serving as researchers. In some cases ABCS involves participatory planning with West Philadelphia schools and/or community organizations and programs to put plans into action. To date, approximately two hundred ABCS courses, seminars, and internship programs have been developed de novo or through the redesign of existing courses in thirty departments and programs in all of Penn's twelve schools—Annenberg School for Communication, Arts and Sciences, Dental Medicine, Design, Education, Engineering, Law, Medicine, Nursing, Social Policy and Practice, Veterinary Medicine, and the Wharton School.

In local public schools, ABCS courses have contributed to curricular and co-curricular activities in such areas as reading, nutrition and disease detection/prevention, dance and physical activity, urban environmental issues (including lead toxicity and brownfields), urban gardening and landscaping (vest-pocket park design, for example), housing renovation, music, social-base mapping, transit-oriented development, African American culture and history, and the STEM disciplines: science, technology, engineering, and math. ABCS courses have also supported professional development for teachers, college-access programs, and community arts, including, for example, a historical play memorializing the Black Bottom neighborhood, researched, staged, and performed by undergraduate and high school students at a packed local church and at Penn's Annenberg Center for the Performing Arts. When the Netter Center began operation in 1992, only four ABCS courses were offered. That number has grown to approximately sixty-five, taught each academic year. In 2015–2016, approximately 1,600 graduate and undergraduate students and fifty standing and associated faculty were involved in ABCS courses.

Three members of the Penn faculty working with the Netter Center—Professor of History Michael Zuckerman, Professor of Classics Ralph Rosen, and Professor of Earth and Environmental Science Robert Giegengack—and Harkavy and Puckett authored chapters in two of the volumes sponsored by the American Association for Higher Education on the uses of service learning in a range of academic disciplines, and Harkavy co-edited the volume on history.[9] Nonetheless, while supportive of the integration of service learning in the disciplines, the Netter Center has sustained a central focus on real-world, collaborative problem solving to benefit the wider community.

The Netter Center maintains that the principal benefit of service learning should not be its "trickle-down effect," a process in which a critical mass of students is educated for citizenship to improve society at some distant time in the future.[10] The primary aim of academically based community service is the well-being of community members now *and* in the future. Although the impact on Penn student learning is important—indeed, critical—if university-community partnerships are to be mutually beneficial, there must be genuine, democratic change in the conditions in the community. As noted above, we define academically based community service as service rooted in and intrinsically tied to research, teaching, and learning; it is service designed to advance structural community improvement (for example, effective public schools, neighborhood economic development, and strong community organizations) rather than simply to alleviate individual misery (for example, feeding the hungry, sheltering the homeless).[11]

The Access Science program exemplifies the reciprocal relationships centered on structural community improvements that Penn is developing through discipline- and field-based partnerships in West Philadelphia. Begun in 1999 with initial support from the National Science Foundation (NSF), Access Science works to improve STEM education for both K–12 students and undergraduate and graduate students at Penn. Renamed Moelis Access Science in 2006 to acknowledge a gift from Ronald and Kerry Moelis, a Penn alumnus and his spouse, the program involves faculty and students from six Penn schools who work with West Philadelphia public schools. Undergraduates in Moelis Access Science–affiliated ABCS courses provide content-based professional development for teachers and direct classroom support for implementing high-quality, hands-on laboratory exercises and small-group activities. Approximately a dozen ABCS courses related to the program are now offered each year in the Departments of Biology, Mathematics, Environmental Science, Physics, Education, Chemistry, Electrical and Systems Engineering, and Computer and Information Science, among others. "Community Physics Initiative," taught by Professor Larry Gladney, associate dean for the Natural Sciences, is illustrative. Aligned with the School District of Philadelphia's curriculum for introductory high school physics, Gladney's course links the practical and theoretical aspects of foundational physics. By developing and teaching weekly laboratory exercises and classroom demonstrations at a nearby high school, Penn students learn science by teaching it.

The various ABCS courses in environmental studies at Penn provide another example. The bellwether for this outreach was the Lead Exposure Risk Reduction program, directed in the mid-1990s by Professor Robert Giegengack. Penn undergraduates in ABCS environmental studies courses were taught the principal environmental risks faced by children in urban-core neighborhoods, particularly exposure to the lead found in layers of old paint on the interior and exterior walls of homes. Exposure to lead can cause mental retardation and damage to the immune system. The Penn students in turn provided education and outreach activities at local schools. Middle school students became co-researchers on the distribution of lead, taking samples from inside their homes as well as exterior surfaces. They also worked with the Penn students to disseminate information on reducing lead exposure.[12] Today, six ABCS courses in the Earth and Environmental Science Department focus on environmentally based and environmentally triggered diseases, particularly those related to asthma, tobacco, lead poisoning, air quality, water quality, and community health.

Organizing for Communal Participatory Action Research: Theory into Practice

The Netter Center has developed a body of theoretical and empirically grounded literature to advance its agenda.[13] One of the early theoretical breakthroughs was inspired by the work of the distinguished Cornell sociologist William Foote Whyte, who introduced Benson, Harkavy, and Puckett in the mid-1980s to his participatory action research (PAR) projects. Whyte's research focused on labor-management relationships and worker participation at Xerox Corporation and the Fagor cooperative group in Mondragón, a town in Spain's Basque country.[14] Conversations with Whyte and his Cornell colleague Davydd Greenwood about their PAR studies in the labor-managed industrial cooperatives of Mondragón proved particularly useful. Collectively, the 173 Mondragón cooperatives manufactured, among other things, heavy household appliances, electronic components, and automated manufacturing systems while employing more than 19,500 local workers. A research team that included Whyte, Greenwood, and six Mondragón worker-owners focused on the problem of apathy and alienation in the Fagor cooperative. Their study, steeped in organizational theory, combined data from documents, surveys, face-to-face interviews, and roundtable discussions.[15]

Benson, Harkavy, and Puckett began to reconceptualize their work in West Philadelphia as an ongoing participatory action research project.[16] Inspired by Whyte and Greenwood, the Netter Center planners (Benson, Harkavy, and Puckett, as well as Johnston, who began working with WEPIC in 1990) wanted to know more about this approach. At Greenwood's invitation, Puckett affiliated with the Scandinavian Action Research Development Program (ACRES). In 1992 and 1993 he attended five week-long conferences convened by ACRES in Trondheim, Stockholm, and Amsterdam; here he had extensive discussions with action researchers from Norway, Sweden, Finland, and Great Britain. For the book published by ACRES in 1999, Harkavy and Puckett contributed a history of action research in the United States, highlighting the social research of Addams and the women of Hull House, famously published as *Hull-House Maps and Papers* in 1895; Lewin's action research on problems of industrial democracy and ethnocultural conflict in the 1940s and 1950s; and PAR research conducted in the 1980s by Whyte and his associates at Cornell for the Xerox-Amalgamated Job Preservation Program in New York and the Mondragón cooperatives in Spain.[17]

For the past quarter-century, Benson, Harkavy, Johnston, Puckett, and other Netter Center colleagues have been developing a form of PAR that focuses on mobilizing resources and organizing partnership relationships to form a university-wide, community-wide, *communal* PAR project. There is a fundamental difference between PAR as usually practiced and a communal PAR. Both research processes are directed toward problems in the real world, are concerned with application and implementation, and are participatory. They differ in the degree to which they are continuous, comprehensive, beneficial, and necessary to the organization or community being studied and to the university. The effort of Whyte and his associates at Cornell to advance industrial democracy in the worker cooperatives of Mondragón were not an institutional necessity for Cornell. By contrast, the success of the University of Pennsylvania's research efforts in West Philadelphia is in the institution's enlightened self-interest—hence the emphasis on the communal nature of this PAR. Proximity and a focus on problems that are institutionally significant to the university encourage sustained, continuous research involvement.

In October 2004 leaders of the higher education democratic civic engagement movement, including Harkavy, attended the third in a series of conferences sponsored by the Kellogg Forum on Higher Education for the Public Good at the Johnson Foundation's Wingspread Conference Center in Racine, Wisconsin. The conference, "Higher Education Collaboratives for Community Engagement and Improvement," assigned participants to one of several working groups. The "faculty and researcher working group" echoed many of the themes identified in this book.[18] Its report, with Harkavy serving as lead author, identified *democratic purpose, process, and product* as crucial for successful university partnerships with schools and communities.

The principles of democratic purpose, process, and product are succinctly defined as follows:

1. *Purpose:* An abiding democratic and civic purpose is the rightly placed goal if higher education is to truly contribute to the public good.
2. *Process:* The higher education institution and the community, as well as members of both communities, should treat each other as ends in themselves rather than as means to an end. The relationship itself and welfare of the various partners should be the preeminent value, not developing a specified program or completing a research project. These are the types of collaborations that tend to

be significant, serious, and sustained, lead to a relationship of genuine respect and trust, and most benefit the partners and society.

3. *Product:* A successful partnership also strives to make a positive difference for all partners—this is the democratic product. Contributing to the well-being of people in the community (both now and in the future) through structural community improvement should be a central goal of a truly democratic partnership for the public good. Research, teaching, and service should also be strengthened as a result of a successful partnership. Indeed, working with the community to improve the quality of life in the community may be one of the best ways to improve the quality of life and learning within a higher education institution.[19]

These are the guiding principles of communal PAR. Not every research project undertaken under the Netter Center's auspices involves this kind of PAR, but the term *communal PAR* designates the overarching goal of the Netter Center, its university affiliates, and the center's community partners. Center-affiliated research undertaken at a school or community site, even if not conducted by a research team in the Mondragón PAR modality, is participatory in the sense that it is commensurate with the Wingspread principles of democratic purpose, process, and product and works to involve school and community members, including the Netter Center's Community Advisory Board, from project planning through implementation.[20] Though it has a long way to go before it actually achieves its goal, the center's overall effort has been consciously democratic and participatory—to genuinely work *with* and *for* the community, not merely *in* it.

The most comprehensive example of communal PAR is anthropology professor Francis Johnston's citywide Agatston Urban Nutrition Initiative (AUNI), originally called the Turner Nutritional Awareness Project (see Chapter 9). Like AUNI, other faculty research projects have programmatic components that support teaching and learning at the community school sites and contribute to the overall PAR project focused on improving both Penn and West Philadelphia. A major reading improvement program was led by the linguistics professor William Labov, who began the program in 1998 to raise the reading levels of urban elementary school students. Drawing on his decades of research on African American Vernacular English, Labov and his ABCS students created an Individualized Reading Program that isolated common reading errors. ABCS students and additional tutors were trained in Labov's methodology. They then developed culturally appropriate reading manuals that drew from the lives of West Philadelphia children to address these reading issues. The recognition that educators need to value both the context of children's lives and where they are in their learning brought about measurable improvements in reading. Charles R. Drew Elementary School showed greater improvement in its 1999 reading scores than any other school in the state. All seventy-five Drew students who participated in the Individualized Reading Program with Penn tutors from 2001 through 2004 showed improvement in standardized reading scores from pre- to post-tests, approaching national averages. The program proved effective in decreasing errors made in twenty-seven types of sound-to-letter correspondences. In general, the students with the highest initial error rates showed the greatest improvement.[21] Furthermore, there was a 50 percent improvement in the number of proficient readers in the third grade at Drew School from 2003 to 2006.[22] The research was expanded to include Latino youth in North Philadelphia, and the program was adapted to other cities. Now known as the Penn Reading Initiative (PRI), the program is run by students and supported by the Netter Center. PRI tutors use *The Reading Road,* a curriculum that includes lessons, stories, and games designed to engage the interest of struggling readers. This program partners with the Netter Center's university-assisted community schools in West Philadelphia.

Taking Advantage of a Favorable Institutional Climate

In the university's annual report for 1987–1988, *Penn and Philadelphia: Common Ground,* Sheldon Hackney acknowledged that Penn's future and the future of Philadelphia are inextricably joined: "The picture that emerges is one of a relationship in which the University and the City are important to one another. We stand on common ground, our futures very much intertwined."[23] We have noted Hackney's efforts to bind the wounds inflicted on the community by the university's participation in urban renewal, to treat West Philadelphia as an equal partner with Penn, and to create a mediating structure that would align Penn's academic mission with community needs, primarily through the strategy of academically based community service. Mobilizing the campus behind these efforts was not easy, for Hackney's presidency may have been the most turbulent in the university's history. No other Penn administration faced so many problems percolating from the larger society. In the 1980s the Hackney administration had to contend with a crack cocaine epidemic, escalating violence, and a climate of fear in West Philadelphia/University City—and also, following national trends, with campus racial conflict, contentious identity politics, turbulent free-speech controversies, and episodes of fraternity boorishness, misogyny, homophobia, and hooliganism.

In the mid-1990s, when Judith Rodin—a former Yale provost, Penn alumna, and Philadelphia native—began her tenure as Penn's president, campus safety and security were continuing to deteriorate. Two members of the Penn community, a graduate student and an instructor, were murdered on the street. The escalating crisis of the surrounding area was the university's paramount concern. In 1997 Rodin inaugurated a multipronged program of what she termed "urban revival," later to be known as the "West Philadelphia Initiatives," with five categories of engagement: neighborhood safety and cleanliness, housing stabilization and reclamation, neighborhood retail development, locally targeted campus purchasing, and investments in public education.

In her 2007 memoir *The University and Urban Revival*, Rodin writes forcefully, "It boiled down to this: if Penn did not take the lead to revitalize the neighborhood, no one else would." While Rodin and the Office of the President exercised "overall leadership and direction," the university's executive vice president, John Fry (now president of Drexel University), and his chain of command managed the "day-to-day implementation" of the Initiatives. "Official roles were assigned to the deans and leadership of the Graduate School of Education, the Center for Community Partnerships, and Penn Design [formerly the School of Fine Arts]," she writes. "The goals regarding quality public education were implemented with the support of the center and the Graduate School of Education." Harkavy and Susan Fuhrman, dean of the Graduate School of Education (GSE), co-chaired a "West Philadelphia Region" school-improvement coalition, under the auspices of the School District. While continuing to mediate ABCS courses supporting school improvement projects, Netter Center staff assisted in the restructuring of the School District's regional governance in West Philadelphia. The GSE helped to create a new K–8 public school through a partnership with the School District and the Philadelphia Federation of Teachers.[24]

ABCS received a strong endorsement from the Rodin-appointed Provost's Council on Undergraduate Education, which she charged early in her tenure to redesign Penn's undergraduate education program for the twenty-first century; the Provost's Council cited ABCS as a signature pedagogical strategy of the university. As demonstrated in Penn's 1994–1995 annual report "The Unity of Theory and Practice: Penn's Distinctive Character," Rodin recognized that ABCS was not only good for Penn's community relations but also a powerfully integrated strategy to advance university-wide teaching, research, and service.[25] During Rodin's tenure, the university assigned a high priority to what faculty task forces called "the Urban Agenda." In "Building on Excellence," a strategic planning document published in 2003, a faculty task force commissioned by Rodin earmarked the Center for Community Partnerships for the development of an endowment.[26] Endowment funds arrived three years later, secured with the active involvement of President Amy Gutmann, Rodin's successor in College Hall. Under Gutmann's leadership, the university's $4.3 billion "Making History" capital campaign counted as part of its goal of a $10 million endowment gift to the Netter Center in the fall of 2007. (During the campaign, the center raised about $24 million in individual gifts, including the Netter endowment.)

The Penn Compact and the Netter Center:
One University in Practice

In her 2004 presidential inaugural address, Gutmann, a distinguished political theorist, unveiled the "Penn Compact." Gutmann described the Compact as a statement of "our boldest aspirations for higher education," which she enumerated as follows: "to increase access, to integrate knowledge, to engage locally and globally." While all three principles bear directly on the Netter Center for Community Partnerships, the third has been particularly relevant to its growth and development.[27]

A sine qua non for solving the incredibly complex problems of our global era is interdisciplinary research and teaching. In Gutmann's words, "We cannot understand the AIDS epidemic, for example, without joining the perspectives of medicine, nursing, and finance with those of biochemistry, psychology, sociology, politics, history, and literature."[28] The Compact calls on the university not only to view complex social problems as having, inextricably, both local and global dimensions but also to conceptualize Penn's work in West Philadelphia as part of a comprehensive effort to solve universal problems like poverty, inadequate health care, and failing public schools as those problems are manifested locally. Significantly, the Compact recognizes local engagement as a way for Penn to achieve eminence as a research university. Gutmann is the first president to create an *institutional* advancement strategy linked to local engagement.

Calls for integrating knowledge are not new at Penn. Martin Meyerson, president from 1970 to 1981, advanced "One University" as an aspirational goal to guide the physical, intellectual, and general institutional development and improvement of the university. Meyerson inherited from the urban renewal era a physically contiguous campus—all of its schools stood within walking distance of College Hall, without the impediment of city thoroughfares. Meyerson and his leadership team saw a great opportunity in Penn's physical integration, envisioning an intellectually integrated and diverse research university. They called on Penn to take full advantage of the university's unique heritage, physical setting, and intellectual configuration of resources to integrate the production and use of knowledge.

The Meyerson administration enacted several major policies to advance the One University idea: the creation of the Faculty of Arts and Sciences (later renamed the School of Arts and Sciences), the closing or downsizing of weak schools and departments (a policy called "selective excellence"), and the landscaping of the central campus, making it a true pedestrian enclave. Yet how Penn might actually begin to integrate the production and use of knowledge remained a conundrum for a future president to solve. The radical realignment that Meyerson advocated is, of course, much easier said than done. In practice, overcoming Penn's longstanding disciplinary fragmentation, narrow specialization, bureaucratic barriers, and what Franklin stigmatized in 1789 as "ancient Customs and Habitudes" proved enormously difficult to achieve. One University essentially remained an idea, not an action program. The Netter Center's approach, however, of working to help solve locally manifested universal problems has shown promise as a way forward. This has particularly been the case with programs that focus on reducing health inequities.

In 2002 a group of Penn undergraduates participating in an ABCS seminar focused their research and service on one of the most important problems identified by members of the West Philadelphia community—the issue of health. The students' work with the community ultimately led them to propose establishing a center focused on health promotion and disease prevention at a public school in West Philadelphia, the Sayre Middle School. (Sayre completed a three-year district transition and became a high school in 2007.)

From their research the students learned that community-oriented projects often founder because of an inability to secure stable resources. They postulated that they could accomplish their goal by integrating health issues into the curricula of various schools at Penn and at the Sayre School itself. They emphasized that creating a health promotion and disease prevention program at the school could serve as a learning opportunity for Penn students across all disciplines. This program quickly took root at Sayre and helped inform the long-term goal of creating an on-site primary health care center. The Sayre Health Center was formally opened in 2007 as a federally qualified health center and in 2010 was named the Dr. Bernett L. Johnson, Jr. Sayre Health Center, after the senior associate dean of Penn's Medical School who played a crucial role in the center's creation. Today, it is a central component of a university-assisted community school designed both to advance student learning and democratic development and to strengthen families and institutions within the community. Penn faculty members and students in medicine, nursing, dentistry, social policy and practice, arts and sciences, law, business, and design have worked at the Sayre School through newly created and existing courses, internships, and research projects, illustrating how the One University idea might be realized in practice.

Scholars associated with the Netter Center also promote the One University strategy globally through their participation in the International Consortium for Higher Education, Civic Responsibility, and Democracy. This joint effort with the Council of Europe's Committee on Higher Education includes a program of higher education research, practice, and colloquy to advance the "values of democracy, human rights and social, environmental, and economic sustainability" in local, national, and international settings (see Chapter 8).[29]

The theme that links Gutmann's Penn Compact and Meyerson's One University is the integration of knowledge. In contrast to the absence of a cohesive strategy that seriously limited Meyerson's conception, the Penn Compact (and its continuation through Compact 2020) encourages a unifying practical means to integrate knowledge for local and global problem solving. It also provides a powerful platform for stimulating Penn and other institutions of higher education around the world to work to realize in practice the idea of One University.

Thus far we have identified a civic tradition at the University of Pennsylvania that includes Benjamin Franklin, the Progressive Era Wharton School, and the present-day Netter Center for Community Partnerships. We have seen that Franklin proposed to educate youths for lives of useful citizenship and service—a vision that was thwarted by conservative Penn trustees of the Early Republic period. The practical, civic orientation of the pre–World War I Wharton School of Edmund James and Simon Nelson Patten would no doubt have pleased Franklin, but their action-oriented civic education was quashed by Penn trustees whose economic and social interests were threatened by faculty and student investigations. Displaced by the student frivolities and anti-intellectualism that were hallmarks of the collegiate way, Penn's civic tradition receded in the institution's memory until revivified by campus activists in the 1960s and finally given a systematic, institutional form during Sheldon Hackney's presidency.

In the 1980s Hackney tried to set Penn's civic "course aright."[30] He restructured the West Philadelphia Corporation to represent community interests and laid the foundation for a civic revival at Penn in the 1990s by establishing the Center for Community Partnerships. Harkavy and Benson introduced the idea of "academically based community service" (ABCS), calling for the creation or redesign of academic courses and seminars that would make West Philadelphia issues and problems the focus of student learning and problem-solving; these projects would be democratically designed and implemented in partnership with West Philadelphia teachers, students, and community organizations. Deeply cognizant of Penn's history, Benson, Harkavy, and the other authors of this book have come to see ourselves as intellectual and institutional heirs of Franklin and the James-Patten Wharton School, particularly with regard to their common emphasis on education for service and continuous human betterment.

To this point we have focused on the history, theory, and practice of the Netter Center for Community Partnerships as it operates in West Philadelphia. In Chapter 8, we explore the Netter Center's outreach programs and networking activities beyond Penn and West Philadelphia.

8

The Netter Center and
the Global Society

Outreach to the Nation and the World

> As the progress of learning consists not a little in the wise order-
> ing and institutions of each university, so it would be yet much
> more advanced if there were a closer connection and relation-
> ship between all the different universities of Europe than now
> there is.
>
> —FRANCIS BACON, *Advancement of Learning* (1605)

> To be a great university, we must first be a great local university.
>
> —SHIRLEY STRUM KENNY,
> former president, SUNY–Stony Brook (1999)

In Chapter 7 we traced the origins and early growth of the West Philadelphia Improvement Corps (WEPIC) project to create university-assisted
community schools (UACS) in West Philadelphia. We described how historical research informed the theory and practice of the early Netter Center,
and we looked at the organizational innovations and developments at Penn
that facilitated the expansion of WEPIC in the public schools of West Philadelphia and WEPIC's development as a cornerstone of the Netter Center. In
the present chapter, we explore replication and outreach projects that carried
the WEPIC idea and the Netter Center's UACS strategy, as well as related
approaches the center has helped stimulate, to other institutions of higher
education in the greater Philadelphia area, to strategic regional sites within
the United States, and to countries around the globe. We begin our narrative
in the early years of WEPIC's outreach initiatives.

Replicating the WEPIC Idea: From
the Region to the Nation

Within a few years of WEPIC's founding, a number of agencies began to
express interest in the project's approach to collaboration between university,

community, and local schools. In 1987, the U.S. Department of Labor designated a WEPIC program involving high school students in housing construction a National Demonstration Youth Employment and Training Program. In
1988, the German Marshall Fund of the United States sponsored education
study tours in Europe for WEPIC partners, including Penn and WEPIC staff,
West Philadelphia schoolteachers, and local nonprofit, governmental, and
business leaders. These tours resulted in a 1989 publication by the Brookings
Institution, *Schoolworks: Reinventing Public Schools to Create the Workforce
of the Future, Innovations in Education and Job Training from Sweden, West
Germany, France, Great Britain, and Philadelphia*. Its author cited WEPIC as
"one of the nation's leading local education and training initiatives."[1]

In 1987, Penn and two other Philadelphia universities, Temple and La
Salle, founded the Philadelphia Higher Education Network for Neighborhood Development (PHENND), a consortium of colleges and universities in
the greater Philadelphia area dedicated to helping revitalize local communities and schools and to fostering civic responsibility among the region's institutions of higher education. At this writing, PHENND's membership includes
more than thirty colleges and universities.[2]

Having helped to inaugurate PHENND, Harkavy joined forces with like-
minded colleagues around the country to organize a national movement. Over
the next quarter-century, to promote what he called "The Cause," he traveled
the national rubber chicken circuit, gave hundreds of speeches, co-authored
books and book chapters, and published in academic journals. The original reference point for Penn's contribution to this national dialogue was the
WEPIC program, the theory and practice of which Benson, Harkavy, Puckett,
and Hackney discussed in academic journals[3] and Harkavy described in numerous speeches around the country. The next step was to seed WEPIC-style
partnerships at other universities.

In 1992, the year of its official founding, the Netter Center for Community
Partnerships (then the Center for Community Partnerships) entered into discussions with the Wallace Foundation (then the DeWitt Wallace–Reader's Di
gest Fund) about replicating the WEPIC concept, and particularly the center's
work at Turner Middle School, which was the most developed site in West
Philadelphia. The cohort of approximately one hundred Turner students involved in WEPIC's first full-year school-within-a-school in 1990–1991 demonstrated improved academic performance compared with both their own
1989–1990 percentile results and their school's overall results as measured by
the Philadelphia School District's Comprehensive Test of Basic Skills.[4]

Intrigued by these on-site programs, the level of school and community
participation, and more broadly the idea of university-assisted community
schools, the Wallace Foundation awarded an eighteen-month planning grant
to the "WEPIC Replication Project" to explore the feasibility of adapting the

model nationally. On the strength of the feasibility study, the Wallace Foundation awarded the center a $1 million implementation grant that it used to support, through training and technical assistance, replication efforts at three universities, the winners of a competitive review process: Miami University of Ohio (for work in Cincinnati), the University of Kentucky–Lexington (UK), and the University of Alabama–Birmingham (UAB). The three replication sites offered school-day, afterschool, and Saturday programs designed along the lines of Penn's WEPIC program, as well as parent-engagement activities, such as training parents to serve as paraprofessionals within the schools. UAB and UK education faculty also taught their university service learning courses on-site at their partner schools.

Conferences, site meetings, and the center's ongoing journal, *Universities and Community Schools,* publicized and helped to build a national network to expand the WEPIC Replication initiative. Additional grants from the Wallace Foundation and the Learn and Serve America program of the Corporation for National and Community Service funded twenty-three university-assisted community school (UACS) programs at two- and four-year colleges and research universities through 2004. These institutions of higher education provided afterschool programs along WEPIC lines and, with the Learn and Serve America funding, helped incorporate service learning into the curricula of their partner schools.[5]

In 2006 four of the authors—Harkavy, Matthew Hartley, Rita Hodges, and Joann Weeks—undertook a retrospective study of the center's replication efforts. A survey was sent to twenty of the sites, and four sites were selected for on-site interviews by Hartley. At least eight institutions reported "significant growth in university engagement since they began as a replication site, indicating that start-up grants and technical support (through the Replication Project) helped them create a solid foundation on which to build." They reported partnering with local K–12 schools, expanding their range of service learning courses, and establishing campus partnership centers. The schools benefited from a range of academic and enrichment programs that would have been infeasible without these partnerships, including service learning projects, mentoring and exposure to college campuses, and activities open to the wider community along the lines of the WEPIC model.[6] Although many of these WEPIC replication projects have been discontinued—in some cases because of transitions in project or university personnel, in other cases because of partner-school restructuring or school closings—some UACS projects have endured with considerable strength. The University of New Mexico continues to support its network of community schools in Albuquerque; the University of Dayton works with six schools across the city; and Indiana University–Purdue University Indianapolis (IUPUI) maintains extensive support for George Washington Community High School and its feeder schools and has established UACS projects in other areas of Indianapolis (see below).

With the naming gift from Edward and Barbara Netter, a Penn alumnus and his spouse, in 2007, the Netter Center began to target the development of regional (multistate) training centers at other campuses whose service learning programs were already aligned with the UACS framework and whose faculty and staff demonstrated a capacity to provide technical assistance to other institutions. Over the next several years, three regional university centers for UACS were designated, funded, and charged to strengthen the community school partnerships in their immediate localities and to provide regionwide training for institutions of higher education interested in developing UACS programs.

Two of the regional centers, the IUPUI Midwest Center for UACS (established in 2011) and the University of Connecticut New England Center for UACS (established in 2014), are housed on their respective campuses in offices designated for community outreach. They provide academic resources to support UACS programs: in IUPUI's case, in the Indianapolis schools, especially George Washington Community High School; in UConn's case, in the Hartford city schools. In their respective regions, they train university faculty and staff for partnership roles and responsibilities, and they consult with community school coordinators, teachers and administrators, and parent-liaison personnel. The inaugural regional center, the University of Oklahoma–Tulsa Southwest Center for UACS (established in 2007), has a different organizational form than its sister centers. In 2011, the work of the Southwest Center was incorporated into the Higher Education Forum of Oklahoma, a consortium of ten colleges and universities and their community partners in northeastern Oklahoma, housed at Tulsa Community College. As the umbrella for partnerships with eight northeastern Oklahoma school districts, including the Tulsa Public Schools, and eleven community agencies, the Higher Education Forum helps link the area's high schools and colleges through a program that includes higher education–assisted college-readiness and career-exploration programs.

Building a National Infrastructure for University-Community Partnerships

The Netter Center has fostered the development of national and global networks that support university-community partnerships. It has also pioneered the idea of universities and academic medical institutions as essential anchor institutions for such partnerships. We turn now to three national organizations that the Netter Center helped found.

The center is a founding partner of the Coalition for Community Schools, which was established at the Institute for Educational Leadership in Washington, DC, in 1997 (see Chapter 4).[7] At this writing, more than two hundred regional and national organizations (for example, health and social agencies, youth development organizations, and school practitioner associations) are Coalition partners.[8] In 2015 the Coalition, the Netter Center, and Rutgers University–Camden, responding to the growing number of colleges and universities engaged in UACS programs, created the University-Assisted Community Schools Network. Its aim is to build a professional learning community among higher education leaders that shares resources and best practices to advance university-community partnerships and community schools. More than fifty colleges and universities are participants. The range of support provided by these institutions of higher education to schools, students, and families includes academic enrichment, mental and physical health services, youth development programs, dual-enrollment classes and college access, and parent-resource development.

Two examples are the University at Buffalo, SUNY, and Florida International University. The Center for Urban Studies at the University at Buffalo (UB) supports the "Community as Classroom" program at Futures Academy, a preK–8 public school on Buffalo's East Side. As they studied the area's built environment, for instance, the schoolchildren worked alongside UB undergraduates and local residents on the Futures Garden project to transform a vacant, derelict lot near the school into a community garden and art park. In Miami, Florida International University oversees the "Education Effect," FIU's university-assisted community school partnership with Northwestern High School to improve science education and college access. This program includes dual-enrollment classes at Northwestern, an aquaponics science lab, and visits to the FIU campus.

The Department of Housing and Urban Development (HUD) oversees another national project that advances university-community partnerships. The aim of HUD's Office of University Partnerships (OUP), established in 1994, is "to encourage and expand the growing number of partnerships formed between colleges and universities and their communities." OUP's role is to facilitate "the formation of campus-community partnerships that enable students, faculty, and neighborhood organizations to work together to revitalize the economy, generate jobs, and rebuild healthy communities." Until 2012, it provided "grants, interactive conferences, and housing and urban development-related research" to strengthen and expand these collaborations.[9]

Harkavy worked closely with Secretary Henry Cisneros and higher education leaders, including the early directors of the Office of University Partnerships and HUD staff members, in shaping the OUP's early operations, including the Community Outreach Partnership Center (COPC) program.

In 2002, the Urban Institute reported on the progress of COPC: "Since 1994, HUD has invested approximately $45 million in more than 100 colleges, universities and community colleges to support community engagement. Most COPC grantees (77 percent) are public institutions, and an even larger majority (81 percent) are universities; two-year community colleges constitute only six percent of program grantees." The Urban Institute noted, unsurprisingly, considerable variability among the grantees, "from those [institutions] that exhibit a high overall level of integration of community engagement in academic and administrative practices and policies, to those that have more limited resources and are typically dependent on individual faculty members to continue their outreach work."[10]

In a 1995 essay, which Harkavy helped draft, Cisneros forcefully challenged colleges and universities—calling them "great anchoring institutions"—to adopt COPC's aims as part of their social responsibility and dedicate "formidable intellectual and economic resources" to improve the well-being of their cities.[11] In 1999, the Aspen Institute Roundtable on Comprehensive Community Initiatives broadly defined "anchor institutions" as those "that have a significant infrastructure investment in a specific community and are therefore unlikely to move out of that community," applying the term to institutions of higher education, medical centers, and public utilities.[12] According to a 2013 literature review, anchor institutions "emerged [after 2000] as a new paradigm for understanding the role that place-based institutions could play in building successful communities and local economies."[13]

Partnerships between anchor institutions and communities gained increased impetus from the Anchor Institutions Task Force (AITF). Following the 2008 presidential election, the incoming Obama administration asked a group of more than one hundred academics and practitioners calling themselves the "urban and metropolitan policy caucus," led by professor of law Rachel Godsil and community development consultant Paul Brophy, to put together a series of recommendations for Shaun Donovan, President Barack Obama's nominee as secretary of HUD. Godsil and Brophy worked closely with the co-directors of the Penn Institute for Urban Research, Eugenie Birch and Susan Wachter, to organize a series of task force groups that would develop the specific recommendations.[14] After hearing a panel moderated by Harkavy in December 2008 at the Philadelphia-based Foundation for Architecture, Brophy was convinced that recommendations to the incoming HUD secretary should also come from a group that would advise on strategies for mobilizing anchor institutions. A few weeks later, Harkavy was asked to chair and convene a national task force to advise HUD on how the agency could leverage anchor institutions, particularly "eds and meds," to improve communities and help solve significant urban problems. The Task Force on Anchor Institutions report, "Anchor Institutions as Partners in Building Successful

Communities and Local Economies," was published along with nine other reports in a volume entitled *Retooling HUD for a Catalytic Federal Government: A Report to Secretary Shaun Donovan* (2009).[15]

Soon after the report's publication, the ad hoc group convened by Harkavy became a formal organization, the Anchor Institutions Task Force (AITF), with the mission of helping to create and advance democratic, mutually beneficial partnerships between anchor institutions and communities. As we note above (Chapter 5), AITF, an individual membership organization, is guided by the core values of collaboration and partnership, equity and social justice, democracy and democratic practice, and commitment to place and community. Marga Incorporated administers AITF, with Harkavy continuing to serve as chair at the request of task force members. Significantly, the development of this group as a permanent organization, with approximately 700 members as of December 2016, has helped bring the idea of anchor institutions increasingly into national academic and policy discussions. Perhaps even more critical is AITF's unique role as a values-based movement organization, which helps ensure that as institutions increasingly embrace their role as community-minded anchors, they are making, in the words of David Maurrasse, founding president of Marga Incorporated and director of AITF, "an active commitment to reducing disparities and engaging in mutually beneficial, democratic collaboration."[16]

The global reach of the anchor institution concept is also noteworthy. At a 2014 Global Forum hosted in Belfast on "Higher Education and Democratic Innovation," Snežana Samardžić-Marković, director general of democracy for the Council of Europe, called for the creation of a network of anchor institutions in Europe.[17] Responding to that call, the Council of Europe and the AITF are co-sponsoring a European Conference on "Higher Education Institutions as Local Actors," to be held in Rome in June 2017.

Becoming an International Movement

Since the Netter Center's inception, one of its objectives has been to cultivate not only national but also international networks of institutions of higher education committed to democratic civic engagement with their communities. To realize his goal of advancing knowledge to improve the human condition, Bacon called for, among other things, "a closer connection and relationship between all the different universities of Europe."[18] The need for collaboration among universities, of course, is no longer restricted to Europe.

From the early 1990s onward, the Netter Center hosted visitors from across Europe, Africa, Asia, and Australia and invited them to participate in conferences. Harkavy worked closely with a number of international projects, including the Community–Higher Education–Service Partnerships (CHESP) initiative, which South Africa's Joint Education Trust inaugurated in 1999. In post-apartheid South Africa, CHESP's goals were to create partnerships for the reconstruction and development of civil society and transform higher education to meet societal needs. CHESP partnered eight South African universities with eight U.S. colleges and universities for extended study tours by teams composed of faculty and senior administrative staff from each South African university along with local community leaders. Penn's partner was the University of Witwatersrand (Wits). This relationship lasted beyond the study tour and conference, with Penn entering into a formal exchange agreement with Wits and visits by Harkavy, Johnston, and other Penn colleagues to Wits and other South African institutions of higher education.[19]

Connections to South Africa were further developed through a grant from the National Science Foundation (NSF) to the Netter Center to convene a series of workshops for higher education representatives from South Africa (including that country's National Research Foundation), the United States, and China. From 2012 through 2014, workshops hosted at Penn, the Durban University of Technology in South Africa, and NSF focused on the theme of the "Role of Higher Education: Fostering P–20+ Community Engagement through Knowledge Production, Human Capacity Building, Innovation and Social Cohesion."[20]

In a white paper and at the workshops, South African colleagues shared innovative approaches to higher education–community engagement (including programs with dedicated funding) that were under development at South African universities. The authors of the white paper reported specifically on two developments:

- The South Africa Council on Higher Education (formed in 1997) and its quality-assessment unit, the Higher Education Quality Committee (HEQC), established "knowledge based community service" as a requirement for program accreditation and quality assurance and made reporting on community engagement mandatory for institutional audits. "One of the consequences of the HEQC audits has been the institutionalization of community engagement in South African universities," including the establishment of offices of community engagement in all twenty-one universities.
- The National Research Foundation (NRF) of South Africa released its "Vision 2015" strategic plan in 2008, identifying a number of strategic investment areas, including community engagement: "The decision to initiate investment in community engagement signaled the NRF's commitment to better support research . . . [on] community engagement for knowledge production, innovation and human capital development to align more closely with the higher educa-

tion mandate of research, teaching and community service/engagement." The NRF's inaugural Community Engagement Program was launched in 2010 and awarded approximately $116 million to seventeen projects over a three-year period.[21]

The most significant and enduring global organizational development has been the formation of the International Consortium for Higher Education, Civic Responsibility, and Democracy (IC) in 1999. Its purpose is to advance the contributions of institutions of higher education to democratic development on campus, as well as in local communities and the wider society. The IC works in collaboration with the Council of Europe (COE) and its Steering Committee on Educational Policy and Practice. The COE, established in 1949, defends human rights, democracy, and the rule of law; develops continent-wide agreements to standardize member countries' social and legal practices; and promotes awareness of a European identity across cultures based on shared values. It is Europe's oldest existing political organization, with a total membership of forty-seven countries, including twenty-one countries from central and eastern Europe. Three other countries are party to the European Cultural Convention, which provides the framework for the COE's work in education policy and practice.[22]

The IC/COE collaboration undertakes cross-national research projects, joint meetings, and the sharing of best practices as part of its efforts to advance higher education's contribution to building democratic societies. The Netter Center houses the executive offices of the IC, and Associate Director Joann Weeks serves as its executive secretary. Membership in the IC is by country. Each country is represented by a small delegation or a steering committee formed by the leaders of the country's higher education associations; these delegates and steering committee members constitute the IC. Harkavy chairs the U.S. steering committee, which includes leaders from the American Council on Education, the American Association of State Colleges and Universities, the Association of American Colleges and Universities, Campus Compact, the Democracy Commitment, and NASPA (an organization of student-affairs professionals in higher education). Australia has joined through Engagement Australia, the United Kingdom is represented by the National Co-ordinating Centre for Public Engagement, Ireland has joined through Campus Engage Ireland, and South Africa is represented by Universities South Africa.

Complementary developments in the United States and Europe laid a strong foundation for the IC/COE collaboration, including the Council of Europe's *Budapest Declaration for a Greater Europe without Dividing Lines,* adopted on the organization's fiftieth anniversary (May 1999), which designated the education system as the major societal means for democratic development. And in July 1999 fifty-one college and university presidents in the United States signed a *Presidents' Declaration on the Civic Responsibility of Higher Education*, sponsored by Campus Compact (see Chapter 5). Nearly six hundred universities have now signed the declaration, which highlights the university's central role in citizenship education.[23]

The IC/COE collaboration first launched a cross-national research project on "Universities as Sites of Citizenship and Responsibility." Beginning in 1999 a team of European and U.S. researchers assessed the activities of institutions of higher education that supported democratic values and practices, and also helped to disseminate those activities. Working groups were established to develop the methodology and protocols for the research. Fourteen European and fifteen U.S. universities completed the pilot study, whose U.S. component was funded by NSF. The COE published the research findings in *The University as Res Publica: Higher Education Governance, Student Participation and the University as a Site of Citizenship* (2004).

The collaboration has hosted four global forums, and the COE has published monographs on the conference themes, including *Higher Education and Democratic Culture: Citizenship, Human Rights, and Civic Responsibility* (2008), *Higher Education for Modern Societies: Competencies and Values* (2010), *Reimagining Democratic Societies: A New Era of Personal and Social Responsibility* (2013), and *Higher Education for Democratic Innovation* (2016). Additional partners joined in planning the conferences, among them the International Association of Universities, the European Wergeland Centre, the European Students' Union, and the University of Oslo and Queen's University–Belfast, which hosted the 2011 and 2014 forums, respectively.

Other major global networks promote the civic and social responsibilities of institutions of higher education. The Talloires Network, for example, has 350 institutional members representing seventy-seven countries. The Global University Network for Innovation (GUNi) has 208 institutional members representing seventy-eight countries.[24]

Among the major defects Bacon attributed to universities, their internal divisions and their failure to collaborate closely ranked high. We quote this passage from his great work *The Advancement of Learning*:

As the progress of learning consists not a little in the wise ordering and institutions of each university, so it would be yet much more advanced if there were a closer connection and relationship between all the different universities of Europe than now there is. For we see there are many orders and societies which, though they be divided under distant sovereignties and territories, yet enter into and maintain among themselves a kind of contract and fraternity, in so much that they have governors (both provincial and general) whom they all obey. And surely as nature creates brotherhood in families, and arts mechanical contract brotherhoods in societies, and the anointment of God superinduces a brotherhood in kings and bishops, and vows and regulations make a brotherhood in religious orders; so in like manner there cannot but be a noble and generous brotherhood contracted among men by learning and illumination, seeing that God himself is called "the Father of Lights."[25]

In our judgment, the International Consortium, as well as networks such as Talloires and GUNi, is a positive response to Bacon's proposal that institutions of higher education collaborate across cultures and national boundaries to advance learning and human welfare.

In describing the Netter Center's regional, national, and global initiatives, we have argued that the *collaborative approach* embedded in the higher education projects, coalitions, networks, and task forces it has helped catalyze exemplifies Bacon's insightful proposition that the true advancement of learning is contingent on "a closer connection and relationship between the universities." Writing in the early seventeenth century, Bacon's frame of reference was limited to "the universities of Europe," but his proposition provides a strong, logically powerful, and quintessentially pragmatic rationale for collaboration between and among universities in today's global society. The more contemporary universities combine insights, ideas, and resources to focus on and help solve multifaceted community and societal problems, the greater the likelihood of advances in learning and human well-being.

Against the backdrop of this essential Baconian proposition, we have delineated several significant developments over the past quarter-century. Having played an instrumental role in organizing the multi-institutional Philadelphia Higher Education Network for Neighborhood Development in 1987, Harkavy and his colleagues were primed to build or contribute to numerous national projects, organizations, and networks: the WEPIC Replication Project, the Coalition for Community Schools, the Community Outreach Partnership Center of HUD's Office of University Partnerships, Netter Center–sponsored regional centers for university-assisted community schools, and the Anchor Institutions Task Force. And true to the Penn Compact, the Netter Center has adopted *an explicit global agenda* through its development and leadership of networks that engage U.S. colleges and universities with the Council of Europe through the International Consortium for Higher Education, Civic Responsibility, and Democracy, as well as through other global collaborations that advance higher education's social responsibilities.

While this is a propitious beginning on an international scale, it is still only a beginning. As in the United States, realizing the goal of embedding democratic civic engagement in the academic programs of a range of colleges and universities around the globe will necessitate a "long march" of dedicated, resilient, activist academics through historically conservative institutions. As in the United States, these global long-marchers will need effective approaches if they are to move higher education from *here* (being a source of the problem of nondemocratic education and schooling) to *there* (being a contributor to solving that problem). Our experiences have convinced us that academically based community service and university-assisted community schools are promising and effective approaches that can be translated into and effectively adapted to diverse national and international settings. We now turn to the most developed academically based community service project: the Agatston Urban Nutrition Initiative, created and led since 1991 by Francis Johnston.

9

Solving Complex Real-World Problems through Academically Based Community Service

The Agatston Urban Nutrition Initiative

If you want truly to understand something, try to change it.
—Maxim widely attributed to Kurt Lewin

To say that obesity is caused by merely consuming too many calories is like saying that the only cause of the American Revolution was the Boston Tea Party.
—Observation widely attributed to Adelle Davis

The growth of children amongst the various groups which make up a contemporary society reflects rather accurately the material and moral condition of that society.
—James M. Tanner, *Growth as a Mirror of the Condition of Society* (1986)

The Agatston Urban Nutrition Initiative (AUNI) is a comprehensive, academically based community service (ABCS) program of the Netter Center for Community Partnerships. AUNI emerged from requests from West Philadelphia school and community partners to collaborate on health improvement projects. It has achieved its present organization and implementation through several conceptual shifts over the past two decades. Today, AUNI integrates research, teaching, learning, and service in an approach that brings together a range of Penn's social science, health, and medical resources, as well as the resources of community partners at the Netter Center's five university-assisted community schools (UACS) sites in West Philadelphia, at approximately fifteen other Philadelphia schools, and at various West Philadelphia community centers and locations, to improve health and nutrition and reduce obesity.

Francis Johnston, a Penn anthropology professor, and his undergraduate and graduate students have worked over the past two and a half decades on solutions to the problem of childhood and youth obesity in collaboration with West Philadelphia community members, teachers, students, and administrators in local public schools. We begin this chapter with a discussion of obesity as an ill-structured problem and describe the pedagogy that underlies the reconstruction of education as problem-solving learning, a hallmark of academically based community service at Penn. We then delineate the problem of childhood and youth obesity in West Philadelphia. We look next at how AUNI utilizes a neo-Deweyan problem-solving approach to address poor nutrition and obesity. We trace the program's history, both chronologically and conceptually, from its origins in a single middle school in the early 1990s to its expansion to other West Philadelphia schools in the mid-1990s, to its citywide adoption as a public health initiative of the School District of Philadelphia in the early 2000s, and finally to its current, multifaceted operation.

Obesity as a Complex, Ill-Structured Problem

The risks to health that are associated with obesity are clear and significant. Extensive research identifies obesity as a national—even international—epidemic, perhaps the greatest public health failure of recent decades.[1] The increase in the prevalence of obesity among adults as well as children and youth became a public health issue in the 1970s, as did the growing incidence of type 2 diabetes among children and youth. One well-established research finding is that obesity in childhood and youth, which is associated with type 2 diabetes, tends to predict adult obesity and the health problems that accompany that condition.[2] Cheryl Fryar, Margaret Carroll, and Cynthia Ogden's graph (Figure 9.1), using data from the Centers for Disease Control (CDC), shows the dramatic increase in the percentage of overweight and obese American children from the 1970s to 2009–2010.[3]

The CDC reports that "among preschool children ages two to five years, obesity increased from 5.0 percent to 12.1 percent between 1976–1980 and 2009–2010; it increased from 6.5 percent to 18.0 percent among those ages six to eleven. Among adolescents ages twelve to nineteen, obesity increased from 5.0 percent to 18.4 percent during the same period." Racial and ethnic disparities are prevalent in the data for 2009–2010: 17.5 percent for non-Hispanic white boys versus 22.6 percent for non-Hispanic black boys and 28.9 percent for Mexican American boys; 14.7 percent for non-Hispanic white girls versus 18.6 percent for Mexican American girls and 24.8 percent for non-Hispanic black girls.[4]

It is equally clear that obesity is more than just a health-related condition: it is an indicator of a complex interaction of a broad range of social and cultural factors that two of the authors of this book, Harkavy and Johnston, elsewhere

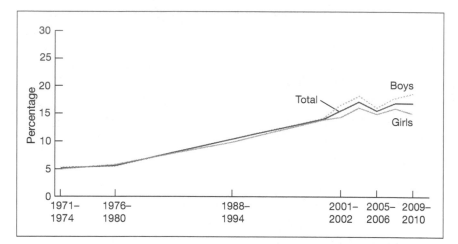

Figure 9.1. Trends in obesity among children and adolescents two to nineteen years old, by sex, in the United States, 1971–1974 through 2009–2010. (U.S. Centers for Disease Control and Prevention, "Prevalence of Obesity among Children and Adolescents: United States, Trends 1963–1965 through 2009–2010," by Cheryl D. Fryar, Margaret D. Carroll, and Cynthia L. Ogden, available at http://www.cdc.gov/nchs/data/hestat/obesity_child_09_10/obesity_child_09_10.pdf.)

have termed the "obesity culture," an ill-defined, complex, and poorly understood problem that can be solved only through effective and sustainable efforts.[5]

Obesity is not simply the result of an absence of willpower or the overfeeding of children, corporate evildoing, or lack of exercise. It is in a category of contemporary social and health dilemmas that fit the description of complex, ill-defined or ill-structured problems. That is, they cannot be specified with any certainty, nor can their parts be related to each other in any clearly structured framework. In a 1997 paper, Shelagh Gallagher discusses how ill-structured problems differ from ones that are well defined:

- More information than is initially available is needed to understand the problem and decide what actions are required for its resolution.
- No single formula exists for conducting an investigation to resolve the problem.
- As new information is obtained, the problem changes.
- One can never be sure that the "right" decision has been made.[6]

As Dewey persuasively argued, a problematic situation whose dimensions are not self-evident (an ill-structured problem, in our terms) is ripe with opportunities for thinking. In *How We Think* (1910), *Democracy and Education* (1916), and later related works such as *Logic: A Theory of Inquiry* (1937), Dewey brilliantly explicated the role of an ill-structured problem in stimulating purposeful, productive (reflective) thinking. A committed Darwinist, he described a biologically formed, discursive problem-solving mode that productive human beings apply in their daily lives in all manner of problematic situations. He sketched out a heuristic for reflective thinking, a process he called "the complete act of thought," which he loosely associated with the method of science: (1) an ongoing activity that is not problematic, representing in biological terms a state of equilibrium; (2) a meaningful problem that arises within the course of this activity, creating a state of dissonance or disequilibrium and stimulating further thought; (3) refinement of the difficulty or perplexity to specify precisely its dimensions; (4) the formulation and elaboration of an idea or suggestion into a tentative solution to the problem, a hypothesis; (5) testing the validity of the hypothesis by an application—by visible action and observation of results or by mental action and contemplation of results; and (6) a review or summary of the entire process that results in a conclusion or course of action to determine what was positive, negative, or nugatory, constructing a cognitive steppingstone for dealing effectively with future problems in analogous situations.

Trying to solve the complex, ill-structured problem of obesity in West Philadelphia results in significant thinking, planning, and activity. Consistent with Dewey's pedagogical theory,[7] part of students' learning is achieved through traditional didactic means: classroom lectures and assigned readings. Yet, contrary to the neo-Platonic, essentialist model of academic learning, our neo-Deweyan model treats disciplinary subject matter not as an end in itself but as a *means* for productive thinking. ABCS students apply their new (new to them) knowledge and skills to the real-world obesity problem as manifested locally. Penn students work with Penn faculty, AUNI staff, community partners, and public school teachers and students. In Deweyan terms, the prospect of solving the obesity problem of West Philadelphia schoolchildren constitutes an "end-in-view"; students' interest in the end-in-view provides the motivation that suffuses every phase of the project, from the university-classroom component to the planning and on-site implementation of AUNI. Reasoned speculation leads us to believe that this Deweyan (testable) hypothesis explains in no small way the interest and energy the AUNI project evokes in idealistic undergraduates. Dewey's idea of end-in-view is embedded in the process of continuous, iterative institutional learning and flexible planning characteristic of AUNI's growth since 1990–1991. The following sections describe the main turning points and conceptual developments of the program.

Origins and First Decade's Growth

The community health project that evolved into the Netter Center's Agatston Urban Nutrition Initiative originated in the fall of 1990 at the John P. Turner Middle School in West Philadelphia. Located about 2.5 miles from the Penn campus, the Turner School was the site of a pilot community school launched in 1989 by the West Philadelphia Improvement Corps (WEPIC), a coalition of Penn faculty, staff, and students and West Philadelphia teachers, middle and high school students, school administrators, and community leaders (see Chapter 7). WEPIC worked with the Penn Program for Public Service (PPPS), the predecessor of the Netter Center for Community Partnerships. In the summer of 1990, WEPIC organized a School of Medicine–supported summer institute that involved Turner Middle School pupils and their teachers working alongside Penn medical students and undergraduates in the PPPS Summer Internship program; their collaboration centered on the development and operation of a community health–centered curriculum and hypertension screening program—a program that included, among other activities, a health-risk survey, focused medical histories, and blood-pressure testing by the (supervised) middle school children.

Johnston, a specialist in nutritional anthropology, helped move the community health project into the Turner School's regular curriculum. In the fall of 1990, Harkavy and Benson met with Johnston, whose career to that point had focused on nutritional problems in Latin America, the United States, and other parts of the world. Specifically, he focused on the negative impact of poor nutrition on children and youth and the development and application of interventions to mitigate these health threats.[8] Although he was committed to the core premises underlying ABCS and had been working with Harkavy on the Turner School community health project, Johnston had no prior experience with ABCS-related programming. His subsequent meetings with Benson and Harkavy resulted in the development of an undergraduate ABCS anthropology course that was a restructured version of Anthropology 210: "Anthropology and Biomedical Science," a course originally developed to link premedical training at Penn with the Department of Anthropology and the field of biomedical science.

First offered in the fall of 1991, Johnston's new ABCS course was listed as Anthropology 310: "Nutrition, Health, and Community Schools." The initial class of eighteen Penn students worked with Turner sixth-grade students on a range of small-scale participatory action research projects dealing with healthy foods, physical growth, dietary intake, and obesity status. The results were used in planning subsequent activities. Over the next decade, Anthropology 310 operated more or less according to the following format:

> For their work at Turner, the Penn students are divided into four groups. One group, about half of the class, is responsible for teaching nutrition to Turner students on a weekly basis throughout the semester. Under the guidance of a graduate teaching assistant, lesson plans are discussed and formulated. This group of Penn students uses the

lesson plans to teach about nutrition, food, and the health outcomes of the Turner students' dietary choices. A second group of Penn students is charged with carrying out the collection and analysis of dietary data at Turner; in this activity, they interview individual students, collect 24-hour recalls of food intake, and enter the data into computers for analysis using appropriate software. A third group carries out an anthropometric determination of nutritional status, focusing on physical growth, body fatness, and the prevalence of obesity, which is a major problem among the urban poor. The fourth group (the smallest) involves students in related research on topics including observational studies of the local school lunchroom, type and distribution of restaurants and grocery stores in the area, children's attitudes about food, and other issues important in a nutritional ecosystem. Data collection and analysis are presented as an ongoing research project subject to the principles of research design, reliability and validity, and both quantitative and qualitative analysis.[9]

Turner School teachers participated in the design and preparation of the nutrition education component. Penn students and Turner sixth graders worked side by side to access the adequacy of the children's dietary intakes and the nutrients they contained. The Turner students also learned and practiced techniques of measuring height and body weight, as well as calculating and assessing body mass index (BMI) as an indicator of nutritional status. As seventh graders, these same youngsters presented their research findings to their peers and taught nutrition and healthy eating behaviors to elementary school children. By the mid-1990s, Anthropology 310, with increasing enrollments (capped at twenty five), had diversified to feature a broader range of food- and nutrition-related activities. After 1992, the program was called the Turner Nutritional Awareness Project (TNAP).

To carry out the nutrition project, Penn undergraduates and Turner middle school students had to collect, organize, and interpret a relatively large and complex body of data directly relevant to Johnston's longstanding research interests. In the process of carrying out their work, the Penn and Turner students functioned as his research assistants, collaborating members of a research team that he supervised and directed. The project recorded a high rate of obesity among the middle school students. Analysis of dietary intakes showed that the consumption of fat, saturated fat, protein, and carbohydrates exceeded not only recommended daily allowances (RDA) but also the consumption levels for their age peers nationally. Deficiencies were found in the intakes of calcium, zinc, fiber, and vitamins A and D.[10] A study of 392 West Philadelphia school students (ages eleven to fifteen) conducted by one of Johnston's doctoral students found that 31 percent were obese.[11]

Danny Gerber and Tamara Dubowitz, Penn students, took Johnston's course in the mid-1990s. Both worked for several years in TNAP and served as Johnston's teaching assistants. Under Gerber's leadership, the Turner School and Penn students designed and established a student-operated school garden—the first of its kind in Philadelphia (see below). It soon became, and it remains, a signature activity of AUNI. In 1995, Dubowitz, working with Turner sixth graders and Penn undergraduates in Anthropology 310, launched the "Fruits R Us (and Vegetables Too)" fruit stand at Turner. The garden and the fruit and vegetable stand supplied Turner students, teachers, staff, and parents with fresh produce in a community-oriented setting. In 1995, TNAP was renamed the Youth Empowerment Nutrition Initiative (YENI).

TNAP's Expansion: UNI and AUNI

An extraordinarily civic-minded activist, Gerber led the expansion of TNAP/YENI from the Turner School to two other West Philadelphia public schools: University City High School (UCHS) and the Charles R. Drew Elementary School (K–8). These schools were located on adjacent sites a block north of Market Street and east of 38th Street, a three-block walk from the Penn campus, providing easy access for Penn students.[12] They assisted in the urban garden directed by Gerber and shared by the two schools, a co-curricular afterschool program for UCHS students, and a fruit and vegetable stand at Drew. With this expansion, TNAP/YENI was renamed the Urban Nutrition Initiative (UNI) in 1996. Edward and Barbara Netter provided significant financial support in 2001, challenging UNI to broaden its scope.

As part of their work helping to build and implement UNI programs, Penn undergraduates participated in small-scale research activities that were also core components of their ABCS coursework. For example, they analyzed the impact of UNI on dietary intake, nutrition, and health-related behavior, which provided affirmative (though by no means definitive) testimony for the general efficacy of Dubowitz and Gerber's approach. Johnston and his students base their work on the assumption that behavioral change associated with improved nutrition and overall healthier lifestyles is more likely to take place when all stakeholders, including the schoolchildren and youth, are involved in planning and implementing the program.

In one undergraduate study, schoolchildren demonstrated positive changes in afterschool snacking associated with the fruit and vegetable stand. On the day when the stand was open, the consumption of fruits almost doubled (from 39 percent of pupils to 68 percent), and consumption of vegetables almost tripled (from 13 percent to 38 percent), compared with snacking on other school days. The snacks of children at the UNI-supported school were also healthier than those at a control school, indicating the influence of the fruit stand beyond the day of operation.[13]

Another study looked at the effects of participation in UNI activities among sixth graders. The number of visits and purchases by the students in the weeks following the opening of the stand were compared with those of two classes that had not taken part in the planning. (All students had been exposed to schoolwide announcements about the stand and its hours of operation.) Those who participated in planning and implementation were significantly more likely than nonparticipants to visit the stand in the following several weeks and to make purchases.[14]

In another study, 200 twelfth-grade high school students who had been part of UNI programming for four years completed twenty-four-hour recalls of their diets, with the nutrient intakes calculated by appropriate software. The nutrient intakes of these high school seniors were healthier than those of ninth graders who were in their first year of UNI programming. Twelfth graders, for example, consumed twice as many daily servings of fruits and vegetables as the ninth graders did.[15] Participation in UNI was also shown to be associated with more positive attitudes and beliefs about oneself, as well as a greater willingness to try new foods. And, finally, the parents of first and second graders were more likely to know about and make purchases from the fruit stand if their children were involved in it.[16]

UNI also began to look at exercise habits among the families it worked with in West Philadelphia. Lack of exercise is widely recognized as a major contributor to obesity in children and adults, especially among the poor, as well as a risk factor for other diseases. Programs to decrease obesity through exercise, however, have had disappointing results. Physical fitness has become a commodity that is exploited by the diet, food processing, and fashion industries, manufacturers of increasingly sophisticated fitness equipment, and advertisers. The commodification of physical fitness diminishes opportunities for exercise among the urban poor, who cannot afford fees for a gym membership (even if a facility is available in their neighborhood) or equipment for the home. Crime and violence in their communities often curtail opportunities to simply walk, jog, or play outside, while urban schools are increasingly unable to support and maintain physical education programs because of budget cuts and a narrowing of the curriculum to emphasize subjects covered on standardized state assessments, among other reasons.[17]

In the early 2000s UNI initiated a weekly fitness night. It began as free program for local community residents to participate in such activities as swimming, basketball, weightlifting, and aerobic dancing. The program's success, supplemented with input from community participants, led UNI to add a range of lessons in yoga, fitness for asthmatics, and various dance styles (line dancing, salsa, ballet), as well as activities not directly related to exercise, like healthy cooking, adult computer literacy, music lessons, and more. Penn students became involved as teachers and as part of their service learning experience.[18]

After graduating from Penn, Gerber spent several years as a teacher in the Philadelphia public schools. In 1999, he returned to the university and joined the Netter Center as director of UNI, a position he held until 2012 while leading the continued growth of the program. In the year of Gerber's return, UNI received its initial grants. One was a Community Food Project grant from the U.S. Department of Agriculture (USDA), awarded under the umbrella of the West Philadelphia Partnership (see Chapters 6 and 7), which supported a paid internship program that involved high school students teaching after-school healthy-cooking workshops. The other was UNI's first grant from the Pennsylvania Nutrition Education Program (PANEP), which was funded in turn by the USDA's Supplemental Nutrition Assistance Program (SNAP).

In 1999 UNI launched the Powelton Village Farmers Market (PVFM) on a sidewalk near 37th Street and Lancaster Avenue, a block north of UCHS and the Drew School. This farmers market filled a need for fresh produce, which was lacking in most of the grocery stores north of Market Street. According to a reporter for the *Daily Pennsylvanian*, Penn's independent student newspaper:

> Every Saturday from May to October, farmers line up tables of colorful fruits and vegetables as passersby peruse the selection of food. . . . Operated by a group of University City High School students called the University City Farmers' Collective, the operation is not just about buying and selling fresh produce grown in rural areas. . . . Yes, there are a few farmers from Lancaster County who trek into the city with truckloads of fruits and vegetables [dispersing to several sites, as well as the PVFM]. . . . As members of UNI's Roots Program—a curriculum based around the development of agriculturally-based businesses at public schools in West Philadelphia—the students involved with the market participate in an after-school program that is centered around learning basic entrepreneurial skills in a hand's on [sic] environment.
>
> During the week, they get ready for Saturday's operation by planting and harvesting vegetables in a garden near their school, ordering bread, yogurt and cheese from local food vendors and learning the financial background needed to maintain a successful business.
>
> In addition, they are also responsible for larger-scale publicity and marketing projects geared toward retaining a basis of regular customers and, in the process, making sure that the other vendors keep coming back on Saturdays to set up shop. . . . Based around the

concept of a collective—an alternative form of operating a company that doesn't employ the standard hierarchical system—the program requires the students themselves to take responsibility for every aspect of how their business runs.

The students, who receive a salary on top of a percentage of the sales from the market, work as a team as they make decisions about what they are going to sell, how much it will cost and how best to market their products.[19]

In the early 2000s the project gained national recognition as a bellwether educational and health innovation. Awards and citations included the following:[20]

- In 2003, the Robert Wood Johnson Foundation cited UNI as one of the four promising models for improving health and nutrition among children in the United States.
- In 2003, the National Academies named the university-assisted community school programming of the Netter Center, of which UNI is a core component, the winner of the inaugural W. T. Grant Foundation Youth Development Prize. This award honored the UACS program for its "high-quality, evidence-based collaborative efforts that generate significant advances in knowledge while increasing the opportunities for young people to move successfully through adolescence with ample support and care." The prize was sponsored in collaboration with the National Academy of Sciences' Board on Children, Youth and Families.
- In 2003, the Pennsylvania State Horticultural Society recognized the UNI school garden at University City High School and Drew K–8 school as the best school garden in Philadelphia. UNI received this award several more times through 2013.
- In 2004, the Community Outreach Partnership Centers program of HUD cited UNI for its collaboration with the local community, helping to improve it through empowering residents and the organizations that serve them, and strengthening relationships between campus and community.
- In 2005, Campus Compact recognized UNI as one of eight exemplary Campus-Community Partnerships in the United States.

Over the next several years, UNI expanded from its original base in three schools to twenty public schools in West and North Philadelphia. In 2005, to support this expansion, UNI received a larger grant from PANEP.[21] A significant gift from the Agatston Family Foundation followed in 2007, and UNI became the Agatston Urban Nutrition Initiative (AUNI). A major grant from the U.S. Department of Health and Human Services (HHS), also awarded in 2009, funded the expansion of the Youth Empowerment Program (YEP), the student-internship program at UCHS, which helped provide paid internships to over one hundred fifty high school students in West Philadelphia for work in peer education and urban agriculture projects and participation in regional and national networks and conferences. The internship program engaged students in working after school for ten hours weekly to organize better food choices in their communities. It combined various direct-service approaches, such as teaching healthy-cooking classes and growing healthy foods in school gardens for sale at farmers markets. In 2009 AUNI student interns were also teaching nutrition and healthy cooking in five community health and senior centers in West Philadelphia.

Through all of these changes, AUNI's founding purposes remained unaltered:[22]

- To help students from kindergarten through the postgraduate years enhance their nutritional well-being and develop healthy lifestyles;
- To improve their educational experiences and increase learning by means of a curriculum that involves active, hands-on, service-centered learning;
- To instill a greater civic awareness and participation in society through working to help solve the problems that afflict modern urban society;
- To enhance specialized training in academic disciplines and research methods through a curriculum that is rooted in problem-solving learning;
- To develop models for change that can be extrapolated, with appropriate modifications, to other settings nationally and internationally.

AUNI initiated a significant pilot project in 2011 to establish the Community Farm and Food Resource Center in partnership with historic Bartram's Garden, Philadelphia's Parks and Recreation Department, and the Pennsylvania Horticultural Society. The Community Farm comprises a two-acre farm and a half-acre fruit orchard, as well as a solar-powered greenhouse—an enterprise that more than doubled AUNI's total food production in its first year of operation. Youths from John Bartram High School are employed in all aspects of running the farm and community garden, including crop planning, supporting community gardeners, teaching workshops, managing the farm stand, and growing, harvesting, and selling produce. In June 2016, after the completion of the five-year pilot, the project was renamed "the Farm at Bartram's Garden" and began operating independently.

The school gardens and community farm together produced more than ten thousand pounds of fresh produce in 2015–2016. With this produce, AUNI students operated farm stands at three farmers markets in West and Southwest Philadelphia. Markets at Clark Park and Bartram Village operated weekly; and a market at the Women, Infants and Children (WIC) office in Southwest Philadelphia was open on average twice monthly. About one-third of the produce was sold at farm stands, one-third used for an AUNI-operated Community Supported Agriculture (CSA) program,[23] and one-third used for AUNI educational programming, both as ingredients in AUNI programs and as a basis for teaching business and entrepreneurial skills through students' sales to local vendors.

Today, the Netter Center's AUNI is among Penn's largest community outreach programs, with a full-time staff of about twenty in 2015–2016. More than two hundred Penn students work with AUNI each year under the auspices of approximately ten ABCS courses (see below) and through volunteer and work-study internship opportunities. For fiscal year 2016, the program's total budget, funded by individual donors and grants and gifts from five agencies and foundations, was $1,741,431. Penn was one of only six universities to receive five additional years of funding from the HHS Youth Empowerment Program, beginning in 2012–2013. AUNI's outreach includes nutrition education programs at more than twenty elementary, middle, and high schools. Three West Philadelphia schools operate fruit and vegetable stands; AUNI-supported gardens operate at two West Philadelphia schools, and staff provide technical assistance to a few others. AUNI offers nutrition education for adult community members and caregivers (ages eighteen years and older) at twelve community agencies, as well as to staff and parents at our UACS sites through the Adult Senior Nutrition Program.

School Gardens and School-Based Small Businesses, ABCS and AUNI

The goals of AUNI school gardens align well with those of the various agencies—nonprofit, municipal, faith-based, governmental, and so on—that provide healthy foods to Philadelphia's working poor, unemployed, and homeless through a variety of mechanisms. AUNI is school-based: Public school students and teachers work jointly with Penn students, faculty, and staff to change food systems.

As we have emphasized, AUNI is a partnership between the schools, the community, and the University of Pennsylvania. While AUNI staff members learn from the "insider knowledge" and expertise of classroom teachers, they assist teachers in the implementation of a problem-solving curriculum leading to a healthier lifestyle, avoiding the limitations of an educational program that focuses didactically on nutrition. AUNI's work operating fruit stands and school gardens has both school-day and afterschool components, with a hands-on, active learning approach. The curriculum is adapted accordingly. At the elementary school level, the design, construction, and operation of a small business is a basis for improving mathematics, social studies, and reading skills. University students serve as peer educators and supervisors as part of their ABCS coursework in, for example, urban health, community nutrition, or public health. The school-based fruit and vegetable stands increase access to and consumption of fresh fruits and vegetables through their design as child-friendly venues where children can readily purchase fruits and vegetables as afterschool snacks in convenient and affordable portions. The stand becomes part of the afterschool ritual and competes with traditional unhealthy patterns of afterschool snacking.

At the secondary-school level AUNI extends the themes of agriculture, nutrition, and entrepreneurial education and further develops its approach to school-based microbusiness—for example, cultivating vegetables in school and community gardens for sale to local markets. AUNI also engages high school students after school hours through community cooking programs. These activities provide students with opportunities to gain tangible skills in horticultural science and small-business management and allow teachers to link more complicated theoretical subject matter to students' real-world experiences.[24]

Along with specific educational and nutritional benefits, participating students have adopted a socially responsible approach to business development. These businesses will directly benefit their school and community. Profits generated through these entrepreneurial projects help support AUNI activities, including funding for secondary school students to give formal presentations at public health, nutrition, and education conferences and workshops.

AUNI projects are supported by several ABCS courses in the Netter Center's multidisciplinary portfolio. AUNI-related ABCS has come a very long way since its inception in a single course, Anthropology 310, over twenty-five years ago. ABCS courses contribute greatly to AUNI's ability to implement its approach and generate innovative lesson plans and curricula. Integrating this focus across the curriculum from kindergarten through graduate school and beyond distinguishes AUNI from other food systems–education programs. Its expansion has opened new opportunities for Penn professors and students to connect courses and research to meaningful service experiences with food systems. AUNI facilitates field placements for students enrolled in ABCS courses in the School of Arts and Sciences, the School of Nursing, the School of Social Policy and Practice (formerly Penn's School of Social Work), the Graduate School of Education, the Master of Public Health Program, and the Wharton School. In 2011 AUNI hired its first director of student and academic engagement, who is supported by a leadership team consisting of student volunteers. More than twenty-three ABCS courses have been linked to AUNI since that time. AUNI has also formed partnerships with the Penn Entrepreneurial Law Clinic and the Wharton Social Impact Center. AUNI staff members work closely with leading nutrition and obesity prevention experts at Penn. A partnership with the Children's Hospital of Philadelphia (CHOP) supported the launch of a longitudinal impact evaluation of the high school internship program and AUNI's urban gardens, which is continuing under the direction of the Netter Center's evaluation office.

ABCS courses taught by two Penn colleagues, one in the School of Arts and Sciences and the other in Nursing, illustrate AUNI's multipronged, campus-wide approach. Scott Poethig, a biology professor specializing in cell and developmental plant biology, began working with AUNI in the early 2000s and has taught ABCS biology classes designed for both majors and nonmajors. Biology 17, "The Biology of Food," presents central themes in biology for non-science-majors by examining the nature of food and the ways in which humans modify, and have been modified by, the organisms they eat. The class helps to support and further develop AUNI programs such as school gardens, cooking crews, fruit stands, and the Farm at Bartram's Garden. For example, Penn students working at elementary schools teach science through cooking In other afterschool programs in the Philadelphia public schools, the snack is typically provided by the school's food services department and consists of a vacuum-sealed tray with a sandwich, fruit cocktail, bag of chips, and milk. In the AUNI program, in contrast, a cooking crew cooks a meal from scratch, using fresh ingredients from the school garden, to serve to their peers as the afterschool snack. Penn students not only help the K–8 students improve the supply of healthy foods and learn healthy cooking habits but also use this opportunity to improve science education. The Penn students take the labs and demonstrations Poethig introduces in the course and transform them into lessons appropriate for middle school students: cheese making, tofu making, bread baking, and lacto-fermenting. The Penn students' final deliverable is a series of lesson plans that incorporate science experiments and cooking. In addition to integrating science education into the cooking process, they are also responsible for joining a cooking crew on a weekly basis to assist in the implementation of the food education program. Another project focuses on school gardens, where Penn students and middle school students plan spring plantings, create scientifically accurate garden art and plant labels, and develop a school composting system.

Terri Lipman, a professor in Penn's School of Nursing, has offered service learning opportunities with AUNI for nurse practitioner (NP) students. Since 1989 Lipman's research has focused on identifying children with diabetes and increasing the physical activity of underserved populations. In 2005 she began teaching a clinical practicum, Nursing 723: "Nursing of Children II," as an ABCS course. The NP students received classroom content on diabetes in children, racial disparities in children with endocrine disorders, and key aspects of community engagement. In the clinical component of the course, NP students trained Sayre High School students to obtain accurate assessments of height and weight, evaluate growth disorders, and identify diabetes risk factors. NP and high school students together assessed growth and risk factors in elementary school–aged children from the community. The first year of the project, the students worked together to compile the data and submitted two abstracts to the National Pediatric Nursing Conference in Dallas, Texas. High school students presented alongside NP students and won first prize for research and third prize for their clinical poster presentations. From 2005 to 2009, fifty NP students collaborated with thirty-six high school students to assess 240 elementary school children. Thirty percent of the children were found to be at risk for type 2 diabetes based on obesity, high waist circumference, linear growth failure, and/or the presence of acanthosis nigricans (a skin finding associated with insulin resistance).[25]

In 2011 Lipman launched the free Dance for Health program at the Sayre Recreation Center. NP students in her ABCS course (now called Nursing 735: "Pediatric Acute Care Nurse Practitioner: Professional Role and Intermediate Clinical Practice: Dance for Health") look at dance as a culturally relevant, enjoyable, and easily accessible form of physical activity and means of obesity reduction. For the first part of the semester, NP students provide an interactive curriculum for Sayre High School students who participate in AUNI, based on the needs identified by AUNI staff and Sayre students. Subsequently, the NP and high school students work as a team to implement the Dance for Health project, which is directed toward increasing physical activity in the Sayre community. NP and high school students evaluate participants' height, weight, heart rate, and pedometer readings and survey their perception of endurance and enjoyment of activity. In addition, they survey a sample of the participants to determine their assessment of the Dance for Health project.[26]

The evolution of Johnston's Anthropology 310 seminar, which launched AUNI over two decades ago, is noteworthy. Johnston has taught several iterations of this course in the Anthropology Department, focusing on nutritional anthropology as well as on the anthropology of sports and well-being. Penn undergraduates have been able to select their work from options that include the fruit stand, school garden, school lunchroom, and community food education project, as well as other health and wellness programing led by the Netter Center. In the 2015–2016 academic year, when Johnston focused his course on the interactions of physical activity, obesity, and nutrition, his students supported the development and evaluation of several sports and fitness partnerships at UACS, including Young Quakers Community Athletics, a program operated in partnership with Penn's Department of Recreation and Intercollegiate Athletics.[27]

AUNI was developed to cope with the growing problem of obesity in the United States, especially among schoolchildren. Its global perspective is informed by its local activity in West Philadelphia. In its earliest stages, AUNI was an ABCS program that emphasized innovative approaches to nutrition education, with a reduction in body mass index as the goal. Within a few years, however, participants had come to understand the obesity problem in terms far more complex than simply "calories-in/calories-out." Increasingly, they recognized that basic changes in lifestyle were necessary to meet the challenges posed by obesity, which they now conceptualized as a response to systemic social conditions, not the least of which are racial and ethnic disparities in health education and access to affordable healthy foods.

AUNI seeks to reverse a major public health failure by attacking the cause, not the result. The approach of attacking the cause of the problem has been a hallmark of the Netter Center's work. In the concluding chapter we describe that work as part of a literally radical attempt to advance a "democratic devolution revolution."[28] We also identify obstacles to transforming universities into progressive, civically engaged anchor institutions—a transformation that is essential for our democratic devolution revolution. Finally, we propose strategies for reducing these obstacles.

10

Universities, Local Engagement, and Achieving a Democratic Devolution Revolution

> The social philosopher, dwelling in the region of his concepts, "solves" problems by showing the relationship of ideas, instead of helping men solve problems in the concrete by supplying them hypotheses to be used and tested in projects of reform.
>
> —JOHN DEWEY, *Reconstruction in Philosophy* (1920)

> Democracy must begin at home, and its home is the neighborly community.
>
> —JOHN DEWEY, *The Public and Its Problems* (1927)

> The great universities of the twenty-first century will be judged by their ability to help solve our most urgent social problems.
>
> —WILLIAM R. GREINER, "In the Total of All These Acts: How Can American Universities Address the Urban Agenda?" *Universities and Community Schools* (1994)

It is axiomatic, we think, that in the global era the schooling system increasingly functions as the core subsystem—the strategic subsystem—of modern information societies. Contrary to the position of orthodox Marxists, schooling, more than any other subsystem, now influences the functioning of the societal system as a whole. Viewed systemically, it has on balance the greatest "multiplier" effects, direct and indirect, short term and long term. To restate these points somewhat differently, we strongly agree with the Chilean sociologist Eugenio Tironi that the answer to the question "What kind of education do we need?" is to be found in the answer to the question "What kind of society do we want?"[1] Education and society are dynamically interactive and interdependent. If human beings hope to maintain and develop a particular type of society, they must develop and maintain the particular type of education system conducive to it. As Dewey in effect argued: *No effective democratic schooling system, no democratic society.*

We also think it axiomatic that universities—particularly research universities—are the primary shapers of the American schooling system overall. To a significant extent they function as the "reference institution" that other higher education institutions and preK–12 schools imitate and look to for approval.[2] A proposition central to Harper's vision for the University of Chicago (discussed in Chapter 3) was that universities primarily determined the character of the schooling system: "Through the school system, the character of which, in spite of itself, the university determines and in a large measure controls . . . through the school system every family in this entire broad land of ours is brought into touch with the university; for from it proceed the teachers or the teachers' teachers."[3]

Universities' societal—indeed, global—reach also makes them particularly important partners in school-system reform, as well as in community-wide improvement efforts in areas such as health, education, and economic development. In this era of global information and communication, local school systems are powerfully affected by national and global schooling systems. Local changes cannot be sustained if they remain only local and unconnected to broader national and global developments. Not only must significant systemic change be locally rooted and generated; it must also be part of a national and global movement for change. For that to occur, an agent is needed that can function simultaneously on the local, national, and global levels. Universities are, as we have argued, that agent. They are simultaneously preeminent local institutions (embedded anchors in their communities) and national/global ones (part of an increasingly interactive worldwide network).

For nearly a generation, John Gardner, arguably the leading spokesperson for what we call the "new democratic cosmopolitan civic university," thought deeply and wrote cogently about organizational devolution and the university's potential role. For Gardner, the effective functioning of organizations required the planned and deliberate, rather than haphazard, devolution of functions.

> We have in recent decades discovered some important characteristics of the large-scale organized systems—government, private sector, whatever—under which so much of contemporary life is organized. One such characteristic—perhaps the most important—is that the tendency of such systems to centralize must be countered by deliberate dispersion of initiative downward and outward through the system. The corporations have been trying to deal with this reality for almost 25 years and government is now pursuing it. . . . What it means for government is a substantially greater role for the states and cities. And none of them are entirely ready for that role. . . . Local govern-

ment must enter into collaborative relations with non-governmental elements. . . . So how can colleges and universities be of help?[4]

Gardner powerfully extended the Harper-Dewey vision by proposing a multisided involvement in "contemporary life" for institutions of higher education, including initiating community building, convening public discussions, educating public-spirited leaders, offering continuing civic and leadership seminars, and providing a wide range of technical assistance. The effective, compassionate, democratic devolution revolution we call for requires much more than practicing new forms of interaction among federal, state, and local governments and among agencies at each level of government; it requires, to use Gardner's phrase, "the deliberate dispersion of initiative downward and outward through the system." For Gardner, government integration by itself does not advance meaningful change. New forms of interaction among the public, for-profit, and nonprofit sectors are also necessary. Government must be a collaborating partner, effectively facilitating cooperation among all sectors of society, including higher education, to support and strengthen individuals, families, and communities.[5]

A Strategy to Bring About a Democratic Devolution Revolution

The strategy we propose requires creatively and intelligently adapting the work and resources of a wide variety of local institutions—universities, hospitals, faith-based organizations, and more—to the particular needs and resources of local communities. It assumes, however, that universities and colleges, which are simultaneously preeminent international, national, and local institutions, *potentially* represent by far the most powerful partners, anchors, and creative catalysts for change and improvement in the quality of life in American cities and communities.

For universities and colleges to fulfill their great potential as anchor institutions and really contribute to a democratic devolution revolution, they will have to do things very differently from the way they do them now. To begin with, changes in "doing" will require them to recognize that as they now function, they—particularly research universities—constitute a major part of the problem, not a significant part of the solution. To become part of the solution, they must give full-hearted, full-minded devotion to the painfully difficult task of transforming themselves into socially responsible *civic* universities and colleges. To do so, they will have to radically change their institutional cultures and structures, democratically realign and integrate themselves, and develop a comprehensive, realistic strategy.

To extend Gardner's observations about universities and colleges (and similar observations by such highly influential thinkers as Ernest Boyer, Derek Bok, Lee Shulman, and Alexander Astin), we propose a democratic devolution revolution.[6] In our proposed "revolution," government serves as a powerful catalyst, largely by providing the funds needed to create stable, ongoing, effective partnerships. But government would be a second-tier deliverer of services, with institutions of higher education, community-based organizations, unions, faith-based communities, other voluntary associations, schoolchildren and their parents, and other community members functioning as the first-tier operational partners. That is, various levels and departments of government would guarantee aid and significantly finance welfare services. Local personalized care, however, would actually be delivered by the third tier of society (private, nonprofit, and voluntary associations) and the fourth tier (personal connections—family, kin, neighbors, and friends). Government would not be primarily responsible for the delivery of services; it would instead have macrofiscal responsibilities, including fully adequate provision of funds.

The Netter Center and Penn have developed and implemented a strategy focused on university-assisted community schools designed to help educate, engage, activate, and serve *all* members of the community in which the school is located. We emphasize *university assisted* because community schools require far more resources than traditional schools and because we have become convinced that universities constitute the strategic sources of broadly based, comprehensive, sustained support for community schools.

Dewey emphasized that since public schools "belong" to all members of the community, they should "serve" all members of the community (see Chapter 4). (Clearly public schools are not the only community places where learning takes place; ideally, libraries, museums, private schools, and other "learning places" in a community would collaborate.) For public schools to actually function as integrating community institutions, however, local, state, and national governmental and nongovernmental agencies must be effectively coordinated to help provide the myriad resources community schools need to play the greatly expanded roles we envision for them in American society. How to conceive that organizational revolution, let alone implement it, poses extraordinarily complex intellectual and social problems. But as Dewey forcefully argued, working to solve complex, real-world problems is the best way to advance knowledge and learning, as well as the general capacity of people and institutions to advance them.

We contend, therefore, that American universities should give a very high priority—arguably their highest priority—to solving the problems inherent in the organizational revolution we have sketched above. If universities were to do so, they would demonstrate in concrete practice their self-professed theoretical ability to simultaneously advance knowledge and learning. They would then satisfy the critical performance test proposed in 1994 by the president of the University at Buffalo, SUNY, William R. Greiner—namely, that "the great universities of the twenty-first century will be judged by their ability to help solve our most urgent social problems."[7]

By that real-world Baconian performance test, American colleges and universities, including our own, are falling short. Government at all levels should and could use the bully pulpit and financial incentives to encourage institutions of higher education to do well by doing good—that is, to realize their missions by contributing *significantly* to developing and sustaining democratic schools and communities. Specifically, government could support higher education–community partnerships that demonstrate genuine community benefit, not simply benefit to the college or university, as well as transparent and democratic collaborations with local partners. Federal support would be based on what we call the "Noah Principle"—give funds for building arks (producing real change), not for predicting rain (describing the problems that exist and will develop if actions are not taken).

Instituting the Noah Principle in practice will have only limited impact if institutions of higher education continue to treat community engagement largely as an add-on and fail to change their core teaching and research functions. They will need to make significant internal changes, including identifying and reducing obstacles to effective university-community-school partnerships, so that they can work effectively with government, foundations, and other organizations to "help solve our most urgent social problems."

Obstacles to Developing and Sustaining University-Assisted Community Schools and Achieving a Democratic Devolution Revolution

Our own work serves as an example. Partnerships with schools and communities in West Philadelphia date back more than thirty years; a developing and expanding critical mass of faculty and students participates in academically based community service teaching and learning; and Penn's current president, Amy Gutmann, has given the Netter Center visible and sustained support. Yet serious obstacles have prevented Penn from realizing the potential of university-assisted community schools and slowed Penn's development as a truly democratic, cosmopolitan, engaged, civic university dedicated to realizing Franklin's vision for the university: to educate students with "an *Inclination* join'd with an *Ability* to serve Mankind, one's Country, Friends and Family."[8] The obstacles are not unique to Penn. They affect, we believe, nearly all institutions of higher education in the United States to some extent.

What Franklin termed a "Prejudice in favour of ancient Customs and Habitudes" continues to impede the radical transformation of research universities into civic institutions committed to the advancement of learning and knowledge for "the relief of man's estate." And this is by no means the only obstacle, in our judgment. Commercialism and commodification, misplaced nostalgia for traditional, elitist, "ivory tower" liberal arts education, and intellectual and institutional fragmentation also get in the way of needed change.

Education for profit, not virtue; students as consumers, not producers of knowledge; academics as individual superstars, not members of a community of scholars—all of these developments reflect the commercialization of higher education, which contributes to an overemphasis on institutional competition for wealth and status and has a devastating impact on the values and ambitions of college students.[9] When institutions openly pursue commercialization, their behavior legitimizes and reinforces the pursuit of economic self-interest by students and amplifies the widespread sense that they are in college *exclusively* to gain career-related skills and credentials. Student idealism and civic engagement are strongly diminished when students see their universities abandon academic values and scholarly pursuits to function as competitive, profit-making corporations. Commercialism and the development of the entrepreneurial university foster an environment in which higher education is seen as a private benefit, not a public good.[10]

Partly in response to galloping commercialism, some make a case for a return to traditional liberal arts education—an essentialist approach with roots in Plato's antidemocratic, elitist theory of education.[11] What is needed instead is, to quote Carol Geary Schneider, "a new liberal art" involving "integrative learning—focused around big problems and new connections between the academy and society."[12] The concept of a new liberal art resonates with Dewey's rejection of abstract contemplation and his call for an engaged, problem-solving approach to scholarship and learning. In *Reconstruction in Philosophy,* he wrote: "The social philosopher, dwelling in the region of his concepts, 'solves' problems by showing the relationship of ideas, instead of helping men solve problems in the concrete by supplying them hypotheses to be used and tested in projects of reform."[13]

"Communities have problems, universities have departments," stated a report published by the Organisation for Economic Co-operation and Development titled *The University and the Community* (1982).[14] Beyond being a criticism of universities, that statement neatly indicates another major reason why colleges and universities have not contributed as they should. Quite simply, their unintegrated, fragmented, internally conflictual structure and organization impede understanding and developing solutions to highly complex human and societal problems. Colleges and universities need to significantly decrease the fragmentation of disciplines, overspecialization, and division between and among the arts and sciences and the professions, since these departmental and disciplinary divisions have increased the isolation of higher education from society itself. Compounding this problem is what might be called the "disciplinary fallacy" afflicting American universities— namely, the misconception that faculty members are duty-bound to serve only the scholastic interests and preoccupations of their disciplines and have neither the responsibility nor the capacity to help their universities keep their longstanding promise to prepare undergraduates for lives of moral and civic responsibility.[15]

Reducing Obstacles to Developing and Sustaining University-Assisted Community Schools and Achieving a Democratic Devolution Revolution

So what is to be done to reduce the negative effects of dysfunctional traditions, commercialism and commodification, ivory tower nostalgia, and intellectual and institutional fragmentation? The first step is to clarify and even redefine the purpose of undergraduate education.

In the foreword to *Educating Citizens: Preparing America's Undergraduates for Lives of Moral and Civic Responsibility,* Lee Shulman emphasizes colleges' crucial role in the development of the virtues and understanding vital for democratic citizenship. Observing that a democratic society requires an "educated citizenry blessed with virtue as well as wisdom," Shulman hailed the book's demonstration that achieving the requisite

> combination of moral and civic virtue accompanied by the development of understanding occurs best when fostered by our institutions of higher education. It does not occur by accident, or strictly through early experience. Indeed, I argue that there may well be a critical period for the development of these virtues, and that period could be the college years. During this developmental period, defined as much by educational opportunity as by age, students of all ages develop the resources needed for their continuing journeys through adult life.[16]

Shulman's astute observation helps us see the important, diverse roles that institutions of higher education play in the lifelong, all-encompassing development of the different types of educators and other personnel who directly and indirectly control and operate the American schooling system. If their formative years at college neither contribute to their own growth as democratic citizens nor concretely demonstrate to them how schools can function to produce democratic citizens, they will necessarily reproduce what they have learned—or failed to learn—in college. As a result of that flawed reproductive process, the schooling system will be incapable of developing an effective program for democratic citizenship.

Five of the authors (Benson, Harkavy, Hartley, Johnston, and Puckett) have devoted thought and hard work to the question of how best to create a democratic classroom. Besides trying to function more as "a guide on the side" than a "sage on the stage," each of them has encouraged students to work in collaborative groups with community members on community-identified problems that are of deep personal interest. We have tried to put into practice Dewey's insight that individuals learn best when they are driven by "a real motive behind and a real outcome ahead."[17] Harkavy has organized his seminars (including one on university-community relationships that he has taught since 1985) so that at a relatively early point in the semester, students in the seminar collaboratively design the syllabus and take an increasing (and, over time, primary) responsibility for the organization and operation of the seminar itself.[18] It would require another book to describe in detail the steps, both useful and "false," we have taken to advance genuinely democratic learning at Penn, including practices in the seminars we teach. Although we believe we have made progress, particularly during the past ten years, we still have a long way to go to realize Dewey's democratic vision in practice.

What strategic step might help engage Penn, as well as other universities, to embrace that democratic vision actively as well as rhetorically? To repeat one of Dewey's most significant propositions, "Democracy must begin at home, and its home is the neighborly community."[19] Democracy, he emphasized, has to be built on face-to-face interactions in which human beings work together cooperatively to solve the ongoing problems of life. We are updating Dewey and advocating the following proposition: *Democracy must begin at home, and its home is the engaged neighborly college or university and its local community partners.* Neighborliness, we contend, is the primary indicator that an institution is working for the public good.

The benefits of a local community focus for college and university civic engagement programs are manifold. Ongoing, continuous interaction is facilitated through work in an easily accessible location. Relationships of trust, so essential for effective partnerships and effective learning, are also built through day-to-day work on problems and issues of mutual concern. In addition, the local community provides a convenient setting in which service learning courses, community-based research courses, and related courses in different disciplines can work together on a complex problem to produce substantive results. Work in a university's local community, since it facilitates interaction across schools and disciplines, can also create interdisciplinary learning opportunities. Finally, the local community is a democratic real-world learning site in which community members and academics can pragmatically determine whether the work is making a real difference and whether *both* the neighborhood and the institution are better as a result of common efforts.

For Dewey, knowledge and learning are most effectively advanced when human beings work collaboratively to solve specific, important real-world problems in "a *forked road* situation, a situation that is ambiguous, that presents a dilemma, which poses alternatives."[20] Focusing on universal problems—for example, poverty, poor schooling, and inadequate healthcare—that are manifested locally is, in our judgment, the best way to apply Dewey's brilliant proposition. A focus on local engagement is an extraordinarily promising strategy for realizing institutional mission and purpose. As elegantly expressed by Paul Pribbenow, president of Augsburg College, the "intersections of vocation and location" provide wonderful opportunities for both the institution and the community.[21]

"Only connect!" The powerful, evocative epigraph to E. M. Forster's *Howards End* captures the essence of our argument[22]—namely, that the necessary revolutionary transformation of research universities is most likely to occur in the crucible of significant, serious, sustained engagement with local public schools and their communities. Abstract, solipsistic, contemplative, ivory tower isolation will neither shed intellectual light on our most significant societal problems nor produce positive democratic change. It will not get us where we need to go. To put it more positively, we conclude this book as we began, by calling on democratic-minded academics to create and sustain a global movement to radically transform research universities to realize Bacon's goal of advancing knowledge for "the relief of man's estate," as well as Dewey's vision of an organic "Great Community" composed of participatory, democratic, collaborative, and interdependent societies.

Acknowledgments

Our acknowledgments must begin with Lee Benson, co-author of *Knowledge for Social Change*, who continued to make indispensable contributions to the conceptualization, research, and writing of this book until a week before his death, at age ninety, in 2012. A generous and brilliant scholar, Lee taught and mentored each of us as we worked together on this project, as he had done for so many other colleagues throughout the years.

We also wish to express our gratitude to Michael Zuckerman, Professor Emeritus of History at the University of Pennsylvania, for his extraordinarily insightful, critical reading of the manuscript, and to the following Netter Center colleagues: Associate Director Cory Bowman, for his review of various drafts of the book and his many valuable suggestions; Sonya Ann Dryz, for her careful proofreading; and Tina Ciocco, for her exceptional assistance in preparing the book for publication.

We are especially indebted to our many Netter Center colleagues; our school and community partners; the Netter Center's community, faculty, and national and student advisory boards; and numerous University of Pennsylvania faculty, students, and staff working in West Philadelphia. Without their extraordinary collaborative work, this book would not have been possible. Nor could it have come to fruition without the generosity of many organizations, foundations, agencies, and individual donors that have supported the Netter Center's local, national, and global projects.

For permission to republish in Chapters 3, 4, and 10, with modifications, parts of *Dewey's Dream: Universities and Democracies in an Age of Education*

Reform (2007), by Lee Benson, Ira Harkavy, and John Puckett, we thank Temple University Press. For permission to republish in Chapter 6, with modifications, parts of John L. Puckett's "University City Science Center," *Encyclopedia of Greater Philadelphia* (2016), we thank Charlene Mires, editor-in-chief of the *Encyclopedia*.

We owe special thanks to Barbara Netter and her late husband, Edward, for the generous endowment that has so powerfully contributed to advancing and sustaining our work for the past decade.

Philadelphia, Pennsylvania
June 2017

Notes

PREFACE

    1. John Dewey, *Reconstruction in Philosophy*, in *The Middle Works of John Dewey, 1899–1924*, vol. 12, ed. Jo Ann Boydston (Carbondale: Southern Illinois University Press, 1978), 96; digitally reproduced in Larry Hickman, ed., *The Collected Works of John Dewey, 1882 1953: The Electronic Edition* (Charlottesville, VA: InteLex, 1996).

    2. Robert B. Westbrook, *John Dewey and American Democracy* (Ithaca, NY: Cornell University Press, 1991), xiv–xv.

    3. Lee Benson, Ira Harkavy, and John Puckett, *Dewey's Dream: Universities and Democracies in an Age of Education Reform* (Philadelphia: Temple University Press, 2007), ix–x.

    4. Each of the authors of this book has made distinct and important contributions to the development and operation of the Netter Center.

    5. John Dewey, *The Public and Its Problems*, in *The Later Works of John Dewey, 1925–1953*, vol. 2, ed. Jo Ann Boydston (Carbondale: Southern Illinois University Press, 1981), 368; digitally reproduced in Hickman, *The Collected Works of John Dewey, 1882–1953*.

INTRODUCTION

    1. For discussion, see Lee Benson, Ira Harkavy, and John Puckett, *Dewey's Dream:* ness, 2007), 3–7.

    2. Darnell Rucker, *The Chicago Pragmatists* (Minneapolis: University of Minneapolis Press, 1969), 3.

    3. Harper's 1899 Charter Day address at the University of California, "The University and Democracy," reprinted in William Rainey Harper, *The Trend in Higher Education* (Chicago: University of Chicago Press, 1905), 19, 21, 28–29.

    4. William Rainey Harper, "The University and Democracy," in Harper, *The Trend in Higher Education*, 12, 25, 32; Harper, "The Urban University," reprinted in Harper, *Trend in Higher Education*, 158.

    5. Harper, "The University and Democracy," 12.

CHAPTER 1

1. John Dewey, *Reconstruction in Philosophy*, in *The Middle Works of John Dewey, 1899–1924*, vol. 12, ed. Jo Ann Boydston (Carbondale: Southern Illinois University Press, 1978), 96–97; digitally reproduced in Larry Hickman, ed., *The Collected Works of John Dewey, 1882–1953: The Electronic Edition* (Charlottesville, VA: InteLex Corporation, 1996).

2. Ibid., 98–99, 101.

3. The quotation is from Perez Zagorin, *Francis Bacon* (Princeton, NJ: Princeton University Press, 1988), 30.

4. John E. Leary Jr., *Francis Bacon and the Politics of Science* (Ames: Iowa State University Press, 1994), 22–23.

5. Ibid., 28–29.

6. Ibid., 34.

7. Ibid., 37–38.

8. Francis Bacon, *Advancement of Learning*, Book 1, in *Francis Bacon: Selected Philosophical Works*, ed. Rose-Mary Sargent (Indianapolis: Hackett, 1999), 29.

9. Zagorin, *Francis Bacon*, 29–39, 57–68; quotations on 29, 57.

10. Ibid., 26.

11. Ibid., 29.

12. Ibid., 25–39, 86–89.

13. Ibid., 58.

14. Rose-Mary Sargent, "Advancement of Learning and Division of the Sciences," in *Bacon: Selected Philosophical Works*, 1.

15. Ibid., 1; "General Introduction," ibid., xi.

16. Leary, *Bacon and the Politics of Science*, 39.

17. Zagorin, *Francis Bacon*, 59–61.

18. Francis Bacon, *Advancement of Learning*, Book 2, "Dedication," in *Bacon: Selected Philosophical Works*, 49–55.

19. Ibid., 50–51.

20. Ibid., 51–52.

21. Ibid., 53–54.

22. Ibid., 54.

23. Zagorin, *Francis Bacon*, 61–68.

24. Leary, *Bacon and the Politics of Science*, 131.

25. Ibid., 39.

26. Francis Bacon, *Advancement of Learning*, Book 2, "Dedication," in *Bacon: Selected Philosophical Works*, 54–55.

27. Ibid.

28. Rose-Mary Sargent, "Great Instauration, New Organon, and Preparative," in *Bacon: Selected Philosophical Works*, 63.

29. Zagorin, *Francis Bacon*, 76.

30. Leary, *Bacon and the Politics of Science*, 39.

31. Joel J. Epstein, quoted ibid., 41.

32. Ibid., 47. See also and cf. Benjamin Farrington, *The Philosophy of Francis Bacon: An Essay of Its Development from 1603 to 1609, with New Translations of Fundamental Texts* (Liverpool: Liverpool University Press, 1964), which brackets the years 1603 to 1609 as "decisive in the evolution of . . . [Bacon's] thought" (11).

33. Leary, *Bacon and the Politics of Science*, 53–54.

34. Sargent, "Great Instauration," 63.

35. Zagorin, *Francis Bacon*, 74–75.

36. Leary, *Bacon and the Politics of Science*, 57–58.

37. Ibid., 56–57.

38. Ibid., 63–72.

39. Ibid., 153.

40. William Rawley, quoted ibid., 247.

41. Ibid., 147–148.

42. Ibid., 6–7.

43. Ibid., 6.

44. Ibid., 6–7.

45. Ibid., 106.

46. Zagorin, *Francis Bacon*, 60.

47. Leary, *Bacon and the Politics of Science*, 106.

48. Ibid., 231.

49. Ibid., 148.

50. Ibid., 252–253.

51. Ibid., 253.

52. Ibid., 253–254.

53. Ibid., 145–158, quotation on 158.

54. Ibid., 148.

55. Ibid.

56. Zagorin, *Francis Bacon*, 29.

57. Sargent, "General Introduction," xxix.

58. William Whewell, quoted ibid.

59. Ibid.

60. Zagorin, *Francis Bacon*, 125.

61. Leary, *Bacon and the Politics of Science*, 223.

CHAPTER 2

1. Benjamin Franklin, *Poor Richard Improved, 1749*, in *Writings*, ed. J. A. Leo Lemay (New York: Literary Classics of the United States and Library of America, 1987), 1252.

2. Quoted ibid. It is an excerpt from James Thomson's *The Seasons*, lines 1538–1549 49 (London: Printed by Henry Woodfall for A. Millar, in the Strand, 1744), 118, reprinted in Gale/Cengage, *Eighteenth Century Collections Online*, ESTC number T141533. The passage comes from a revised version of the "Summer" section of Thomson's long poem *The Seasons* and seems to have made its first appearance in the 1744 revision of the work. The original version of "Summer" was published in 1727, and the first version of *The Seasons* was published in 1730.

3. Whitfield J. Bell quoted in James Campbell, *Recovering Benjamin Franklin: An Exploration of a Life of Science and Service* (Chicago: Open Court, 1999), 78.

4. Francis Bacon, preface to *The Great Instauration*, in *The Works of Francis Bacon, Baron of Verulam, Viscount St. Alban, and Lord High Chancellor of England*, ed. James Spedding, Robert Leslie Ellis, and Douglas Denon Heath, vol. 1: *Translations of the Philosophical Works* (London: Longman, 1858), 20–21.

5. Michael Zuckerman, "An Inclination Joined with an Ability to Serve," in *The Autobiography of Benjamin Franklin*, Penn Reading Project edition, ed. Peter Conn (Philadelphia: University of Pennsylvania Press, 2005), 156.

6. Quoted in Campbell, *Recovering Benjamin Franklin*, 68.

7. Quoted in Zuckerman, "An Inclination," 156. Edmund S. Morgan, *Benjamin Franklin* (New Haven, CT: Yale University Press, 2002), 5, cites Franklin's "most conspicuous virtue, the thing that would earn him world-wide fame in his own lifetime: his insatiable curiosity."

8. For a fuller discussion of Bacon's emphasis on the need to integrate the production and use of knowledge, see Lee Benson and Ira Harkavy, "Progressing Beyond the Welfare State," *Universities and Community Schools* 2, nos. 1–2 (1991): 6–8.

9. Campbell, *Recovering Benjamin Franklin*, 86, 260–261.

10. Quoted ibid., 87. For an insightful discussion of Franklin's capacity to identify and propose organizational solutions to strategic problems, see ibid., 76–89.

11. Benjamin Franklin to Samuel Johnson, Philadelphia, 23 August 1750, in *Benjamin Franklin on Education*, ed. John Hardin Best, Classics in Education 14 (New York: Bureau of Publications, Teachers College, Columbia University, 1962), 163. This very important letter on education can be found on pages 162–164. Best's volume is a valuable source for Franklin's writings on education, and we have benefited from his thoughtful and stimulating commentaries on them.

12. Benjamin Franklin, *Proposals Relating to the Education of Youth in Pensilvania*, in Best, *Franklin on Education*, 129.

13. Charles A. Beard and Mary R. Beard, *The Rise of American Civilization* (New York: Macmillan, 1930), 173.

14. Franklin's paper "Idea of the English School, Sketch'd Out for the Consideration of the Trustees of the Philadelphia Academy," is conveniently reprinted in Best, *Franklin on Education*, 165–171.

15. John Hardin Best, "Franklin and the Enlightened Education in America," ibid., 13–14.

16. Ibid., 14–15.

17. Franklin, *Proposals*, 128. For an insightful analysis of Franklin's compromises on the vernacular language and other issues, see Lorraine Smith Pangle and Thomas L. Pangle, "Benjamin Franklin and the Idea of a Distinctively American Academy," in *The Learning of Liberty: The Educational Ideas of the American Founders*, American Political Thought Series (Lawrence: University Press of Kansas, 1993), 75–90. Our understanding of Franklin's educational ideas has benefited from this perceptive chapter. Our appreciation of the numerous intense conflicts in Philadelphia that powerfully worked against the full realization of Franklin's vision of higher education also benefited from J. David Hoeveler's chapter, "The College of Philadelphia: The Perils of Neutrality," in *Creating the American Mind: Intellect and Politics in the Colonial Colleges* (Lanham, MD: Rowman and Littlefield, 2002), 155–180.

18. Benjamin Franklin quoted in Campbell, *Recovering Benjamin Franklin*, 197, 99; and in Zuckerman, "An Inclination," 154.

19. Elizabeth Flower and Murray G. Murphey, *A History of Philosophy in America*, vol. 1 (New York: Capricorn Books and G. P. Putnam's Sons, 1977), 110.

20. Ibid., 109–110, quotation on 109.

21. Franklin, *Proposals*, 128.

22. Ibid., 150–151n30.

23. Ibid., 149–150.

24. Ibid., 150n30. For Locke's influence and Franklin's specification of his primary goal for the education of American youth, see Best, "Franklin and the Enlightened Education," 12; Franklin, *Proposals*, 127, 149–151.

25. For Franklin's conviction that the college he envisioned should "not be a religiously affiliated, elite bastion like the four colleges (Harvard, William and Mary, Yale, and Prince-

ton) that already existed in the colonies," see Walter Isaacson, *Benjamin Franklin: An American Life* (New York: Simon and Schuster, 2003), 146–147.

26. Best neatly summarizes Franklin's educational views: "The educational thought of the Enlightenment made a profound impression on Franklin, and much of his greatness lay in a characteristic ability to translate European ideas into American designs for action." "Franklin and the Enlightened Education," 12.

27. Two leading historians of eighteenth-century Philadelphia evoke the environment in which Franklin envisioned a radically new kind of college for the "rising middle class" developing in America: "Much of what we call the Enlightenment was merely the intellectual and philosophical expression of the practical, secular, humane genius of the rising middle class. Hence the accomplishment of many of its objectives was the greater in what was probably the leading, certainly the most unfettered, middle-class community of the Western world, the city on the Delaware, where admission to the middle class was freest, its opportunities and privileges greatest, and the literate base of society most broad. . . . There was here no accumulated rubbish of ideas and institutions which, gathering for centuries, had to be swept aside before progress and enlightenment could begin." Carl Bridenbaugh and Jessica Bridenbaugh, *Rebels and Gentlemen: Philadelphia in the Age of Franklin* (New York: Reynal and Hitchcock, 1942), 363–364.

28. Benjamin Franklin, "Observations Concerning the Increase of Mankind, Peopling of Countries, &c.," in *Writings*, 373.

29. Ibid., 367.

30. Ibid., 368.

31. Ibid., 368–369.

32. Ibid., 369.

33. For an illuminating analysis of the English classical colleges that the colonial colleges imitated, see Bruce A. Kimball, *Orators and Philosophers: A History of the Idea of Liberal Education* (New York: Teachers College Press, Columbia University, 1986), 114–141. To explain why students attended the colonial colleges, Kimball quotes the historian Daniel H. Calhoun: "For many [colonial] students, perhaps for most, liberal education served no functions of any specific use to society. Latin and Greek and philosophy, and the having attended some higher school, were marks of prestige and breeding" (138).

34. Ibid., 138–139.

35. Benjamin Franklin, "Observations Relative to the Intentions of the Original Founders of the Academy in Philadelphia," in Best, *Franklin on Education*, 173.

36. Platonic thought has had perhaps its greatest impact on Western education. For Plato, learning occurred through contemplative thought, not through action and reflection. Dividing the world into ideal and material universes, Plato viewed knowledge as deriving from the ideal, spiritual universe of permanent and fixed ideas. He conceptualized the material world of objects and actions as merely "a shadowy, fleeting world" of imperfect imitations. Quotation from R. Freeman Butts, *A Culture History of Western Education: The Social and Intellectual Foundations*, 2nd ed. (New York: McGraw–Hill, 1955), 46.

37. Flower and Murphey, *Philosophy in America*, 1:110.

38. Franklin, *Proposals*, 126–152.

39. Dr. George Turnbull, quoted ibid., 142n18.

40. Ibid., 142.

41. Turnbull, quoted ibid., 142n18.

42. Ibid., 143.

43. Ibid., 141–142.

44. Ibid., 149.

45. Ibid., 146–148.

46. Ibid., 148.

47. Franklin, "Idea of the English School," 170.

48. Ibid., 168–169.

49. Ibid., 169–170.

50. Edward Potts Cheyney, *History of the University of Pennsylvania, 1740–1940* (Philadelphia: University of Pennsylvania Press, 1940), 29.

51. Bacon, preface to *The Great Instauration*, 20–21.

52. Benjamin Franklin, "On the Need for an Academy," in Best, *Franklin on Education*, 124–126.

53. Franklin, "Observations Relative to the Intentions of the Original Founders," 171–174.

54. Ibid., 173.

CHAPTER 3

1. Carl Sandberg, "Chicago," in *Chicago Poems* (New York: Henry Holt, 1916), available at http://carl-sandburg.com/index.htm/.

2. U.S. Bureau of the Census, "Nativity of the Population of the 50 Largest Urban Places: 1870 to 1890," available at https://www.census.gov/population/www/documentation/twps0029/tab19.html, accessed 26 February 2016.

3. Sandberg, "Chicago."

4. Charles W. Anderson, *Prescribing the Life of the Mind: An Essay on the Purpose of the University, the Aims of Liberal Education, the Competence of Citizens, and the Cultivation of Practical Reason* (Madison: University of Wisconsin Press, 1993), 7–8, quotation on 8.

5. Ibid., 8.

6. Daniel Coit Gilman quoted in Edward LeRoy Long Jr., *Higher Education as a Moral Enterprise* (Washington, DC: Georgetown University Press, 1992), 184.

7. Charles W. Eliot quoted in Laurence R. Veysey, *The Emergence of the American University* (1965; reprint ed., Chicago: University of Chicago Press, 1970), 119.

8. Thorstein Veblen's scathing critique of "captains of erudition" can be found in his influential *The Higher Learning in America: A Memorandum on the Conduct of Universities by Business Men*, American Century Series S-7 (New York: B. W. Huebsch, 1918; reprint ed., New York: Sagamore Press, 1957). For a much more positive view of these entrepreneurial university presidents as well as Progressive Era academics, see Steven J. Diner, *A City and Its Universities: Public Policy in Chicago, 1892–1919* (Chapel Hill: University of North Carolina Press, 1980).

9. Jessica Ivy Elfenbein, "To 'Fit Them for Their Fight with the World': The Baltimore YMCA and the Making of a Modern City, 1852–1932" (Ph.D. diss., University of Delaware, 1996), quotations on 73, 78.

10. For a discussion of the Progressive Era as a golden age of university-community relationships, see Sheldon Hackney, "The University and Its Community: Past and Present," *Annals of the American Academy of Political and Social Science* 488 (1986): 135–147; Richard Mayo-Smith quoted in Barry D. Karl, *Charles E. Merriam and the Study of Politics* (Chicago: University of Chicago Press, 1974), 31.

11. Hackney, "The University and Its Community," 145.

12. For an excellent discussion of Seth Low's Columbia, see Thomas Bender, *The New York Intellect: A History of Intellectual Life in New York City, from 1750 to the Beginnings of Our Time* (Baltimore, MD: Johns Hopkins University Press, 1987), 279–284, quotations on

282, 283. Also see Ira Harkavy and Lee Benson, "De-Platonizing and Democratizing Education as the Bases of Service Learning," in *Academic Service Learning: A Pedagogy of Action and Reflection*, ed. Robert A. Rhoads and Jeffrey Howard (San Francisco: Jossey–Bass, 1998), 11–20.

13. Low quoted in Gerald Kurland, *Seth Low: The Reformer in an Urban and Industrial Age* (New York; Twayne, 1971), 53.

14. Quoted ibid., 55.

15. Bender, *New York Intellect*, 282.

16. Low quoted in Edward Cary, "Seth Low: A Character Sketch," *American Monthly Review of Reviews* 16 (July–December 1897): 40.

17. Cary, "Seth Low," 40, 41.

18. Bender, *New York Intellect*, 284.

19. Kurland, *Seth Low*, 60–61, quotation on 61.

20. Ira Harkavy and John L. Puckett, "Lessons from Hull House for the Contemporary Urban University," *Social Service Review* 68 (1994): 299–321; Jane Addams quoted in Lela B. Costin, *Two Sisters for Social Justice: A Biography of Grace and Edith Abbott* (Urbana: University of Illinois Press, 1983), 45.

21. Jane Addams, *Twenty Years at Hull-House* (New York: Macmillan, 1910), 118, 120.

22. Kathryn Kish Sklar, "Hull House in the 1890s: A Community of Women Reformers," special issue, "Communities of Women," *Signs: Journal of Women in Culture and Society* 10 (1985): 658–677; Stanley Wenocur and Michael Reisch, *From Charity to Enterprise: The Development of American Social Work in a Market Economy* (Urbana: University of Illinois Press, 1989), 26–29.

23. Addams quoted in John H. Ehrenreich, *The Altruistic Imagination: A History of Social Work and Social Policy in the United States* (Ithaca, NY: Cornell University Press, 1985), 35.

24. Ellen Gates Starr quoted in Gertrude Himmelfarb, *Poverty and Compassion: The Moral Imagination of the Late Victorians* (New York: Knopf, 1991), 241n.

25. Addams quoted in Allen F. Davis, *American Heroine: The Life and Legend of Jane Addams* (New York: Oxford University Press, 1973), 65. For Toynbee Hall, see Himmelfarb, *Poverty and Compassion*, 235–243.

26. Jane Addams, prefatory note to Residents of Hull-House, *Hull-House Maps and Papers* (Boston: Thomas Y. Crowell, 1895; reprint ed., New York: Arno Press, 1970), viii.

27. Kathryn Kish Sklar, "Hull-House Maps and Papers: Social Science as Women's Work in the 1890s," in *The Social Survey in Historical Perspective 1880–1940*, ed. Martin Bulmer, Kevin Bales, and Kathryn Kish Sklar (New York: Cambridge University Press, 1991), 122. The key volume, which included Booth's "Descriptive Map of London Poverty," was Charles Booth, ed., *Labour and Life of the People in London*, vol. 2 (London: Williams and Norgate, 1891).

28. Residents of Hull-House, *Hull-House Maps and Papers*, 41. This volume was published as part of the series Library of Economics and Politics, edited by Richard Ely of the University of Wisconsin–Madison.

29. Our understanding of Addams's work and contributions, as well as the significance of Hull House as an organizational model that effectively integrated knowledge production and social change, was significantly advanced by the following works by Louise W. Knight: *Citizen Jane Addams and the Struggle for Democracy* (Chicago: University of Chicago Press, 2005); *Jane Addams: Spirit in Action* (New York: W. W. Norton, 2010); "John Dewey and Jane Addams Debate War," in *Trained Capacities: John Dewey, Rhetoric, and Democratic Practice*, ed. Brian Jackson and Gregory Clark (Columbia: University of South Carolina Press, 2014), 106–124.

30. Mary Jo Deegan, *Jane Addams and the Men of the Chicago School, 1892–1918* (New Brunswick, NJ: Transaction, 1988), 5, 24.

31. Ellen Fitzpatrick, *Endless Crusade: Women Social Scientists and Progressive Reform* (New York: Oxford University Press, 1990), 39. As Fitzpatrick indicates, this commitment was shared by the Departments of Political Science and Political Economy at Chicago: "They stressed the importance of using scholarship to advance both knowledge and civic-mindedness" (41).

32. The quotation appears in a different context in Fitzpatrick's introduction to *Endless Crusade* (xv), but our research indicates that it aptly describes the first generation of Chicago sociologists. For Social Gospel influences in American social science in its formative period, see Arthur S. Link and Richard L. McCormick, *Progressivism* (Arlington Heights, IL: Harlan Davidson, 1983), 23–24. In the early 1890s, Small, Vincent, and Edward Bemis (whom Harper would fire in 1895 because of Bemis's support for the 1894 Pullman strike) worked with Addams, Kelley, and community leaders to help secure legislation eliminating sweatshops and regulating child labor. In the winter of 1910, Henderson and Mead joined the women of Hull House in supporting 40,000 striking garment industry workers; in 1915, Mead participated in another garment union strike.

33. See Martin Bulmer, *The Chicago School of Sociology: Institutionalization, Diversity, and the Rise of Sociological Research* (Chicago: University of Chicago Press, 1984), 45–63, 238n1. The most important research study of the early Chicago School was *The Polish Peasant in Europe and America* (Chicago: University of Chicago Press, 1918), a 2,232-page study co-authored by William I. Thomas and Florian Znaniecki.

34. Addams quoted in Deegan, *Jane Addams and the Men of the Chicago School,* 38.

35. Jane Addams, "A Function of the Social Settlement," reprinted in *Jane Addams on Education,* ed. Ellen C. Lagemann, Classics in Education 51 (New York: Teachers College Press, 1985), 78, 90–91.

36. Ibid., 76–77.

37. Ibid., 90.

38. Darnell Rucker, *The Chicago Pragmatists* (Minneapolis: University of Minnesota Press, 1969), 9–10.

39. James P. Wind, *The Bible and the University: The Messianic Vision of William Rainey Harper* (Atlanta: Scholars Press, 1987), 5.

40. Ibid., 4–5.

41. William Rainey Harper, "The University and Democracy," 1899 Charter Day address at the University of California, in *The Trend in Higher Education* (Chicago: University of Chicago Press, 1905), 1–34, quotation on 19.

42. Ibid., 21.

43. Ibid., 27–28.

44. Ibid., 19–20.

45. William Rainey Harper, "The Urban University," in *The Trend in Higher Education,* 158.

46. Ibid., 158–160.

47. Clark Kerr, *The Uses of the University* (Cambridge, MA: Harvard University Press, 1963).

48. Harper, "The University and Democracy," 12.

49. Daniel Lee Meyer, "The Chicago Faculty and the University Ideal, 1891–1929," vol. 1 (Ph.D. diss., University of Chicago, 1994), 65.

50. Woodie Thomas White, "The Study of Education at the University of Chicago: 1892–1958" (Ph.D. diss., University of Chicago, 1977), 11–247, quotations on 13, 24. This

dissertation is a valuable source of information and insights about Harper's creation of the Department of Pedagogy, accelerating interest in public schools, and changing views on the importance of the academic study of education to the University of Chicago. White also provides valuable quotations from the correspondence between Harper and Bulkley while she was in Europe (24–28).

51. James H. Tufts's letter to Harper is conveniently printed in William W. Brickman and Stanley Lehrer, eds., *John Dewey: Master Educator*, rev. ed. (New York: Atherton Press, 1965), 167–168. In that volume, however, Tufts's letter does not include the list of "more important publications of Professor Dewey." We found that list when we tracked down Tufts's original letter in Collection of Presidents Papers, 1889–1925, Department of Special Collections, Joseph Regenstein Library, University of Chicago. Highly informative accounts of the relationship between Harper and Dewey at Chicago are Hobert L. McCaul, "Dewey, Harper, and the University of Chicago," in Brickman and Lehrer, *John Dewey: Master Educator*, 31–92; and Robert B. Westbrook, *John Dewey and American Democracy* (Ithaca, NY: Cornell University Press, 1991), 59–113, esp. 83, which emphasizes the impact on Dewey of the move from Ann Arbor to Chicago.

52. Harper quoted in White, "Study of Education at University of Chicago," 15. For the Harper-Dewey relationship at the University of Chicago, see Lee Benson and Ira Harkavy, "University-Assisted Community Schools as Democratic Public Works," *Good Society* 9, no. 2 (1999): 14–20; Lee Benson and Ira Harkavy, "Integrating the American System of Higher, Secondary, and Primary Education to Develop Civic Responsibility," in *Civic Responsibility and Higher Education*, ed. Thomas Ehrlich (Phoenix: Oryx Press, 2000), 174–196.

53. Harper, "The University and Democracy," 32.

54. Ibid., 25.

55. Ibid., 12.

56. Harper, for example, chaired the group that produced the "Report of the Educational Commission of the City of Chicago" (1898), which was authorized by the city council and approved by the mayor and the board of education. The report lists Daniel Coit Gilman of Johns Hopkins and Seth Low of Columbia as advisors to the commission. Nicholas Murray Butler, who would succeed Low as Columbia's president in 1902, called the Harper Report "the most complete and most illuminating document on the organization and administration of a school system of a large American city that has ever been published"; cited in Marvin Lazerson, "If All the World Were Chicago: American Education in the Twentieth Century," *History of Education Quarterly* 24, no. 2 (1984): 169.

57. Westbrook, *Dewey and American Democracy*, 83.

CHAPTER 4

1. Dewey's analysis of Bacon is quoted at greater length in Chapter 1. The source of this chapter's epigraph, "The School as Social Centre," is reprinted in *The Middle Works of John Dewey, 1899–1924*, vol. 2, ed. Jo Ann Boydston (Carbondale: Southern Illinois University Press, 1978), 80. *The Collected Works of John Dewey, 1882–1953*, edited by Boydston, were published in three series (*Early Works, Middle Works, Later Works*) by the Southern Illinois University Press and are digitally reproduced in Larry Hickman, ed., *The Collected Works of John Dewey, 1882–1953: The Electronic Edition* (Charlottesville, VA: InteLex, 1996).

2. Steven M. Cahn, "Introduction," in *The Later Works of John Dewey, 1925–1953*, vol. 13, ed. Jo Ann Boydston (Carbondale: Southern Illinois University Press, 1981), xvi–xvii.

3. Ibid., xvii–xviii.

4. Ira Harkavy and Lee Benson, "De-Platonizing and Democratizing Education as the Bases of Service Learning," in *Academic Service Learning: A Pedagogy of Action and Reflection*, eds. Robert A. Rhoads and Jeffrey Howard (San Francisco: Jossey–Bass, 1998), 11–12.

5. It is generally agreed that the term *participatory democracy* was coined in 1960 by Arnold Kaufman, a philosopher at the University of Michigan, and popularized in 1962 by Tom Hayden, Kaufman's student, in the extraordinarily influential Port Huron Statement of the radical Students for a Democratic Society. For the term's coining and Deweyan inspiration, see the brilliant review essay on the history of the general theory of participatory democracy by Jane Mansbridge, "On the Idea That Participation Makes Better Citizens," in *Citizen Competence and Democratic Institutions*, ed. Stephen L. Elkin and Karol Edward Soltan (University Park: Pennsylvania State University Press, 1999), 311–315. Also see Robert B. Westbrook, *John Dewey and American Democracy* (Ithaca, NY: Cornell University Press, 1991), 549–550. Dewey was of course only one of a number of theorists who, for a variety of reasons, strongly advocated some form of participatory democracy.

6. John Dewey, "Ethical Principles Underlying Education," in *The Early Works of John Dewey, 1882–1898*, vol. 5, ed. Jo Ann Boydston (Carbondale: Southern Illinois University Press, 1972), 54–83, quotations on 59–63.

7. For an insightful analysis of the school, see Westbrook, *John Dewey and American Democracy*, 96–113.

8. John Dewey, *The School and Society*, in *The Middle Works of John Dewey, 1899–1924*, vol. 1, ed. Jo Ann Boydston (Carbondale: Southern Illinois University Press, 1978), 1–110, quotation on 23.

9. Lee Benson and Ira Harkavy, "School and Community in the Global Society: A Neo-Deweyan Theory of Community Problem-Solving Schools, Cosmopolitan Neighborly Communities, and a Neo-Deweyan Manifesto to Dynamically Connect School and Community," *Universities and Community Schools* 5 (1997): 16–71, quotation on 32.

10. Dewey, *School and Society*, 21–38.

11. Ibid., 7–8.

12. For a detailed analysis of Wundt's influence on Dewey, see the chapter on "Wundtian Voluntarism," in John R. Shook, *Dewey's Empirical Theory of Knowledge and Reality* (Nashville, TN: Vanderbilt University Press, 2000), 71–120, quotation on 71.

13. For a fuller and much more detailed critique of Dewey's 1899 lectures on *School and Society* and the scientistic character of his laboratory school, see Benson and Harkavy, "School and Community in the Global Society," 23–28. For the definition of scientism, see *Merriam–Webster Dictionary*, http://www.merriam-webster.com/dictionary/scientism.

14. Dewey, *School and Society*, pts. 1 and 2, quotation on 8; Dewey, *The Child and the Curriculum*, in *Middle Works*, 2:273–291.

15. Dewey, *School and Society*, 12.

16. See Philip Jackson's incisive critique of the Laboratory School in his introduction to the centennial edition of Dewey's *"The School and Society" and "The Child and the Curriculum"* (Chicago: University of Chicago Press, 1990), ix–xli, esp. xxix–xxxiii.

17. Westbrook, *John Dewey and American Democracy*, 97–101, quotations on 97, 100, 101.

18. For an illuminating discussion of Addams's profound influence on Dewey and his thinking, see Louise W. Knight, "John Dewey and Jane Addams Debate War," in *Trained Capacities: John Dewey, Rhetoric, and Democratic Practice*, ed. Brian Jackson and Gregory Clark (Columbia: University of South Carolina Press, 2014), 106–124. Charlene Haddock Siegfried provides a particularly insightful and persuasive analysis of the "contributions of Jane Addams and the women of the Hull House Settlement to pragmatist theory, particularly as formulated by John Dewey," in "Socializing Democracy: Jane Addams and John

Dewey," *Philosophy of the Social Sciences* 29 (1999): 207–230. See also Ira Harkavy and John L. Puckett, "Lessons from Hull House for the Contemporary Urban University," *Social Service Review* 68 (1994): 299–321.

19. John Dewey, "The Ethics of Democracy," in *Early Works*, 1:227–250. For a discussion of this essay as Dewey's democratic manifesto, see Lee Benson, Ira Harkavy, and John Puckett, *Dewey's Dream: Universities and Democracies in an Age of Education Reform* (Philadelphia: Temple University Press, 2007), 3–7.

20. In *Middle Works*, 2:80–93.

21. Ibid., 82, 89–90, 93.

22. Ibid., 92.

23. Ibid., 80, 82, 83.

24. Ibid., 89–92.

25. Ibid., 91.

26. Ibid., 93.

27. Ibid.

28. Ibid., 82.

29. Ibid.

30. Ibid., 90.

31. Edward J. Ward, "The Rochester Civic and Social Centers," in *The City School as a Community Center*, pt. 1 of *Tenth Yearbook of the National Society for the Study of Education*, ed. Chester W. Parker (Chicago: University of Chicago Press, 1911), 51–57; William J. Reese, *Power and the Promise of School Reform: Grass-Roots Movements during the Progressive Era* (Boston: Routledge and Kegan Paul, 1986), 177–208; Kevin Mattson, *Creating a Democratic Public: The Struggle for Urban Participatory Democracy during the Progressive Era* (University Park: Pennsylvania State University Press, 1998), 51–65.

32. Edward J. Ward, ed., *The Social Center* (New York: D. Appleton, 1913), 204–206; Edward W. Stevens Jr., "Social Centers, Politics, and Social Efficiency in the Progressive Era," *History of Education Quarterly* 12 (Spring 1972): 16–33; Robert Fisher, "The People's Institute of New York City, 1897–1934: Culture, Progressive Democracy, and the People" (Ph.D. diss., New York University, 1974); Robert Fisher, "From Grass Roots Organizing to Community Service: Community Center Movement, 1907–30," in *The Roots of Community Organizing, 1917–1939*, ed. Neil Betten and Michael J. Austin (Philadelphia: Temple University Press, 1990), 76–93.

33. Eleanor T. Glueck, *The Community Use of Schools* (Baltimore, MD: Williams and Wilkens, 1927), 32–36; Fisher, "People's Institute," 310–318, 333–352; Clarence A. Perry, *Educational Extension* (Cleveland, OH: Survey Committee of the Cleveland Foundation, 1916), 94–96, 108–113; Fisher, "Community Center Movement," esp. 85–88; Robert Fisher, "Community Organizing and Citizen Participation: The Efforts of the People's Institute in New York City, 1910–1920," *Social Service Review* 51 (1977): 474–490; George Butler, *Introduction to Community Recreation* (New York: McGraw-Hill, 1949); New York City Board of Education, *Annual Report of the Superintendent of Schools, 1938–1939* (New York: Board of Education, 1939).

34. Michael C. Johanek and John L. Puckett, *Leonard Covello and the Making of Benjamin Franklin High School: Education as if Citizenship Mattered* (Philadelphia: Temple University Press, 2007), 32–33.

35. The major archival repositories are the Leonard Covello Papers, Historical Society of Pennsylvania (Balch Institute Collections), Philadelphia; and the Elsie Ripley Clapp Papers, Special Collections Research Center, Morris Library, Southern Illinois University, Carbondale. The *Journal of Progressive Education* featured articles by Covello and Clapp.

36. The federal subsistence homestead (the name was a misnomer) sluggishly outlasted the community school by about seven years, perennially in the red. Small-farm (subsistence) production was never meant to be a principal support of the project; the lynchpin was to be the operations of diverse branch industries that would invest in the community and employ the homestead's families. Having failed to recruit or hold the industries necessary to sustain the project on an independent footing, the federal government, from 1942 to 1947, liquidated and sold off its properties at fire-sale prices to individual householders and speculators.

37. Johanek and Puckett, *Leonard Covello*, 41. For Arthurdale's curriculum, see Elsie Ripley Clapp, *Community Schools in Action* (New York: Viking, 1939), and *The Use of Resources in Education* (New York: Harper Brothers, 1952).

38. For the curriculum see Clapp, *Community Schools in Action*, chap. 9. The quotation is on p. 3, as cited in Sam F. Stack, *The Arthurdale Community School: Education and Reform in Depression-Era Appalachia* (Lexington: University Press of Kentucky, 2016), 53.

39. Stack, *The Arthurdale Community School*, chaps. 3–7.

40. John Dewey, foreword to Clapp, *Community Schools in Action*, in *Later Works*, 14:352–355.

41. Daniel Perlstein, "Community and Democracy in American Schools: Arthurdale and the Fate of Progressive Education," *Teachers College Record* 97 (1996): 625–650.

42. Dewey, foreword to *Community Schools in Action*, 354.

43. Leonard Covello, *The Heart Is the Teacher* (New York: McGraw-Hill, 1958); Johanek and Puckett, *Leonard Covello*, chaps. 3–7.

44. Johanek and Puckett, *Leonard Covello*, chaps. 4–5.

45. Ibid., chap. 5.

46. Ibid., 182–193.

47. Ibid, 194–197.

48. Ibid., 206–224. After a sixty-year hiatus, Mayor Bill de Blasio and the Department of Education revisited the idea in the form of a strategic plan, unveiled in 2015, to transform one hundred city schools into community schools by 2017. Exceeding the original goal, 128 community schools are under development at this writing, although it is too soon to know if this large-scale implementation will be successful. Office of the Mayor et al., *New York City Community Schools Strategic Plan: Mayor Bill de Blasio's Strategy to Launch and Sustain a System of Over 100 Community Schools across NYC by 2017* (New York: Office of the Mayor, 2015), available at http://www1.nyc.gov/assets/communityschools/downloads/pdf/community-schools-strategic-plan.pdf, accessed 26 August 2016.

49. Johanek and Puckett, *Leonard Covello*, 233.

50. Lee Benson, Ira Harkavy, Michael Johanek, and John Puckett, "The Enduring Appeal of Community Schools," *American Educator* 33, no. 2 (Summer 2009): 28; see also John Puckett, review of *Full-Service Schools: A Revolution in Health and Social Services for Children, Youth, and Families*, by Joy G. Dryfoos, and *Urban Sanctuaries: Neighborhood Organizations in the Lives and Futures of Inner-City Youth*, by Milbrey W. McLaughlin, Merita A. Irby, and Juliet Longman, *Teachers College Record* 96 (1995): 584–590.

51. C. Warren Moses, "History of the Children's Aid Society Model," in *Community Schools in Action: Lessons from a Decade of Practice*, ed. Joy G. Dryfoos, Jane Quinn, and Carol Barkin (New York: Oxford University Press, 2005), 13–15. For New York City's Beacon programs, see Johanek and Puckett, *Leonard Covello*, 243–245. For a short history of the Beacons, see Jennifer LaFleur, Christina A. Russell, Troy A. Scott, and Elizabeth R. Reisner, *Evaluation of the Beacon Community Centers Middle School Initiative: Report on the First Year*, prepared for the Department of Youth and Community Development and the Wal-

lace Foundation (New York: Department of Youth and Community Development, 2009), 2, available at http://www.nyc.gov/html/dycd/downloads/pdf/beacon_middle_school_initia tive_report0609.pdf.

52. Johanek and Puckett, *Leonard Covello*, 244–245.

53. Harkavy served as chair of the Coalition from 1997 to 2012, when he became emeritus chair; Joann Weeks has served on the steering committee since 2012.

54. Martin J. Blank, "Reaching Out to Create a Movement," in Dryfoos, Quinn, and Barkin, *Community Schools in Action*, 243–244, 246.

55. See the Coalition's strategic plan for 2015–2020, *Growing a Strong Community Schools Field*, internal document, Institute for Educational Leadership, 2015, 1; *Coalition for Community Schools 4.0: Operating Principles*, internal document, Institute for Educational Leadership, 2015, 2–3.

56. Institute for Educational Leadership (IEL) Coalition for Community Schools, "What Is a Community School?" Coalition for Community Schools website, available at http://www.communityschools.org/aboutschools/what_is_a_community_school.aspx, accessed 21 July 2015.

57. IEL Coalition for Community Schools, "FAQs," Coalition for Community Schools website, available at http://www.communityschools.org/aboutschools/faqs.aspx, accessed 27 July 2015.

58. IEL Coalition for Community Schools, "Community Schools Leadership Network (CSLN)," Coalition for Community Schools website, available at http://www.communi tyschools.org/about/community_schools_leadership_network_csln.aspx, accessed 27 July 2015.

59. Community schools representatives from over fifty institutions of higher education and several nonprofits are engaged in this network. In winter 2016, staff from the Mayor's Office of Education, which is developing community schools in Philadelphia, joined the network. See the Coalition for Community Schools website, http://www.com munityschools.org/about/universityassistedcommunityschoolsnetwork.aspx, accessed 19 December 2016.

CHAPTER 5

1. Derek C. Bok, *Universities and the Future of America* (Durham, NC: Duke University Press, 1990), 3.

2. David P. Baker, *The Schooled Society: The Educational Transformation of Global Culture* (Stanford, CA: Stanford University Press, 2014), 1–19, 58–121.

3. Rita Axelroth Hodges and Steve Dubb, *The Road Half Traveled: University Engagement at a Crossroads* (East Lansing: Michigan State University Press, 2012).

4. The analysis presented in this chapter draws in part on research informed by a number of data sources, including a review of documents from the Association of American Colleges and Universities (AAC&U), the American Association for Higher Education (AAHE), Campus Outreach Opportunity League (COOL), and the National Association of State Universities and Land Grant Colleges (NASULGC) from 1980 to the present. It also draws on a review of archival materials from Campus Compact, which is the most extensive network involved in advancing this work. Further, its organizational structure, with a network of thirty-one state offices, has enabled it to gather information on a wide range of engagement efforts across the United States. The materials include quarterly newsletters, annual reports, member survey data, interoffice memoranda, minutes from board meetings, presidential addresses, and state compact reports. This research is also

informed by interviews with 123 individuals who have been involved in advancing civic engagement on their campuses and nationally. These semistructured interviews were conducted between June 2004 and May 2007 by Matthew Hartley. The majority were conducted in the 2006–2007 academic year with the support of a National Academy of Education/ Spencer Foundation post-doctoral fellowship.

5. Paulo Freire, *Pedagogy of the Oppressed*, trans. Myra Bergman Ramos (New York: Herder and Herder, 1970).

6. Quoted in Ernest L. Boyer, "Creating the New American College," *Chronicle of Higher Education*, 9 March 1994, A48.

7. bell hooks, *Teaching to Transgress: Education as the Practice of Freedom* (New York: Routledge, 1994).

8. Christopher C. Morphew and Matthew Hartley, "Mission Statements: A Thematic Analysis of Rhetoric across Institutional Type," *Journal of Higher Education* 77 (2006): 456–471; Alexander W. Astin, "Liberal Education and Democracy: The Case for Pragmatism," in *Education and Democracy: Re-imagining Liberal Learning in America*, ed. Robert Orrill (New York: College Board, 1997), 210–211.

9. Benjamin Franklin, *Proposals Relating to the Education of Youth in Pensilvania*, in *Benjamin Franklin on Education*, ed. John Hardin Best, Classics in Education 14 (New York: Bureau of Publications, Teachers College, Columbia University, 1962), 150–151.

10. Frederick Rudolph, *The American College and University: A History*, Knopf Publications in Education (New York: Alfred A. Knopf, 1962), 58–67.

11. Harry C. Boyte and Nancy N. Kari, "Renewing the Democratic Spirit in American Colleges and Universities," in *Civic Responsibility and Higher Education*, ed. Thomas Ehrlich (Phoenix: Oryx Press, 2000), 47.

12. Jack Stark, "The Wisconsin Idea: The University's Service to the State," in *State of Wisconsin Blue Book 1995–1996*, ed. Lawrence S. Barish (Madison: Wisconsin Legislative Reference Bureau, 1995), 101–102, available at http://digital.library.wisc.edu/1711.dl/ WI.WIBlueBk1995.

13. Quoted in Robert S. Maxwell, *La Follette and the Rise of the Wisconsin Progressives* (Madison: State Historical Society of Wisconsin, 1956), 147–148.

14. Ira Harkavy and John L. Puckett, "Lessons from Hull House for the Contemporary Urban University," *Social Service Review* 68 (1994): 299–321.

15. Dorothy Ross, *The Origins of American Social Science* (New York: Cambridge University Press, 1991), 321.

16. Quoted in Martin Bulmer, *The Chicago School of Sociology: Industrialization, Diversity, and the Rise of Sociological Research* (Chicago: University of Chicago Press, 1984), 182.

17. Ellen Condliffe Lagemann, *The Politics of Knowledge: The Carnegie Corporation, Philanthropy, and Public Policy* (Middletown, CT: Wesleyan University Press, 1989), chap. 3; Martin Bulmer and Joan Bulmer, "Philanthropy and Social Science in the 1920s: Beardsley Ruml and the Laura Spelman Rockefeller Memorial, 1922–29," *Minerva* 19 (1981): 347–407.

18. For a painstakingly detailed analysis of the advent and expansion of scientism in academic social science from the 1920s, see Ross, *Origins of American Social Science*, 390–470.

19. Sheldon Hackney, "The University and Its Community: Past and Present," *Annals of the American Academy of Political and Social Science* 488 (1986): 135–147. For discussion of the strengthening of disciplinary communities, see Daniel Alpert, "Performance and Paralysis: The Organizational Context of the American Research University," *Journal*

of Higher Education 56 (1985): 241–281; Christopher C. Jencks and David Riesman, *The Academic Revolution* (New York: Doubleday, 1968).

20. Page Smith, *Killing the Spirit: Higher Education in America* (New York: Penguin Books, 1990), 131–135. For the origins of the collegiate way, see Rudolph, *The American College and University*, 86–109.

21. David R. Thelin, *A History of American Higher Education* (Baltimore, MD: Johns Hopkins University Press, 2004), 155–156.

22. Jonathan Zimmerman, "The Context of Undergraduate Teaching and Learning," Springer Science and Business Media, 13 January 2015, available at http://link.springer.com/article/10.1007%2Fs12115-014-9856-0#/p, accessed 19 March 2016. See also Lee Benson and Ira Harkavy, "Saving the Soul of the University: What Is to Be Done?" in *The Virtual University? Knowledge, Markets, and Management*, ed. Kevin Robbins and Frank Webster (New York: Oxford University Press, 2002), 169–209.

23. For the Movement's descent into factionalism and underground violence, see Terry H. Anderson, *The Movement and the Sixties* (New York: Oxford University Press, 1995); Mark Rudd, *My Life with SDS and the Weathermen* (New York: HarperCollins, 2009); Todd Gitlin, *The Sixties: Days of Hope, Years of Rage* (New York: Bantam, 1987; rev. ed. 1993); Bryan Burrough, *Days of Rage: America's Radical Underground, the FBI, and America's Forgotten Age of Revolutionary Violence* (New York: Penguin, 2015).

24. Robert A. Rhoads, *Freedom's Web: Student Activism in an Age of Cultural Diversity* (Baltimore, MD: Johns Hopkins University Press, 1998), 54.

25. John H. Pryor, Sylvia Hurtado, Victor B. Saenz, José Luis Santos, and Williams S. Korn, *The American Freshman: Forty Year Trends, 1966–2006* (Los Angeles: Cooperative Institutional Research Program, Higher Education Research Institute, University of California, Los Angeles), 72. In his meticulous study of the decade's collegiate culture, *When Dreams and Heroes Died: A Portrait of Today's College Student* (San Francisco: Jossey-Bass, 1980), Arthur Levine reports "an ethic of 'looking out for number one' and an almost single-minded concern with material success" (xvii).

26. Levine, *When Dreams and Heroes Died*, 39–42; John L. Puckett and Mark Frazier Lloyd, *Becoming Penn: The Pragmatic American University, 1950–2000* (Philadelphia: University of Pennsylvania Press, 2015), 167–169. This is not to dismiss the campus activism associated with identity politics, which was not mainstream and made impressive headway on ethnic and gender studies.

27. M. G. Lord, "Greek Rites of Exclusion," *The Nation*, 4–11 July 1987, 10–13; for discussion of widespread fraternity gang rape, see Julie K. Ehrhart and Bernice R. Sandler, *Campus Gang Rape: Party Games?* (Washington, DC: Association of American Colleges and Universities, 1985), ERIC ED 267 667; for a detailed explication of a highly publicized case at a major research university, see Peggy Reeves Sanday, *Fraternity Gang Rape: Sex, Brotherhood, and Privilege on Campus* (New York: New York University Press, 1990); see also William A. Bryan, "Contemporary Fraternity and Sorority Issues," in *Fraternities and Sororities on the Contemporary College Campus: New Directions for Student Services*, ed. Roger B. Winston, William R. Netter III, and John II. Opper Jr. (San Francisco: Jossey-Bass, 1987).

28. Wayne Meisel, interview by Matt Hartley, 17 May 2007.

29. Ibid.

30. Wayne Meisel and Robert Hackett, *Building a Movement: A Resource Book for Students in Community Service* (Washington, DC: Campus Outreach Opportunity League, 1986.

31. Frank Newman, *Higher Education and the American Resurgence: A Carnegie Foundation Special Report* (Princeton, NJ: Carnegie Foundation for the Advancement of Teaching, 1985), 31.

32. Coalition of College Presidents for Civic Responsibility, *Transcript of Proceedings: First Meeting of the Coalition of College Presidents for Civic Responsibility, Washington, D.C., January 16, 1986* (Washington, DC: Miller Reporting, 2002), quotation on 32. This transcript names the group the "Coalition of College Presidents for Civic Responsibility."

33. Ibid., 92.

34. The conception of civic engagement that emphasized volunteerism led the national leadership of Campus Compact to encourage the development and passage of George H. W. Bush's National and Community Service Act in 1990 and Bill Clinton's National and Community Service Trust Act of 1993; the latter established the Corporation for National and Community Service in 1994.

35. Timothy K. Stanton, *Integrating Public Service with Academic Study: The Faculty Role* (Denver, CO: Education Commission of the States, 1990).

36. Ernest L. Boyer, *Scholarship Reconsidered: Priorities of the Professoriate* (Princeton, NJ: Carnegie Foundation for the Advancement of Teaching, 1990), 3.

37. Ernest L. Boyer, "The Scholarship of Engagement," *Journal of Higher Education Outreach and Engagement* 1, no. 1 (1996): 11–20, quotation on 14. From 1996 to 2000, this journal was titled *Journal of Public Service and Outreach*.

38. Boyer, "Creating the New American College," A48.

39. KerryAnn O'Meara and R. Eugene Rice, *Faculty Priorities Reconsidered* (San Francisco: Jossey-Bass, 2005), 259–262, quotations on 260–262.

40. Ellen Porter Honnet and Susan J. Poulsen, *Principles of Good Practice for Combining Service and Learning*, report prepared for the Johnson Foundation (Racine, WI: Johnson Foundation, 1989), quotation on 1, available at http://www.coastal.edu/media/academics/servicelearning/documents/Principles%20of%20Good%20Practice%20for%20Combining%20Service%20and%20Learning.pdf. In 1991 two authors of this volume, Harkavy and Puckett, attended a related Wingspread Conference on developing a service learning research agenda, and Harkavy and Hartley participated in other meetings on service learning and related topics at the Wingspread Conference Center. These conferences played a powerful role in developing and shaping the movement for democratic civic engagement in higher education.

41. One indication of the influence of ISAS that is particularly relevant to this volume is that three of the authors, Harkavy, Johnston, and Puckett, attended the first Campus Compact faculty institute during the summer of 1991 at Stanford. It was at that institute that the plan for creating Penn's Center for Community Partnerships (later the Netter Center for Community Partnerships) was developed.

42. Sandra Enos, phone interview by Matthew Hartley, 10 April 2007.

43. Maryann Jacobi Gray, Elizabeth Heneghan Ondaatje, and Laura Zakaras, *Combining Service and Learning in Higher Education: Summary Report* (Santa Monica, CA: RAND, 1999), v, available at http://www.rand.org/pubs/monograph_reports/MR998z1.

44. *Michigan Journal of Community Service Learning*, description available at https://ginsberg.umich.edu/mjcsl/about, accessed 8 March 2016.

45. Henry Taylor and Linda McGlynn claim that the democratic, engaged civic university was born in 1968 in the wake of the assassination of Martin Luther King Jr. Although we see it as developing some two decades later, we strongly agree with their claim that "changes in higher education, brought about by the confluence of the black presence on white campuses and white [and minority] student unrest, led to *internal* changes in higher education which paved the way for the emergence of the civic engagement movement among higher eds after 1989." Henry Lewis Taylor and Linda McGlynn, "Solving the Dewey Problem: What Is to Be Done?" *Good Society* 17, no. 2 (2008): 56–62, quotation on 58. For a

more recent discussion of how black college students of the late 1960s and early 1970s dramatically changed higher education, see Martha Biondi, *The Black Revolution on Campus* (Berkeley: University of California Press, 2012).

46. Adapted from Oliver Goldsmith, "The Deserted Village" (1770), line 17: "Ill fares the land, to hastening ills a prey." Available at Poetry Foundation, https://www.poetryfoun dation.org/poems-and-poets/poems/detail/44292.

47. Nida Denson, Lori J. Vogelgesang, and Victor Saenz, "Can Service Learning and a College Climate of Service Lead to Increased Political Engagement After College?" paper presented at the Annual Meeting of the American Educational Research Association, Montreal, Canada, 14 April 2005. Such debates continued into the next decade. As Denson, Vogelgesang, and Saenz observe: "There is not agreement within the service learning field that social justice ought to be an intended outcome of service learning participation" (6).

48. Enos interview; John Wallace, interview by Matthew Hartley, 13 December 2007; Timothy K. Stanton, Dwight E. Giles Jr., and Nadinne I. Cruz, *Service Learning: A Movement's Pioneers Reflect on Its Origins, Practice, and Future* (San Francisco: Jossey–Bass, 1999); Edward Zlotkowski, "Does Service Learning Have a Future?" *Michigan Journal of Community Service Learning* 2, no. 1 (1995): 123–133.

49. Wallace interview. Ira Harkavy, a member of the Invisible College, has a similar recollection.

50. Zlotkowski, "Does Service Learning Have a Future?" 123.

51. Ira Harkavy and Bill M. Donovan, eds., *Connecting Past and Present: Concepts and Models for Service-Learning in History*, Series on Service-Learning in the Disciplines (Washington, DC: American Association for Higher Education, 2000). Although the illumination of disciplinary concepts was a predominant emphasis, it was not the only one. For example, Harkavy and Donovan's volume contains a number of chapters, including one by Elisa von Joeden-Forgey and John Puckett, "History as Public Work" (117–138), that focus on both disciplinary concepts and history as crucial for social change. As Dewey powerfully wrote: "The true starting point of history is always some present situation with its problems." John Dewey, *Democracy and Education* (1916), in *The Middle Works of John Dewey, 1899–1924*, vol. 9, ed. Jo Ann Boydston (Carbondale: Southern Illinois University Press, 1978), 222.

52. Sandra Enos, memorandum, 26 March 1996, "Concept Paper: ISAS," in Matthew Hartley's possession.

53. Jonathan Eisenberg, *1990–1991 National Member's Survey and Resource Guide*, report prepared for Campus Compact (Providence, RI: Campus Compact, Brown University, 1990), 1; Marshall Miller, Melissa Smith, and Lockhart Steele, *Service Counts: Lessons from the Field of Higher Education* (Providence, RI: Campus Compact, 1995), 6; Matthew Hartley, "Reclaiming the Democratic Purposes of American Higher Education: Tracing the Trajectory of the Civic Engagement Movement," special issue, "Perspectives on Citizenship Education, Learning and Teaching," *International Journal of Higher Education in the Social Sciences* 2, no. 3 (2009): 20; Campus Compact, *2002 Service Statistics: Highlights of Campus Compact's Annual Membership Survey* (Providence, RI: Campus Compact, 2002), 4, available at http://compact.org/resource-posts/2002-annual-membership-survey/.

54. Stanton, Giles, and Cruz, *Service Learning: A Movement's Pioneers*, 235.

55. John Saltmarsh, interview by Matthew Hartley, 2 October 2006.

56. Elizabeth Hollander, "Civic Education: Is Higher Ed Losing?" *Compact Current* 12, no. 4, Campus Compact newsletter (October–November 1998): 2.

57. National Commission on Civic Renewal, *A Nation of Spectators: How Civic Disengagement Weakens America and What We Can Do about It*, Final Report (College Park, MD: National Commission on Civic Renewal, University of Maryland, 1997), esp. 12–13.

58. Harry Boyte and Elizabeth Hollander, *Wingspread Declaration on Renewing the Civic Mission of the American Research University*, report prepared on behalf of participants at December 1998 and July 1999 Wingspread conferences (Boston: Campus Compact, June 1999), available at http://www.compact.org/initiatives/trucen/wingspread-declaration-on-the-civic-responsibilities-of-research-universities/. "The conference was coordinated by the University of Michigan Center for Community Service and Learning, with sponsorship by the Association of American Universities, American Association for Higher Education, American Council on Education, Association of American Colleges and Universities, Campus Compact, New England Resource Center for Higher Education, University of Pennsylvania Center for University [*sic*] Partnerships, and the Johnson Foundation, with support from the W. K. Kellogg Foundation" (p. 3 of PDF). (The name of the center at Penn should be University of Pennsylvania Center for Community Partnerships.) For the "filled with the democratic spirit" questions posed to students, faculty, staff, administrators, and the institution, see 9–14 (pp. 6–11 of PDF).

59. Thomas Ehrlich and Elizabeth Hollander, *Presidents' Declaration on the Civic Responsibility of Higher Education* (Providence, RI: printed by Campus Compact, December 2000), quotation on 1, available at http://kdp0l43vw6z2dlw631ififc5.wpengine.netd na-cdn.com/wp-content/uploads/2009/02/Presidents-Declaration.pdf. See also Matthew Hartley and Elizabeth L. Hollander, "The Elusive Ideal: Civic Learning and Higher Education," in *Institutions of American Democracy: The Public Schools*, ed. Susan Fuhrman and Marvin Lazerson (New York: Oxford University Press, 2006), 260. For the current number of signatories, see Campus Compact, *Presidents' Declaration on the Civic Responsibility of Higher Education*, Campus Compact website, available at http://compact.org/resources-for-presidents/presidents-declaration-on-the-civic-responsibility-of-higher-education/, accessed 22 October 2015.

60. Ehrlich and Hollander, *Presidents' Declaration*.

61. Kellogg Commission on the Future of State and Land-Grant Universities, *Returning to Our Roots: The Engaged Institution*, Third Report (Washington, DC: National Association of State Universities and Land Grant Colleges, 1999), quotations on 9, 12, available at http://www.aplu.org/library/returning-to-our-roots-the-engaged-institution.

62. Morphew and Hartley, "Mission Statements."

63. Kellogg Commission, *Returning to Our Roots*; Boyte and Hollander, *Wingspread Declaration*.

64. Mary Jane Brukardt, Barbara Holland, Stephen L. Percy, and Nancy Zimpher, *Calling the Question: Is Higher Education Ready to Commit to Community Engagement?* report prepared on behalf of participants at Wingspread Conference, 18–19 April 2004 (Milwaukee: Milwaukee Idea Office, University of Wisconsin–Madison, 2004).

65. John Saltmarsh and Matthew Hartley, eds., *"To Serve a Larger Purpose": Engagement for Democracy and the Transformation of Higher Education* (Philadelphia: Temple University Press, 2011).

66. AASCU Task Force on Public Engagement, *Stepping Forward as Stewards of Place* (Washington, DC: American Association of State Colleges and Universities, 2002), 7, available at http://www.aascu.org/WorkArea/DownloadAsset.aspx?id=5458; American Association of State Colleges and Universities, "The American Democracy Project," informational handout (Washington, DC: American Association of State Colleges and Universities, n.d.), available at http://www.aascu.org/programs/ADP/InformationalHandout, accessed 16 October 2015 (the American Democracy Project now has over 250 members); Carol Geary Schneider, "Making Excellence Inclusive: Liberal Education and America's Promise," *Lib-*

eral Education 91, no. 2 (2005), quotations on 11–12; Maureen F. Curley and Timothy K. Stanton, "The History of TRUCEN," special issue, "The Research University Civic Engagement Network (TRUCEN)," ed. Trish Kalivoda, Maureen F. Curley, Ira Harkavy, Kathy O'Byrne, and Timothy K. Stanton, *Journal of Higher Education Outreach and Engagement* 16, no. 4 (2012): 3–4, available at http://openjournals.libs.uga.edu/index.php/jheoe/article/view/896/602; "The Democracy Commitment Fact Sheet," under "Resources," the Democracy Commitment website, available at http://thedemocracycommitment.org/wp-content/uploads/2013/01/TDC-Fact-Sheet1.pdf, accessed 14 July 2015; National Task Force on Civic Learning and Democratic Engagement, *A Crucible Moment: College Learning and Democracy's Future* (Washington, DC: Association of American Colleges and Universities, 2012), available at http://www.aacu.org/civic_learning/crucible/.

67. For example, see Anne Colby, Thomas Ehrlich, Elizabeth Beaumont, and Jason Stephens, *Educating Citizens: Preparing America's Undergraduates for Lives of Moral and Civic Responsibility* (San Francisco: Jossey-Bass, 2003); Brukardt et al., *Calling the Question*; Saltmarsh and Hartley, *"To Serve a Larger Purpose."*

68. Alexander W. Astin and Linda J. Sax, "How Undergraduates Are Affected by Service Participation," *Journal of College Student Development* 39 (1998): 251–263.

69. John Saltmarsh and Matthew Hartley, "Democratic Engagement," in Saltmarsh and Hartley, *"To Serve a Larger Purpose,"* 14–26; Matthew Hartley, John Saltmarsh, and Patti Clayton, "Is the Civic Engagement Movement Changing Higher Education?" special issue, "Civic Engagement," *British Journal of Educational Studies* 58 (2010): 391–406.

70. Michael C. Johanek and John Puckett, "The State of Civic Education: Preparing Citizens in an Era of Accountability," in Fuhrman and Lazerson, *Public Schools,* 149.

71. Lee Benson, Ira Harkavy, and John Puckett, *Dewey's Dream: Universities and Democracies in an Age of Education Reform* (Philadelphia: Temple University Press, 2007); Saltmarsh and Hartley, *"To Serve a Larger Purpose."*

72. Ira Harkavy et al., "Anchor Institutions as Partners in Building Successful Communities and Local Economies," in *Retooling HUD for a Catalytic Federal Government: A Report to Secretary Shaun Donovan,* ed. Paul C. Brophy and Rachel D. Godsil (Philadelphia: Penn Institute for Urban Research, University of Pennsylvania, 2009), 147–169; quotations from Marga Incorporated, *Anchor Institutions Task Force,* Task Force Statement (New York: Marga, 2010), available at http://www.margainc.com/files_images/general/anchor_task_force_statement.pdf (for the Anchor Institutions Task Force core values, see p. 1); Marga Incorporated, "Annual AITF Conference, October 29–30, 2015," under "Marga News," *Marga INC* website, available at www.margainc.com, accessed 4 September 2015. See the current AITF membership numbers at http://www.margainc.com/news/ (1)

73. Stanton, Giles, and Cruz, *Service Learning: A Movement's Pioneers.*

74. Quoted in Coalition of College Presidents for Civic Responsibility, *Transcript of Proceedings,* 11–12.

75. Stanton, *Integrating Public Service,* 1.

76. Eisenberg, *1990–1991 National Members' Survey and Resource Guide,* 1.

77. Campus Compact, *Three Decades of Institutionalizing Change: 2014 Annual Member Survey* (Boston: Campus Compact, 2014), 2–5, 9. The work has also spread across the range of institutions of higher education. The 2014 survey sample, for example, represents a diverse set of institutions: Of the 434 member institutions responding, almost 50 per-

cent are private, four-year institutions, 37 percent are public four-year institutions, and 15 percent are public two-year institutions; 31 percent identify as commuter institutions; and 20 percent identify as Historically Black Colleges and Universities (HBCUs) or minority-serving or tribal institutions.

78. John Dewey, *How We Think*, revised ed., in *The Later Works of John Dewey, 1925–1953*, vol. 8, ed. Jo Ann Boydston (Carbondale: Southern Illinois University, 1981), 122; digitally reproduced in Larry Hickman, ed., *The Collected Works of John Dewey, 1882–1953: The Electronic Edition* (Charlottesville, VA: InteLex, 1996).

79. Dewey, *Democracy and Education*, 44.

80. The phrase "promise of American life" is taken from Herbert Croly's 1909 progressive manifesto, *The Promise of American Life* (New York: Macmillan, 1909).

CHAPTER 6

1. Edward Potts Cheyney, *History of the University of Pennsylvania, 1740–1940* (Philadelphia: University of Pennsylvania Press, 1940), 29.

2. Benjamin Franklin, "Tract Relative to the English School in Philadelphia," June 1789, Papers of Benjamin Franklin, unpublished, 1778–1792, Packard Humanities Institute, Los Altos, CA.

3. Steven A. Sass, *The Pragmatic Imagination: A History of the Wharton School, 1881–1981* (Philadelphia: University of Pennsylvania Press, 1982).

4. Leo S. Rowe, "University and Collegiate Research in Municipal Government," in *Proceedings of the Chicago Conference for Good City Government and the Tenth Annual Meeting of the National Municipal League*, Chicago, 27–29 April 1904, ed. Clinton Rogers (Philadelphia: National Municipal League, 1904), 242–248.

5. Cheyney, *History of the University of Pennsylvania*, 261.

6. Roger Miller and Joseph Siry, "The Emerging Suburb: West Philadelphia, 1850–1880," *Pennsylvania History* 47, no. 2 (1980): 99–146.

7. E. Digby Baltzell, *Puritan Boston and Quaker Philadelphia: Two Protestant Ethics and the Spirit of Class Authority and Leadership* (New York: Free Press, 1979), 255.

8. Rexford G. Tugwell, *To the Lesser Heights of Morningside: A Memoir* (Philadelphia: University of Pennsylvania Press, 1982), 8–9.

9. Our account of James, Patten, and the early years of the Wharton School draws liberally from Sass, *Pragmatic Imagination*, chap. 3.

10. Quoted in Daniel M. Fox, *The Discovery of Abundance: Simon N. Patten and the Transformation of Social Theory* (Ithaca, NY: Cornell University Press, 1967), 40.

11. Rowe, "University and Collegiate Research in Municipal Government," 242–248.

12. Eliott W. Rudwick, "W. E. B. DuBois: A Study in Minority Group Leadership" (Ph.D. diss., University of Pennsylvania, 1956); W.E.B. DuBois, *The Philadelphia Negro: A Social Study* (1899; reprint ed., Philadelphia: University of Pennsylvania Press, 1996). For an insightful discussion of the relationship between racial discrimination and black criminality, as depicted by Du Bois in *The Philadelphia Negro*, see Khalil Gibran Muhammed, *The Condemnation of Blackness: Race, Crime, and the Making of Modern Urban America* (Cambridge, MA: Harvard University Press, 2010), 62–74. Muhammed's analysis brilliantly contextualizes Du Bois's study in the larger context of Jim Crow–era social science, viewing *The Philadelphia Negro* as a forceful antidote to white-supremacist interpretations of U.S. census data on black criminality, which universally condemned blackness.

13. Elijah Anderson and Douglas S. Massey, "The Sociology of Race in the Unit-

ed States," in *Problem of the Century: Racial Stratification in the United States*, ed. Elijah Anderson and Douglas S. Massey (New York: Russell Sage Foundation, 2001), 3–4.

14. Sass, *Pragmatic Imagination*, 118–119.

15. Ibid., 125–126.

16. John L. Puckett and Mark Frazier Lloyd, *Becoming Penn: America's Pragmatic University, 1950–2000* (Philadelphia: University of Pennsylvania Press, 2015), 9–10.

17. Ibid., 25–87.

18. Ibid., 88, 92–93.

19. Ibid., 98–99.

20. Ibid., 98.

21. Ibid., 103–117, 118–139; see also and cf. Margaret Pugh O'Mara, *Cities of Knowledge: Cold War Science and the Search for the Next Silicon Valley* (Princeton, NJ: Princeton University Press, 2005), 142–181.

22. Puckett and Lloyd, *Becoming Penn*, 118–139.

23. Ibid., quotation on 130.

24. Ibid., 156–173.

25. Ibid., 162–164.

26. Ibid., 177.

27. Kurt Lewin, "Psychology and the Process of Group Living," *Journal of Social Psychology* 17 (1943): 113–131, reprinted in *The Complete Social Scientist: A Kurt Lewin Reader*, ed. Martin Gold (Washington, DC: American Psychological Association, 1999), 333–345, quotation on 336.

28. Richard Allen Swanson, "Edmund James, 1855–1935: A Conservative Progressive in American Higher Education" (Ph.D. diss., University of Illinois, 1966); Fox, *The Discovery of Abundance*.

CHAPTER 7

1. MOVE was a militant, back-to-nature African American cult that had formed in West Philadelphia in the 1970s. The organization first locked horns with the Philadelphia police in a 1977 shootout in Powelton Village. In the weeks leading up to the 1985 fire, MOVE members armed and barricaded themselves in a row house on Osage Avenue just above Cobbs Creek Parkway. On 13 May the arrival of the police to extract MOVE members from the house led to a wild melee of gunfire that lasted through the day and into the evening. At that point, Mayor Wilson Goode authorized a police helicopter to drop a satchel bomb on a bunker atop the house. It was a costly decision. The bomb ignited a fire that exploded into a major conflagration, killing eleven MOVE members and destroying two full blocks of middle-class row houses. For details, see John Anderson and Hilary Hevenor, *Burning Down the House: MOVE and the Tragedy of Philadelphia* (New York: W. W. Norton, 1987).

2. Ira Harkavy and John L. Puckett, "The Role of Mediating Structures in University and Community Revitalization: The University of Pennsylvania and West Philadelphia as a Case Study," *Journal of Research and Development in Education* 25, no. 1 (Fall 1991): 10–25.

3. John L. Puckett and Mark Frazier Lloyd, *Becoming Penn: The Pragmatic American University, 1950–2000* (Philadelphia: University of Pennsylvania Press, 2015), 138.

4. The Netter Center director reports to Penn's president through the vice president for government and community affairs.

5. Puckett and Lloyd, *Becoming Penn*, 143–173.

6. Paul R. Hanna and Robert A. Naslund, "The Community School Defined," in *Fifty-Second Yearbook of the National Society for the Study of Education, part II: The Community School*, ed. Nelson B. Henry (Chicago: University of Chicago Press, 1953), 52. See Chapter 4 in this book and also Michael C. Johanek and John L. Puckett, *Leonard Covello and the Making of Benjamin Franklin High School: Education as if Citizenship Mattered* (Philadelphia: Temple University Press, 2007), which traces the 120-year history of the community school idea in the United States, giving particular attention to Benjamin Franklin High School in East Harlem, 1934–1956. Chapter 8 locates Penn's community school initiative within this broader historical context.

7. Ira Harkavy and John L. Puckett, "Toward Effective University–Public School Partnerships: An Analysis of a Contemporary Model," *Teachers College Record* 92 (1991): 564–565. For a project funded by the Spencer Foundation in 1991–1992, Puckett traced the community school idea in the United States from its roots in the Progressive Era settlement house movement to the present. Noting the episodic rise and fall of community school movements in the twentieth century, he advised Benson, Harkavy, and other Netter Center colleagues on the lessons of this history, particularly the critical importance of an institutional anchor for community schools. For a history and critique of America's community schools in their varied forms, see Johanek and Puckett, *Leonard Covello*.

8. Robert G. Bringle, Patti H. Clayton, and Julie A. Hatcher, "Research on Service Learning: An Introduction," in *Research on Service Learning: Conceptual Frameworks and Assessment*, vol. 2B: *Communities, Institutions, and Partnerships* (Sterling, VA: Stylus, 2013), 6.

9. Michael Zuckerman, "The Turnerian Frontier: A New Approach to the Study of Character," in *Connecting Past and Present: Models of Service-Learning in History*, ed. Ira Harkavy and Bill M. Donovan, Series on Service-Learning in the Disciplines (Washington, DC: American Association for Higher Education, 2000), 83–102; Ralph M. Rosen, "Classical Studies and the Search for Community," ibid., 173–188; Ira Harkavy, "Service-Learning, Academically Based Community Service, and the Historic Mission of the American Research University," ibid., 27–42; Elisa von Joeden-Forgey and John Puckett, "History as Public Work," ibid., 117–138; Robert Giegengack, Walter Cressler, Peter Block, and Joanne Piesieski, "An Educational Strategy to Reduce Exposure of Urban Children to Environmental Lead: ENVS 404 at the University of Pennsylvania," in *Acting Locally: Concepts and Models for Service-Learning in Environmental Studies*, ed. Harold Ward, Series on Service-Learning in the Disciplines (Washington, DC: American Association for Higher Education, 1999), 121–132.

10. As examples of this argument, see Ira Harkavy, "Back to the Future: From Service Learning to Strategic, Academically-Based Community Service," *Metropolitan Universities*, Summer 1996, 57–59; Ira Harkavy, "Service Learning and the Democratic Development of Universities, Democratic Schools, and Democratic Good Societies," in *New Perspectives in Service Learning: Research to Advance the Field*, ed. Marshall Welch and Shelly H. Billig (Greenwich, CT: Information Age Publishing, 2004), 5.

11. Lee Benson and Ira Harkavy, "Communal Participatory Action Research and Strategic Academically-Based Community Service: The Work of Penn's Center for Community Partnerships," in *Successful Service-Learning Programs: New Models of Excellence in Higher Education*, ed. Edward Zlotkowski (Bolton, MA: Anker, 1998), 127–128.

12. Giegengack, Cressler, Bloch, and Piesieski, "An Educational Strategy to Reduce Exposure of Urban Children to Environmental Lead."

13. For the theoretical foundations of Penn's approach, see Lee Benson, Ira Harkavy, and John Puckett, *Dewey's Dream: Universities and Democracies in an Age of Education Reform* (Philadelphia: Temple University Press, 2007); Lee Benson and Ira Harkavy, "Saving the

Soul of the University: What Is to Be Done?" in *The Virtual University? Knowledge, Markets, and Management*, ed. Kevin Robbins and Frank Webster (New York: Oxford University Press, 2002), 169–209; Lee Benson and Ira Harkavy, "School and Community in the Global Society: A Neo-Deweyan Theory of Community Problem-Solving Schools, Cosmopolitan Neighborly Communities, and a Neo-Deweyan Manifesto to Dynamically Connect School and Community," *Universities and Community Schools* 5 (1997): 16–71; Ira Harkavy and Lee Benson, "De-Platonizing and Democratizing Education as the Basis of Service Learning," in *Academic Service-Learning: A Pedagogy of Action and Reflection*, ed. Robert A. Rhoads and Jeffrey Howard (San Francisco: Jossey-Bass, 1998), 11–19; Ira Harkavy and John L. Puckett, "Lessons from Hull House for the Contemporary Urban University," *Social Service Review* 68 (1994): 299–321; Harkavy and Puckett, "Toward Effective University–Public School Partnerships," 552–581; Harkavy and Puckett, "Role of Mediating Structures," 225.

14. William F. Whyte, Davydd J. Greenwood, and Peter Lazes, "Participatory Action Research: Through Practice to Science in Social Research," special issue, "Action Research for the 21st Century: Participation, Reflection, and Practice," ed. William F. Whyte, *American Behavioral Scientist* 32 (1989): 513–551; William F. Whyte and Kathleen K. Whyte, *Making Mondragón: The Growth and Dynamics of the Worker Cooperative Complex*, 2nd ed. (Ithaca, NY: ILR Press, 1991).

15. Davydd Greenwood and José Luis González, *Industrial Democracy as a Process: Participatory Action Research in the Fagor Cooperative Group of Mondragon* (Assen–Maastricht: Van Gorcum, 1992).

16. Harkavy co-authored an article with Whyte and Greenwood that featured Penn's work with WEPIC and Whyte's and Greenwood's work with Xerox and the Mondragón cooperatives as ongoing PAR projects. See Davydd J. Greenwood, William F. Whyte, and Ira Harkavy, "Participatory Action Research as a Process and as a Goal," *Human Relations* 46 (1993): 175–192.

17. John Puckett and Ira Harkavy, "The Action Research Tradition in the United States: Toward a Strategy for Revitalizing the Social Sciences, the University, and the American City," in *Action Research: From Practice to Writing in an International Action Research Development Program*, ed. Davyyd J. Greenwood (Amsterdam: John Benjamins, 1999), 147–167.

18. Participants in the faculty and researcher working group at the 2004 Kellogg Forum on Higher Education for the Public Good included Tony Chambers, Arthur Dunning, Ed Fogelman, Richard Guarasci, Ira Harkavy, Jeffrey Higgs, Leonard Ortolano, and Jane Rosser.

19. Ira Harkavy and Matthew Hartley, "University-School-Community Partnerships for Youth Development and Democratic Renewal," *New Directions for Youth Development* 122 (Summer 2009): 11–12.

20. Eleanor Novek's 1993 dissertation study of West Philadelphia High School, a WEPIC site, illustrates the Mondragón PAR modality; see Eleanor M. Novek, "Buried Treasure: The Theory and Practice of Communicative Action in an Urban High School Newspaper," paper presented to the Association for Education in Journalism and Mass Communication, Kansas City, MO, August 1993. A former professional journalist and editor studying at the Annenberg School for Communication, Novek participated as a co-teacher and researcher in an English/journalism class that used "production of a community-focused newspaper as a strategy for the self-determination of young African Americans" (1). Each component of the production of the newspaper, *Q-West*, was adjudicated and carried out by the students. Novek's research on self-determination and student empowerment built on Jürgen Habermas's theory of communicative action, elements of reference group theory

(as described, for example, by Robert Merton), and superordinate goal theory (drawing on work by Muzafer Sherif and Caroline Sherif), not only during the process of interpreting and theorizing from ethnographic data about the students but also, simultaneously, when shaping the intervention strategies, thereby effecting an ebb and flow of theory and action. Novek constructed several criteria for self-determination, such as "providing experiences of mastery, strengthening group bonds and increasing [the students'] influence in social systems" (21). Her description of risk taking and the crossing of social boundaries is a case in point: "A shy young woman who never spoke up in class not only obtained an interview with Ramona Africa, the lone [adult] survivor of the world-infamous MOVE bombing in May 1985, but also brought her to the school to address the whole class. A taciturn young man interested in rap music visited one of the largest African American radio stations in the city and interviewed a popular disc jockey on the air. Another student took it upon himself to develop and distribute an attitude survey about the Q-West project to class members. Two students applied for and won admission to a minority workshop for high school journalists—the first time any students from their school had participated. Another began freelancing sports reports for a community newspaper" (15). These examples suggest that genuine thinking occurred as a result of Novek's project, engendering new ideas, concepts, and approaches to school and community development.

21. William Labov, Drew School Reading Progress, data mailed to Netter Center staff for annual report, 22 February 2006; also see Lee Benson, Ira Harkavy, and John L. Puckett, "An Implementation Revolution as a Strategy for Fulfilling the Democratic Promise of University-Community Partnerships: Penn-West Philadelphia as an Experiment in Progress," *Nonprofit and Voluntary Sector Quarterly* 29 (2000): 39–42.

22. Labov, Drew School Reading Progress.

23. University of Pennsylvania, *Annual Report*, 1987–1988, available at http://www.archives.upenn.edu/primdocs/uph/uph4_5/1988fin_report.pdf.

24. Judith Rodin, *The University and Urban Revival: Out of the Ivory Tower and into the Streets* (Philadelphia: University of Pennsylvania Press, 2007), 46, 48–49, 140–166.

25. Judith Rodin, "The Unity of Theory and Practice: Penn's Distinctive Character," *Almanac Supplement*, 2 April 1996, 9–10, available at http://www.upenn.edu/almanac/v42/n26/presrpt.pdf.

26. "Building on Excellence: The Leadership Agenda: A Strategic Plan for the University of Pennsylvania," *Almanac Supplement*, 23 September 2003, 6.

27. Amy Gutmann, inaugural address, University of Pennsylvania, 15 October 2004, available at http://www.upenn.edu/secretary/inauguration/speech.html.

28. Ibid.

29. International Consortium of Higher Education, Civic Responsibility and Democracy, *Declaration: The Responsibility of Higher Education for a Democratic Culture, Citizenship, Human Rights and Sustainability*, adopted 23 June 2006, https://www.internationalconsortium.org/.

30. Francis Bacon, *The New Organon*, Book 1, in *Francis Bacon: Selected Philosophical Works*, ed. Rose-Mary Sargent (Indianapolis: Hackett, 1999), 117.

CHAPTER 8

1. William E. Nothdurft, *Schoolworks: Reinventing Public Schools to Create the Workforce of the Future*, a German Marshall Fund of the U.S. Book (Washington, DC: Brookings Institution, 1989), viii.

2. The Philadelphia Higher Education Network for Neighborhood Development publishes weekly updates on its members' outreach activities on the website PHENND.org.

3. Ira Harkavy and John L. Puckett, "Toward Effective University–Public School Partnerships: An Analysis of a Contemporary Model," *Teachers College Record* 92 (1991): 552–581; Ira Harkavy and John L. Puckett, "The Role of Mediating Structures in University and Community Revitalization: The University of Pennsylvania and West Philadelphia as a Case Study," *Journal of Research and Development in Education* 25 (1991): 10–25; Sheldon Hackney, "The University and Its Community: Past and Present," *Annals of the American Academy of Political and Social Science* 488 (1986): 135–147. For a nationally circulated paper that appeared in the Netter Center's nonrefereed journal, see Lee Benson and Ira Harkavy, "Progressing beyond the Welfare State," *Universities and Community Schools* 2 (1991): 2–28.

4. School District data cited in memo from Harkavy to Andrew Fisher at the fund, 16 June 1992, submitted in preparation for a full proposal for a planning grant.

5. The Charles Stewart Mott Foundation also made an important contribution to spreading the idea of university-assisted community schools. In 2000, it funded the center to support the foundation's training efforts for 21st Century Community Learning Center programs, particularly to focus on the role of higher education–community–school partnerships. Through 2005, seventy-five partnership teams had received training at Penn, far exceeding the grant's expectation of forty teams.

6. Rita Axelroth Hodges, Matt Hartley, Ira Harkavy, and Joann Weeks, "Catalyzing School Reform: The University-Assisted Community School Approach," internal Netter Center report, October 2006.

7. Joy Dryfoos, a founding member of the coalition, was one of the leading researchers and champions of community schools. In her 1998 book, *Safe Passage: Making It through Adolescence in a Risky Society: What Parents, Schools, and Communities Can Do* (New York: Oxford University Press, 1998), Dryfoos describes the Netter Center's UACS program at Turner Middle School in West Philadelphia as a successful model for working with at-risk youth.

8. For more information on the Coalition for Community Schools, see http://www.communityschools.org/.

9. HUD, "The Office of University Partnerships (OUP)," available at http://www.huduser.gov/portal/oup/home.html, accessed 9 October 2015.

10. Avid Vidal et al., *Lessons from the Community Outreach Partnership Program,* final report prepared for HUD Office of Policy Development and Research (Washington, DC: Urban Institute, 2002), available at http://www.huduser.gov/publications/pdf/lessons_complete.pdf, accessed 9 October 2015.

11. Henry G. Cisneros, "The University and the Urban Challenge" (Washington, DC: U.S. Department of Housing and Urban Development, 1995), 2; see also Ira Harkavy and Harmon Zuckerman, "Eds and Meds: Cities' Hidden Assets," Brookings Institution Center on Urban and Metropolitan Policy, Survey Series 22, August 1999, 1–6.

12. Karen Fullbright-Anderson, Patricia Auspos, and Andrea Anderson. "Community Involvement in Partnerships with Educational Institutions, Medical Centers, and Utility Companies" (Aspen, CO: Annie E. Casey Foundation, Aspen Institute Roundtable on Comprehensive Community Initiatives, 2001), 1.

13. Henry Louis Taylor Jr. and Gavin Luter, *Anchor Institutions: An Interpretative Review Essay* (Buffalo, NY: Anchor Institutions Task Force, 2013), 3–4.

14. Penn Institute for Urban Research sponsored the project with funding from the Rockefeller Foundation.

15. Ira Harkavy et al., "Anchor Institutions as Partners in Building Successful Communities and Local Economies," in *Retooling HUD for a Catalytic Federal Government: A*

Report to Secretary Shaun Donovan, ed. Paul C. Brophy and Rachel D. Godsil (Philadelphia: Penn Institute for Urban Research, 2009), 147–169.

16. David J. Maurrasse, "From the Desk of the Guest Editor," *Journal of Higher Education Outreach and Engagement* 17, no. 3 (2013): 1–6.

17. Snežana Samardžić-Marković, "Higher Education for Democratic Innovation: Challenges and Opportunities for Action," keynote address, opening plenary session, Higher Education for Democratic Innovation Global Forum 2014, Queen's University, Belfast, Northern Ireland, 26 June 2014.

18. Francis Bacon, *Advancement of Learning*, in *Francis Bacon: Selected Philosophical Works*, ed. Rose-Mary Sargent (Indianapolis, IN: Hackett, 1999), 54.

19. For a discussion of the CHESP initiative, see Jo Lazarus, "Embedding Service Learning in South African Higher Education: The Catalytic Role of the CHESP Initiative," special issue, *Education as Change* 11, no. 3 (2007): 91–108.

20. For a summary of the project and its results, see Ira Harkavy, Nancy Cantor, and Myra Burnett, "Realizing STEM Equity and Diversity through Higher Education-Community Engagement," white paper based on work supported by the National Science Foundation under Grant no. 1219996, January 2015, available at https://www.nettercenter.upenn.edu.

21. Andrew M. Kaniki and Candice Steele, "Community Engagement Landscape in South African Higher Education and Critical Issues of Science, Technology, Engineering and Mathematics (STEM)," paper presented at workshop on The Role of Higher Education: Fostering P–20+ Community Engagement through Knowledge Production, Human Capacity Building, Innovation and Social Cohesion, Philadelphia, February 2012.

22. For the International Consortium and the Council of Europe, see www.internationalconsortium.org.

23. In March 2016, as part of its thirtieth anniversary celebrations, more than 350 presidents and chancellors signed the Compact's new Action Statement. The Action Statement advances the "public obligations" of higher education and "commits campuses to specific steps to deepen their engagement for the benefits of students, communities, and the broader public." Each campus will be developing a Campus Civic Action Plan as part of this effort. See http://compact.org/actionstatement/.

24. In 2005 Innovations in Civic Participation worked with Tufts University to organize the Talloires Network, an international consortium of institutions of higher education committed to serving and strengthening the societies of which they are a part. Network members agree to promote the civic roles and social responsibilities of their institutions, as well as to deepen engagement with local and global communities. GUNi formed in 2009 as an international network supported by UNESCO, the United Nations University, and the Catalan Association of Public Universities that emphasizes the social commitment of higher education. See the Talloires and GUNi websites at http://talloiresnetwork.tufts.edu/ and http://guninetwork.org.

25. Bacon, *Advancement of Learning*, 54.

CHAPTER 9

1. Francis E. Johnston and Ira Harkavy, *The Obesity Culture: Strategies for Change: Public Health and University-Community Partnerships* (St. Ives, UK: Smith-Gordon, 2009), 10–19.

2. Ibid.

3. Cheryl D. Fryar, Margaret D. Carroll, and Cynthia L. Ogden, *Prevalence of Obesity among Children and Adolescents: United States, Trends 1963–1965 through 2009–2010*,

report prepared for the U.S. Centers for Disease Control and Prevention (Atlanta: U.S. Centers for Disease Control and Prevention, 2012), 3, fig. 1, available at http://www.cdc.gov/nchs/data/hestat/obesity_child_09_10/obesity_child_09_10.pdf.

4. Ibid., 1–2.

5. Johnston and Harkavy, *Obesity Culture.*

6. Shelagh A. Gallagher, "Problem-Based Learning: Where Did It Come From, What Does It Do, Where Is It Going?" *Journal for the Education of the Gifted* 20 (1997): 332–362.

7. See John Dewey, *Experience and Education,* in *The Later Works of John Dewey, 1925–1953,* vol. 2, ed. Jo Ann Boydston (Carbondale: Southern Illinois University Press, 1981); digitally reproduced in Larry Hickman, ed., *The Collected Works of John Dewey, 1882–1953: The Electronic Edition* (Charlottesville, VA: InterLex, 1996); Dewey, "The Way Out of Educational Confusion," in *Later Works,* 6:76–90; Laurel N. Tanner, "The Meaning of Curriculum in Dewey's Laboratory School (1896–1904)," *Journal of Curriculum Studies* 23 (1991): 101–117.

8. For Johnston's intellectual journey from a research base in Guatemala to West Philadelphia, see Francis E. Johnston, "Academically Based Community Service and the University Curriculum," *Journal of Higher Education Outreach and Engagement* 5, no. 1 (Spring 2000): 17–24. From 1996 to 2000, this journal was titled *Journal of Public Service and Outreach.*

9. Lee Benson, Ira Harkavy, and John Puckett, "An Implementation Revolution as a Strategy for Fulfilling the Democratic Promise of University-Community Partnerships: Penn–West Philadelphia as an Experiment in Progress," *Nonprofit and Voluntary Sector Quarterly* 29 (2000): 38–39.

10. Francis E. Johnston and Robert J. Hallock, "Physical Growth, Nutritional Status, and Dietary Intake of African-American Middle School Students from Philadelphia," *American Journal of Human Biology* 6 (1994): 741–747; also see Penny Gordon-Larsen, Babette S. Zemel, and Francis E. Johnston, "Secular Change in Stature, Weight, Fatness, Overweight, and Obesity in Urban African-American Adolescents from the Mid-1950's to the Mid 1990's," *American Journal of Human Biology* 9 (1997): 675–688.

11. Penny Gordon-Larsen, "Ecology of Obesity in West Philadelphia Adolescents" (Ph.D. diss., University of Pennsylvania, 1997). See esp. v, 79.

12. At the end of the 2011–2012 academic year, the School District of Philadelphia closed six schools. In 2013, it closed twenty-four. In West Philadelphia, three Netter Center partner schools closed, including Drew Elementary School and University City High School.

13. Francis E. Johnston, Ira Harkavy, Frances Barg, Danny Gerber, and Jennifer Rulf, "The Urban Nutrition Initiative: Bringing Academically-Based Community Service to the University of Pennsylvania's Department of Anthropology," special issue, "Service-Learning and Anthropology," *Michigan Journal of Community Service Learning* 10, no. 3 (Summer 2004): 104.

14. Francis E. Johnston, "The Agatston Urban Nutrition Initiative: Working to Reverse the Obesity Epidemic through Academically Based Community Service," special issue, "Universities in Partnership: Strategies for Education, Youth Development, and Community Renewal," *New Directions for Youth Development* 122 (Summer 2009): 77.

15. Johnston, "Agatston Urban Nutrition Initiative," 77.

16. Johnston et al., "Urban Nutrition Initiative," 104.

17. J. Michael Wieting, "Cause and Effect in Childhood Obesity: Solutions for a National Epidemic," *Journal of the American Osteopathic Association* 108 (2008): 545–552, available at http://jaoa.org/article.aspx?articleid=2093529; Paul T. von Hippel and W. Kyle Bradbury, "The Effects of School Physical Education Grants on Obesity, Fitness, and Academic Achievement," *Preventive Medicine* 78 (September 2015): 44–51, doi:10.1016/j.ypmed.2015.06.011; Brad Metcalf, William Henley, and Terence Wilkin, "Effectiveness of Intervention on Physical Activity of Children: Systematic Review and Meta-Analysis of Controlled Trials with

Objectively Measured Outcomes (EarlyBird 54)," *The BMJ* 345, no. 7876 (24–30 September 2012), doi: http://dx.doi.org/10.1136/bmj.e5888.

18. Budget cuts forced schools to close after 6:00 P.M., ending weekly fitness nights at University City High School after three years of operation.

19. Mary Clarke-Pearson, "Cultivating Knowledge: A Local High School's Curriculum Combines Business with Learning," *Daily Pennsylvanian*, 20 June 2002.

20. Francis E. Johnston, "The Obesity Culture: Problem-Solving through University-Community School Partnerships," *Universities and Community Schools* 8, nos. 1–2 (2010): 27.

21. UNI's PANEP grant was coordinated in partnership with Eat.Right.Now, the School District of Philadelphia's comprehensive nutrition education program.

22. Johnston, "Agatston Urban Nutrition Initiative," 72.

23. Locally run CSAs are found all over the country, including many in Philadelphia. A CSA gives city residents direct access to high-quality, fresh produce grown by local farmers. A CSA member purchases a "share" of vegetables from a farmer, who delivers that share of produce to a convenient drop-off location in the member's neighborhood on a weekly or biweekly basis.

24. One of AUNI's classroom-based projects that focused on developing a healthy snack business grew into Rebel Ventures (RV), a youth-run social enterprise. RV engages high school, undergraduate, and graduate students in research and development of healthy recipes, as well as marketing, accounting, and distribution of snacks based on those recipes. Each year the RV Crew produces tens of thousands of healthy snacks, which are provided free to school students and sold at corner stores and university cafes.

25. Terri H. Lipman, Mary McGrath Schucker, Sarah J. Ratcliffe, Tyler Holmberg, Scott Baier, and Janet A. Deatrick, "Diabetes Risk Factors in Children: A Partnership between Nurse Practitioner and High School Students," *American Journal of Maternal Child Nursing* 36, no. 1 (January/February 2011): 56–62, doi: 10.1097/NMC.0b013e3181fc0d06.

26. In five years Dance for Health attracted 358 participants (130 children). Participants showed a significant increase in the average number of steps taken on dancing days versus nondancing days (1,760 versus 851), and women lost an average of 1.2 kg in four weeks. The Penn NP and Sayre High School students have continued to present together each year at the National Pediatric Nursing Conference (a total of twenty poster presentations and two oral presentations) and have received seven national awards. They have also been honored for their service to the community through citations from the Philadelphia City Council and a proclamation from the mayor.

27. Johnston retired from teaching at the conclusion of academic year 2015–2016.

28. The concept of a democratic devolution revolution is presented in testimony by Ira Harkavy before the Subcommittee on Housing and Community Opportunity of the Committee on Banking and Financial Services of the House of Representatives, 105th Cong., 1st sess. (Washington, DC: U.S. Government Printing Office, 1997). Also see Ira Harkavy and Rita A. Hodges, "Democratic Devolution: How America's Colleges and Universities Can Strengthen Their Communities," *Progressive Policy Institute,* October 2012, available at http://www.progressivepolicy.org/wp-content/uploads/2012/10/10.2012_Harkavy-Hodges_Democratic-Devolution.pdf.

CHAPTER 10

1. Eugenio Tironi, *El sueño chileno: Comunidad, familia y nación en el Bicentenario* [The Chilean dream: Community, family and nation at the Bicentenary] (Santiago de Chile: Editorial Taurus, 2005).

2. "Reference institution" is, in our judgment, a logical extension of reference group theory. See Robert K. Merton's brilliant discussion of reference groups in *Social Theory and Social Structure*, enlarged ed. (New York: Free Press, 1968), 279–440.

3. William Rainey Harper, "The University and Democracy," 1899 Charter Day address at the University of California, in *The Trend in Higher Education* (Chicago: University of Chicago Press, 1905), 25.

4. John W. Gardner, "Remarks to the Campus Compact Strategic Planning Committee," San Francisco, CA, 10 February 1998.

5. Ibid.

6. See Ernest L. Boyer, "Creating the New American College," *Chronicle of Higher Education*, 9 March 1994, A48; Derek C. Bok, *Universities and the Future of America* (Durham, NC: Duke University Press, 1990); Lee Shulman, "Professing the Liberal Arts," in *Education and Democracy: Re-imagining Liberal Learning in America*, ed. Robert Orrill (New York: College Board, 1997), 151–173; Alexander W. Astin, "Liberal Education and Democracy: The Case for Pragmatism," in Orrill, *Education and Democracy*, 207–223.

7. William R. Greiner, "In the Total of All These Acts: How Can American Universities Address the Urban Agenda?" *Universities and Community Schools* 4, nos. 1–2 (1994): 12.

8. Benjamin Franklin, *Proposals Relating to the Education of Youth in Pensilvania*, in *Benjamin Franklin on Education*, ed. John Hardin Best, Classics in Education 14 (New York: Bureau of Publications, Teachers College, Columbia University, 1962), 149–150.

9. Derek Bok, *Universities in the Marketplace: The Commercialization of Higher Education* (Princeton, NJ: Princeton University Press, 2003).

10. Although definitions vary, the concept of the entrepreneurial university grew out of the commodification and commercialization that higher education encourages, and the increased impact of the marketplace and the profitmaking motive on university operations and goals. See Sheila Slaughter and Larry L. Leslie, *Politics, Policies, and the Entrepreneurial University* (Baltimore, MD: Johns Hopkins University Press, 1997); Burton R. Clark, *Creating Entrepreneurial Universities: Organizational Pathways of Transformation* (Oxford: Pergamon Press, 1998). For a more recent discussion that highlights the lack of definitional agreement in Europe, where the concept has gained particular currency, see Organisation for Economic Co-operation and Development, *A Guiding Framework for Entrepreneurial Universities* (final version, 18 December 2012), available at https://www.oecd.org/site/cfecpr/EC-OECD%20Entrepreneurial%20Universities%20Framework.pdf, accessed 22 August 2016.

11. For example, James Mulholland, "Academics: Forget about Public Engagement, Stay in Your Ivory Towers," *The Guardian*, 10 December 2015, available at https://www.theguardian.com/higher-education-network/2015/dec/10/academics-forget-about-public-engagement-stay-in-your-ivory-towers, accessed 11 January 2017.

12. Carol Geary Schneider, "Making Excellence Inclusive: Liberal Education and America's Promise," *Liberal Education* 91, no. 2 (2005): 13. See also Andrew Delbanco, *College: What It Was, Is, and Should Be* (Princeton, NJ: Princeton University Press, 2012), 175–176.

13. John Dewey, *Reconstruction in Philosophy*, in *The Middle Works of John Dewey, 1899–1924*, vol. 12, ed. Jo Ann Boydston (Carbondale: Southern Illinois University, 1978), 189–190; digitally reproduced in Larry Hickman, ed., *The Collected Works of John Dewey, 1882–1953: The Electronic Edition* (Charlottesville, VA: InteLex, 1996).

14. Center for Educational Research and Innovation, *The University and the Community: The Problems of Changing Relationships* (Paris: Organisation for Economic Co-operation and Development, 1982), 127.

15. Stanley Fish is arguably the most outspoken proponent of the "disciplinary fallacy." See his *Save the World on Your Own Time* (New York: Oxford University Press, 2008).

16. Lee S. Shulman, "Foreword," in *Educating Citizens: Preparing America's Undergraduates for Lives of Moral and Civic Responsibility*, ed. Anne Colby, Thomas Ehrlich, Elizabeth Beaumont, and Jason Stephens (San Francisco: Jossey-Bass, 2003), viii.

17. John Dewey, *The School and Society*, in *Middle Works*, 1:8.

18. Harkavy co-taught the seminar with Benson from 1985 until Benson's death in 2012.

19. John Dewey, *The Public and Its Problems*, in *The Later Works of John Dewey, 1925–1953*, vol. 2, ed. Jo Ann Boydston (Carbondale: Southern Illinois University, 1981), 368; digitally reproduced in Hickman, *Collected Works of John Dewey*. It perhaps belabors the point to note that technological advances such as the Internet and social media simultaneously connect traditional local communities to universal values and affiliations and weaken those communities. Dewey's argument is that democratic, cosmopolitan, face-to-face, neighborly communities are *necessary* for a democratic society. The formidable challenge is to harness advanced communication technologies to serve participatory, democratic, communal ends rather than individualistic, competitive, or divisive ones.

20. John Dewey, *How We Think*, rev. ed., in *Later Works*, 8:122.

21. Paul Pribbenow, "Lessons on Vocation and Location: The Saga of Augsburg College as Urban Settlement," *World and Word* 34, no. 2 (2014): 158.

22. E. M. Forster, *Howards End* (Toronto: William Briggs, 1911), front matter.

Index

LEE BENSON (1922–2012) was Professor Emeritus of History at the University of Pennsylvania and co-author of *Dewey's Dream: Universities and Democracies in an Age of Education Reform* (Temple).

IRA HARKAVY is Associate Vice President and Founding Director of the Barbara and Edward Netter Center for Community Partnerships at the University of Pennsylvania and co-author of *Dewey's Dream: Universities and Democracies in an Age of Education Reform* (Temple).

JOHN PUCKETT is Professor of Education at the University of Pennsylvania and co-author of *Dewey's Dream: Universities and Democracies in an Age of Education Reform* (Temple).

MATTHEW HARTLEY serves as Associate Dean in the Graduate School of Education and Professor of Education at the University of Pennsylvania. He is also co-editor of *"To Serve a Larger Purpose": Engagement for Democracy and the Transformation of Higher Education* (Temple).

RITA A. HODGES is Assistant Director of the Barbara and Edward Netter Center for Community Partnerships at the University of Pennsylvania.

FRANCIS E. JOHNSTON is Professor Emeritus of Anthropology at the University of Pennsylvania.

JOANN WEEKS is Associate Director of the Barbara and Edward Netter Center for Community Partnerships at the University of Pennsylvania.